THE
MAINE CAPER

THE
MAINE CAPER

John Frisbie

Broadlands Publishing, LLC

Library of Congress Registration 225195E60
Broadlands Publishing, LLC
ISBN 978-0-578-53956-0

CHAPTER 1

Chip sat in the wine cellar with his arm around Sarah Lindeman's shoulder. He smiled. The summer job had gone pretty well so far. It was a great location, an old inn on the coast of Maine. And his little problem hadn't shown itself all summer. Doctor Grubner's counseling, five years of it, seemed to be working. Chip felt good about the improvement in his coping skills. He could sublimate the urges now, mask them, finesse those little slip-ups so no one would notice. It had been years since he'd really hurt anyone.

Chip pulled Sarah onto his lap and leaned back against the old cabinet.

"Eeeh! That tickles," she said.

"Shh. George will hear us."

Sarah snuggled up with her head on his shoulder. "He won't hear that." She diverted his hand away from her thigh. "What's this thing you have about George anyway? The last two dinners you stayed after work buttering him up."

"I need him for a reference." He readjusted the blanket on the stone floor. It wasn't the most comfortable place, but it was the only location at the inn where he could be alone with a date.

"A reference? George? What do you need a reference for?"

"I'm applying to grad school next year."

"More school?"

"MBA."

"Oh, God! George loves you. It seems like he knows you pretty well. You worked here for him last year too didn't you?"

"The last two summers." He moved his hand around her waist and buried his face in her neck, tweaking her skin with his tongue. His left hand cupped her breast.

"Chip, stop that." She moved his hand away again.

He sat up and stared blankly ahead. He grabbed the open bottle of wine and filled his paper cup.

"God, you're aggressive."

He refilled her paper cup. "What do you mean?"

"I don't know. Forget it."

"No, what do you mean, I'm aggressive?"

"Just forget it. Forget I said anything."

"You're crazy; you know that?" He took deep breath. "I mean, I'm probably the most normal person you've ever met. I'm completely normal."

She smiled and took a sip of wine. "Right, you're normal. Sorry."

As she shifted her position again, he realized his left leg had gone numb. She wasn't heavy, but she'd been sitting on a nerve.

"Hold on a second." He slid Sarah off his lap.

"What are you doing?"

He stood up and kicked his foot against the wall. "I'm trying to wake up my leg. It feels like pins and needles."

In an attempt to walk, he collapsed on his numb leg. Reaching for support against the wall, his hand struck a metal serving tray, sending it crashing to the stone floor.

They both froze.

"Damn!" He put his foot on the tray to stop the rattling.

They listened, trying to stay as quiet as possible. There was no sound at first, then quick footsteps pounded overhead straight toward the kitchen and the cellar door.

"George," whispered Sarah.

Chip glanced around. "If he finds us together down here, we're dead. You tell him you were looking for some wine to help out Eugene or something. I'll hide."

"What about you? He'll probably lock the door."

"Don't worry about me. I'll get out of here somehow." He put his finger over his lips and whispered. "Alone you're fine; with both of us here, we're screwed."

They stood in silence as the cellar door opened.

"Who's there?" George's voice echoed down the stairway.

Chip picked up the half-empty wine bottle along with the two cups and hobbled toward the back of the cellar, kicking the blanket along the floor.

"Who's there?" George turned on the stairwell light and walked down the wooden stairs.

Sarah picked up the fallen tray and placed it back on the wall. "Yoo hoo," she yelled. "I'm in here."

Chip pressed against the wall, followed it quietly behind the farthest wine rack, and slowly inched his way into the deepest recesses of the old cellar.

"Sarah?" George walked to the wine cellar entrance.

"George, hey, where's the light switch in this place?"

"Sarah, what are you doing down here?" George reached over and turned on a dull amber light from a switch on the wall. "What are you doing?" He looked around.

"We ran low on burgundy last night, so I thought I'd bring some up for dinner."

"I didn't know you knew where this place was."

"Oh sure. I've been down here with Eugene before to help bring up wine. I just didn't remember where the light switch was."

Eugene was the chef. Everyone at the inn knew she'd been dating him all summer. It had only been a few days since she'd broken up with him. George's look of suspicion disappeared. "Well that's nice of you, Sarah, but I'm not sure I want dining room people down here without checking with me or Eugene first, OK?"

"OK. I was just trying to help."

"I know you were, and I appreciate it." He grabbed three bottles of burgundy from the rack. "I just want you to check with one of us first, so we know when someone's down here. That's why we have a lock on the door—to discourage just anyone from coming down here."

"I hear you," she said, turning out the light. Sarah followed George down the hall and up the cellar stairs to the kitchen.

Chip stood motionless, listening to the cellar door close and the metallic *click* as George turned the lock. He wasn't worried. Sarah would sneak back and unlock the door, or he'd find another way out. Sarah would undoubtedly be grateful, thinking him chivalrous for allowing her the easy explanation and escape. His reputation would remain intact.

He placed the wine bottle on the floor, along with the two paper cups. They and the blanket could be retrieved later. Right now he needed both hands to grope his way through the darkness. He thought of finding the light switch, but decided against it. George might come back, and a light would spell disaster. He felt comfortable the way things were. He knew he'd get out.

The stone wall felt damp and cold against his hands as he fingered his way along the far end of the cellar. The floor took a step down, and the wall turned slightly to the left. He was now in complete darkness. The wine racks he touched were empty. The cobwebs told him he was in a part of the cellar never visited.

Finally, reaching the back wall, he felt a floor-to-ceiling bookcase. His hands explored the wooden frame as he carefully maneuvered in the darkness like a blind man. He counted seven empty shelves. His hand brushed the wall to the left of the case. As it went behind the massive structure, something happened. The wall disappeared. His probing fingers slid back into total emptiness.

He explored the shelves for anything that might weigh them down, but found only cobwebs and dust. He got a firm grip on the old case and pulled with all the muscles in his body, slowly rotating the piece a few inches out from the wall. The last thing he wanted was to make another noise, so he moved slowly. The wood creaked. Two more pulls and he'd opened a gap wide enough to walk through.

Wedging his body behind the case, he felt the floor step down, a single step into a small indentation in the wall, completely hidden by the old shelves. At the far end of the recess his hand felt what seemed to be a half-rotten, wooden door. The wood splintered in his outstretched fingers, and he retracted his hand from the jagged barbs. Carefully feeling across the door, he found the knob. Nothing moved.

Further exploration revealed a hole where the wood had rotted away about a foot above the knob. He reached into the hole and grabbed the knob from the inside. Thick spider webs made him wince as he retrieved his hand, wiping off the strands on his pant leg. Grabbing the inside knob again, he tried turning it only to find it just as stubborn as the outside. Next to the inside knob, he discovered a small lever, which he concluded had to be the locking mechanism. It was rusty but moved ever so slightly. After considerable effort, working the lever up and down, he forced it free.

The hinges squeaked as he opened the door into complete, cold darkness. Slowly, he felt his way forward through the threshold, walking down two steps to a stone floor. He turned right, keeping his right hand on the wall and his left arm in front of his face to protect himself from spider webs and anything else that might crop up. He wondered what kind of space he was in, whether it was a room or a hallway.

It used to bother him, the things he was willing to do to get what he wanted, but those concerns came less and less frequently. He laughed at the term Dr.

Grubner had used; narcissistic aggressive disorder. Whatever it was, Chip was past it. He did what he had to do. It was that simple.

Along the third wall, his right hand groped the stones for guidance. After five paces he stepped on a board, throwing him off balance, forcing his right hand to lean heavily against the wall. A chunk of old cement gave way under the pressure and moved between the stones.

He tore out the cement and felt an odd sensation. It was subtle at first, a freshness against his skin. He held up his palm and felt it again. When he leaned his face in front of the hole, he knew it was oxygen. He breathed in deeply, letting the fresh air wash over his face. He hadn't realized how thin the air was until he had a new supply of oxygen for comparison. After several deep breaths, he pawed at the hole again, removing more chunks of cement and a big stone. He pushed a second stone forward, and it crashed into the emptiness of whatever lay beyond.

Chip inserted his hand, then his whole arm. He felt only emptiness, nothing but fresh air. Bending his elbow and wrist as much as possible, he felt the stones on the other side of the wall, noticing how wet and slimy they were.

He spent the next twenty minutes opening up a hole big enough to crawl through. After several aborted attempts to enter the hole head first, he turned around and backed through it, his feet probing the ground for a solid place to support his weight. Bringing his arms up over his head, he backed through the hole and crouched in the blackness, wondering when the last person before him had occupied this hidden place.

Cool, salty air was the first sensation, a distinct change from the room he'd just left. There was also more light. He could almost see his hands in front of his face. His hand waved through spider webs and quickly smacked the back of his neck as tiny legs scampered across his skin. He felt the perimeter of his new environment, which measured about five feet wide and well over six feet high. Old logs and timbers lined the walls, while the ground was dirt and moist rocks.

Proceeding forward, he realized he was in an underground tunnel. The ground was slick, and he stumbled more than once. At one point he detected movement to his left. He heard a squeaking, cackling sound as something scratched across the tunnel floor. He hated rats almost as much as spiders.

He could sense the ground sloping downward. When the passageway gradually turned to the right, he saw a dull, gray light up ahead. The sound of splashing waves whispered in the background.

Thorny blackberries and vines covered the opening. A quick look at his watch showed fifteen minutes until he was due back at work. He removed his shirt and wrapped it around his forearm to raise the barbed branches. He saw sunlight through the heavy growth and felt cool mist on his skin. With sharp stones cutting into his underbelly and barbs ripping his back, he slowly slithered out to open air, finding himself on a hill with waves lapping ten feet below.

The salt air felt good as Chip stood on the narrow

ledge. He knew he'd discovered a place that hadn't seen human life for decades, maybe a century. His mind raced. Two more weeks before school started. He figured he'd spend his last free afternoons covering his tracks, putting the bookcase snugly in place, locking the old door. He didn't want anyone else to find his tunnel. He knew the value of secret information. He'd read Machiavelli and *The Art of War* by Sun Tzu.

Standing there with the wind blowing in his face, Chip knew he would use the hidden tunnel to his advantage one day. He didn't know how yet, but he knew he'd use it. He looked quickly at his watch, then he picked his way down the hill and swam back to the inn.

CHAPTER 2
Twenty Years Later

Howard Cohen looked through the two-way mirror and breathed heavily. Beads of sweat dribbled across his forehead and under the few wisps of black hair covering his scalp. The woman on the other side of the mirror stared at herself, looking into the specially treated glass. She seemed younger than the other women. She had a pretty face and a sexy figure. Howard glanced at the two engineers sitting beside him in the little room, his subordinates. They were smiling. The woman ran her hand through her hair and returned to the center of the room. Howard adjusted the mechanical pencils in his shirt pocket and re-read the email in his folder.

Howard,

The last of our focus group sessions for the Mustang Oven Project will be held this coming Friday at the United Testing facility in downtown Boston, observation room 27 on the fourth floor. Time, 10:00 AM. I want you to be there. There's no question your presence at sessions one and three was key in working out those early problems with the regulator coil. Gallagher & Associates will be overseeing the session just like they did with all the others. As an FYI Howard, Peter Burke and the rest of top management are firmly behind this project. This new application of our military technology to the consumer market is the wave of the future, so let's put our engineering fingerprints all over this oven and make it a winner.

T. J. Belcher
V. P. Engineering

Howard closed the folder, and reached for his newspaper as Jean Kimer, the moderator, greeted the women, leading each one to a workstation equipped with an ADI ultra sound oven.

"Hey, Howard." Harvey Gallagher walked into the room with a briefcase in one hand and a cup of coffee in the other.

"Harv, good to see you." The engineer took a deep breath and removed a legal pad from his folder. "Are you sure they can't see us in there?"

"No they can't see us." Harvey walked to the other end of the room and set down his coffee and briefcase. He was about six foot one, with sandy brown hair. "I took you in the other room last March, remember?" He took off his sport jacket and rolled up his shirtsleeves. "It looked just like a regular mirror, right?"

"I know, but every time I come in here I feel guilty, like I'm peeking at something I shouldn't be seeing."

Howard and most of the other ADI employees were unfamiliar with sophisticated consumer marketing. The company had functioned primarily as a defense contractor, but when defense budgets began shrinking, management started redirecting their focus to the consumer marketplace. After an extensive search, they hired a well-known marketing guru from New York named Peter Burke to head up the effort.

"Jeez. I feel like a spy," said another of Howard's underlings entering the room.

Howard laughed. "Is this how you guys test shower soap, Harv, put a two-way mirror in a shower?"

Gallagher smiled. "Howard, I think you're a closet voyeur."

"I heard it," said Ted Bass, coming in the door. "I heard it out in the hall: 'A two-way mirror in a shower.' I like it."

Ted was the Marketing Department's second in command after Peter Burke.

"Hey, Ted. Good to see you." Harv raised his hand, slapping his palm against Ted's as he passed.

"That's what we need to liven things up around here." Bass continued his way over to a display of snacks in the corner and grabbed a roast beef sandwich. "There's got to be a way we can incorporate our technology with some kind of shower. Work on it Howard." He patted Cohen on the shoulder and sat down next to Gallagher.

Quickly looking at his watch, Harv began reviewing the discussion guide for his clients, outlining what the women would be doing and what he wanted to accomplish. He had always been intrigued by the product concept. The engineering wizards at ADI had borrowed the wave accelerator from their long range ST-37 rocket over on the military side of the business. They liked the idea that it had the ability to speed up sound waves to a sufficiently high level that heat was produced. The next step was to scale it down and put it into a prototype oven. To everyone's amazement, the newly adapted technology could cook food in a fraction of the time it took microwave or convection ovens and was totally safe.

"You seem to be getting most of our projects these days, Gallagher." Ted Bass stood up and took off his jacket. "You got some inside track or something?"

"I've known Peter Burke for quite a while." said Harv.

Bass sat down and smiled. "I know. Peter told me you guys used to work together before he came here."

"When he was at Pan American Products. I was with the agency that handled one of his coffee brands."

"Listen," Bass slapped Harv on the knee, "you've got most of our business because you're doing a great job, not just because you know Peter."

"Well, I'd like to think so." Harv smiled and removed a folder from his briefcase.

"And this little project." Ted glanced out through the two-way mirror toward the test room. "This baby could be big. If we make this thing happen, there could be some serious bonus money floating around."

"Not bad."

"I mean for employees and consultants alike."

Harv nodded with as much enthusiasm as he could muster. He hadn't taken a vacation since starting his marketing consulting business two years ago and was exhausted. These focus groups were the final task of this phase, and he had promised himself he'd take the next week off.

A uniformed security guard walked into the testing

area as Jean began to speak. "If everyone is ready, we can get started." She explained the new product, told them how to use it, and that she wanted their feedback.

Harv turned on the video camera as the observation crew sat back to watch the session, each with a legal pad and pencil at the ready.

The testing area was a large kitchen with fifteen work stations spread evenly throughout the room, each with an ADI test oven, a sink, a complete supply of cooking ingredients, and a small refrigerator underneath, containing everything they'd need for the test session. The testing area was separated from the smaller observation room by a two-way mirror. From the testing side, it simply looked like a large, decorative mirror on the wall, about five feet wide and three feet high. From the observation side, however, it looked like smoky, transparent glass.

This state-of-the-art test kitchen was one of the reasons Harv had used United Testing's facilities often over the past two years. Located in a five-story brick building, the place occupied one entire block of downtown Boston. The laboratories and testing rooms were equipped to evaluate all kinds of products, from cakes and cookies to laundry detergent, lawn mowers, and toothpaste.

As the session proceeded, Harv noticed one woman at the far side of the room. While the other participants followed along with the moderator, this one appeared to be having some problems with her oven and spent much of the time bending over it, apparently trying to make it work. While the other women talked among themselves, laughing and exchanging ingredients, this one stayed to herself. Harv put her out of his mind and concentrated on the others.

At the session's midpoint, Jean Kimer told the women to take a ten minute break, inviting them to sit down, eat some of their cooking, and generally relax. This planned break allowed her to leave the room. It was an important time to check with the observers to see how they thought things were going and get feedback on directing the remainder of the session.

Jean entered the observation room from the outside hallway. "So, any questions?" She walked over and grabbed a doughnut.

Harv looked surprised. "You mean you're not going to eat any of the food in there prepared in the Ultra 500?"

"No thanks, Harv. I only have so much Alka Seltzer."

"Hey," Bass put down his sandwich and sat up straight, "anything cooked in the Ultra 500 has got to be delicious. I think we ought to make her eat some of that stuff out there."

"Absolutely," said Harv. "I mean to really get a feel for the product."

The engineers chuckled.

"Guys." Jean took her doughnut over and sat on the other side of Harvey. "Guys, I love the product. Everybody loves the product. I'll cook myself something after the session, OK?"

"Well, OK, but I'm going to have Howard stay and watch to make sure you like it," said Bass.

"Seriously," said Harv, "do you think that selection dial might be a problem?"

"I was noticing that." Jean tried to talk while chewing. "It's giving some of them problems. Just like in session three last week."

"I think maybe that touch-sensitive digital approach may be the way to go," said Bass. "Any way you could take a look at that, Howard?"

The engineer talked it over quickly with his colleagues and said he thought it would be quite simple.

As break ended, Harv walked out into the hallway with Jean and mentioned the woman he'd noticed in the corner. He didn't want to talk about it inside and alarm his client. It was most likely nothing, just a communication problem. She probably should have been eliminated in pre-screening when the group was recruited. Harv didn't want to call attention to any screw-ups. He was too tired to deal with it. Jean could take care of it.

The second half proceeded smoothly as the women cooked brownies and muffins, which they sampled. Harv saw Jean walk over to the woman in the corner, who smiled and indicated she was in no need of help. When another participant tapped Jean on the shoulder, the busy moderator redirected her attention and soon became wrapped up in other things.

Harv kept an eye on the woman. The security guard didn't seem to notice anything, and neither did anyone else in the observation room. Ted was clearly pleased. That was the name of the game, keeping the client happy.

After an hour Ted got up to leave. "Looks good, Harv." He closed up his briefcase. "I'll see you tomorrow night then I guess, huh?"

"Yeah, I'll see you tomorrow." Harv knew Ted was referring to the company party Peter Burke was giving Saturday night. He was flattered Peter invited him to his big bashes. Any other party, Harv would stay home and sleep, but a Peter Burke affair for ADI executives and key consultants was a must, no matter how tired he was. He got up and walked Ted to the door. "I'll write up this session over the weekend and have it on your desk Monday."

"Outstanding." Ted said goodbye to everyone and left.

Returning his attention to the focus group, Harv sat down and noticed the woman in the corner was back to her old ways. Her back was turned, so it was difficult to see what she was doing. There was something not quite right about her. Other women experiencing trouble had asked Jean or one of the other participants for help. This woman had avoided all contact and communication. Harv glanced over at Howard, who was busy talking with his engineers, sketching out diagrams on a legal pad.

As Harv stood up and walked to his right to get a better view, he saw the woman give a quick look over her shoulder at the confusion behind her. Then she turned her back completely, and Harv could see both arms moving. He couldn't be sure, but it looked like she was putting something into her purse. He thought of alerting the guard then quickly glanced back at Howard, who was still talking with his technicians. Harv didn't want to create a scene, but he didn't like what he was seeing. He watched closely as the woman turned around, purse in hand, and headed for the exit.

He wasn't sure what to do. She could be going to the rest room as other participants had done during the long session. Maybe she was legitimate, maybe she wasn't. With the metal detector and security guard in the room and x-ray scanner at the main door, he knew she wasn't going to sneak anything out of the building. He tried not to panic. As she walked through the detection devices, Harv watched. The security guard simply smiled. Something was going on; maybe nothing was going on.

Both the test kitchen and the observation room had exit doors out into the hall. When the woman stepped out into the hall, so did Harv. She immediately turned the other way and walked at a measured pace. He thought of getting the security guard but there was no time. Besides, it would be embarrassing to approach a stranger, a woman recruited for his best client, and ask to look in her purse. What if he was wrong? He followed her, wondering why these things always happened on Fridays. He wished he was already on vacation and cursed this woman who apparently was determined to ruin his day.

He hoped she would stop off at the ladies' room and return to the test lab. That would at least be normal, the first normal thing she'd done all day. He thought of Howard back in the observation area, completely oblivious to Harv's mounting crisis, totally engrossed, talking with his technicians about the selector mechanism.

The woman passed the restrooms. Glancing behind her, she saw Harv and picked up her pace.

"Excuse me, madam."

She didn't stop. Instead, she broke out into a slow run. Passing the elevator bank, she opened the door marked *Stairs* and disappeared.

That was all Harv needed. Entering the stairwell, he ran down to the landing and stopped, noticing there were no sounds of footsteps descending the stairs below. Quickly, he opened the door to the third floor. Running footsteps echoed in the hallway to his left, and he took off, bumping into two lab technicians in white coats. Coming to a turn in the hallway, Harv saw a flash of the woman's gray dress head into a room with a big red light over the doorway. The light meant that testing was in progress, but Harv figured the woman probably thought it was some kind of exit.

Inside he saw a reception area with a single door to the right of the desk. The receptionist was on the phone and raised her hand in a stop gesture while Harv dashed passed her through the inner door. He emerged into a large test room with a pleasant per-fumy aroma. Pink walls surrounded white-tiled floors with long sun lamps covering the ceiling. Beneath the giant lamps, some twenty women in bathing suits were stretched out on aluminum lounges. Several were slathering some kind of oil over their bodies. Others, already well oiled, were reclining comfortably. Some had their own individual compartments, created by mobile canvas partitions. Two white-coated female technicians were kneeling on the floor wiping up a puddle of white, creamy oil.

"Excuse me," said Harv as politely as possible, "did a woman in a gray dress just—"

"Hey! You can't come in here." One of the lab

technicians stood up and walked toward Harv while several participants yelled in protest, covering their oily bodies with hands, towels, and anything else they could find.

Spying an open door on the far side of the room, Harv sprang forward in pursuit. Quickly stepping sideways to avoid apprehension by a technician, he slipped on the oily tile and went sliding on his backside into three reclining women. One flimsy chaise lounge careened into another, causing a pile-up of aluminum framing, webbing, skin, and Harvey. Legs, arms, and metal frames were entwined in a massive heap. Every time Harv tried to put his hand down to get up, it slipped on the floor or on someone's greasy skin. One participant in the pile grabbed a plastic bottle and pummeled him on the head as screams echoed throughout the room.

The collision toppled one of the canvas partitions, which in turn knocked over its neighbor, causing all ten to topple over like a row of large, white dominoes, each falling on a confused sunbather.

Two women at the side of the room stood with their hands on their hips laughing.

"Call security," cried a technician. "Where the hell is security?"

"I'm chasing a criminal," yelled Harv, still trying to get up.

"You pervert," shrieked one of the women in his pile as Harv accidentally put his hand on her leg.

He grabbed the plastic bottle away from the woman who was clubbing him and eventually stood up, kicking away an aluminum chaise that entangled his right foot.

"Look what you've done," yelled the technician. "Security is on the way."

"Good." Harv gingerly stepped over the slippery tiles toward the far door. "Tell them to meet me on the ground floor."

Bolting into the hallway, Harv knew he'd lost precious time. He didn't have the luxury of worrying about the grease on his good pants and figured he'd add the cleaning bill to ADI's invoice. The emergency stairway was the most logical target. Even if he guessed wrong, it would lead him to the ground floor, which was the only way out of the building.

Entering the stairwell, he paused and heard the distant pounding of feet echoing up the cement shaft. From the sound, he guessed she'd skipped the second floor and was heading straight down to the first. The hard cement slammed against his feet as he catapulted over the railing to the landing below. He took the remaining stairs three at a time, hoisting himself over hand railings, exploding through the exit door into the first floor hallway. Following the red exit arrow, he sprinted to the right. At the end of the hallway, he could see his mystery woman struggling with a security guard at a turnstile leading out of the building.

She looked at Harv then kicked the guard in his groin, sending him to his knees. She quickly ducked under the turnstile and fled through the main door.

Harv had gained considerable ground. "Coming through," he yelled, leaping over the guard, landing his left foot on top of the turnstile.

"Jesus Christ!" The guard ducked to avoid Harv's flying feet. "What the hell?"

Harvey pushed off the turnstile with his left foot as his momentum carried him deftly to the doorway beyond.

The woman was out on the street when Harv exited the building. About thirty feet down the sidewalk he caught her by the elbow. When she wouldn't stop, he tackled her, sending them both sprawling on the pavement. The purse went flying. As they got up, Harv looked at the woman's face. The features were hard. He couldn't picture her driving kids to Little League in her Volvo.

Instinctively, the woman lunged for her purse, lying on the sidewalk. Harv had instincts too. Four years of ice hockey at Boston University had some lasting influence. As the woman reached for her purse, Harv threw a mean body check, driving her hard into the side of a Buick parked at the curb.

Harv's shoulder hurt as he bent down to retrieve the purse. Looking up, he saw the woman hobble around the back of the Buick and climb into a waiting car. Its tires screeched as it took off down the street.

CHAPTER 3

"The goddamn wave accelerator." Chuck Weitz pointed to the five by two inch electronic object on his desktop.

"Whoever it was knew exactly what they wanted," said Howard Cohen.

Harv had smoothed things over with United's security people, stopped by his apartment to change clothes, and taken the purse directly to Chuck Weitz, executive vice president of ADI's security operation. Chuck had summoned Howard Cohen, and the three of them sat around Chuck's desk, staring at the displayed contents of the flowered, cloth purse.

"Make sure you don't touch anything," said Chuck. "The lab boys'll be here any minute to take this stuff and evaluate every molecule." Chuck was about six feet tall, had a muscular build with broad shoulders, and was probably one of the last ten civilians on the planet to sport a crew cut. Harv had limited involvement with Chuck over the past two years, interacting directly with him on only one other occasion. He had mixed feelings about the guy. There was a little intimidation because of his reputation as an all-seeing, omnipotent security czar and his powerful position in the company. But on the other hand, Harv viewed him as having less status than other V.P.'s at the company. Maybe it had something to do with the fact that his office was in the basement and not up on the fourth floor where Peter Burke and the other top brass lived. Maybe it had to do with the look of Chuck's office, more utilitarian and plain than the stylishly decorated digs upstairs.

"You notice the license plate Harvey?" asked Chuck.

"Only that it looked like a New York plate. It was kind of frantic down there on the street."

"I can't believe I didn't notice anything." Howard Cohen ran his hand through his thinning hair.

"Hey, I wasn't sure exactly what I was seeing," said Harv. "It wasn't until she started running away out in the hall that I knew something was up."

"Anything unusual about her that stands out?" asked Chuck.

"Well just that maybe she was kind of drab looking from a distance, I mean compared to the others and closer up she looked mean. Black eyes, angry, a tough lady."

"So we're definitely not looking for a den mother I guess."

Harv smiled as the door opened. William Cobb, ADI's president, and Roger Cornish, his second in command, walked in. Cobb had a medium build with a ruddy complexion and thick, white hair. Cornish was tall and slim with perfectly combed brown hair and impeccable tailoring. Roger was an executive vice president, the same level as Peter and Chuck. He'd been with ADI for fifteen years, was responsible for the financial side of the business, and was generally considered heir apparent for the presidency when Cobb retired.

"Bill, you know Howard," said Chuck. "And this is Harvey Gallagher, the consultant on the scene."

Cobb smiled and shook Harv's hand, while Roger's handshake was cold with an attitude of aloof contempt.

"So, who knows about this?" asked Cobb.

"Just the five of us and two security guards over at United." Chuck looked at Harvey. "That right, just two?"

"Right, the guard at the door named Wilson and his boss, Jablonski."

As Harv spoke, Cornish took on an expression of arrogant disgust.

"Irv Jablonski," said Chuck. "I just got off the phone with him. I know him. He's assured me he'll keep this under wraps."

"Peter Burke should know," added Cobb.

"Yes I thought about Peter but I wanted to hear it from you," said Chuck.

"Just Peter and that's it. I want this kept as quiet as possible."

Chuck turned on a voice recorder, and they went over the details of the chase and rescue of the purse. Harv described what he'd seen through the two-way mirror. He pointed out how he couldn't really see anything specific but, having monitored many focus groups, he felt there was just something about the woman's behavior that got his attention.

"Why didn't you tell the security guard?" asked Cornish.

"Hindsight's 20/20," said Weitz. "Just because you see something unusual doesn't mean you automatically jump to the conclusion a security breach is about to happen."

"Actually, I did point out the lady to the moderator and asked her to check with the woman to see if there was any problem but nothing came of it." Harv looked over at Chuck. "I wondered if it might be a problem with directions or language." He emphasized that he was apparently the only person to notice anything and didn't want to create a confrontation that might be unwarranted or jeopardize the session. "With the security in place, I felt it best to just keep an eye on the situation."

Roger Cornish threw up his hands. "This is exactly the kind of thing I told you about, Bill. We take some of our prized technology; expose it to the public through some outside consultant and bam! It's gone."

"Now hold it one damn minute," said Weitz. "You want to take pot shots at anybody around here, you aim 'em at me. This is a security issue and I take full responsibility for anything that happens." Cornish shook his head as Chuck continued. "I know you're very protective of the military side of the business around here but the fact remains that nothing's missing. It's sitting right here in front of us thanks to this outside consultant." He nodded in Harv's direction. "And in the second place, all appropriate security precautions were in place. This session was by the book, a level two operation all the way."

"It's not as if this never happens in the military division, Roger," added Cobb.

Cornish backed off, shaking his head.

"What we need to focus on, gentlemen, is how this happened." Chuck put the end of a pencil into the open end of the gray, metallic-looking sack and lifted it off the desk. "Take a look at this. A coated ceramic sack manufactured to accommodate the exact dimensions of our wave accelerator."

"You found it inside that pouch?" asked Cobb.

"Yup. An exact fit. Had to put the white gloves on and touch the sack a little to get the accelerator out but I had to get it out to see what we've got."

"So she knew it'd be x-rayed," said Cobb.

"She knew it would be scanned. She knew the exact dimensions of the accelerator," said Weitz.

"She knew to get the accelerator in the first place," added Howard. "That's our key component. And she apparently knew where to find it in the oven."

"Chuck," Cobb leaned forward in his chair, "are you saying you think this is an inside job?"

"I'm going to wait to answer that when the lab boys get through analyzing this stuff in a day or two. But right now I'd say all indications look that way. I think this lady knew what she was doing all the way. She knew what she wanted, how to get at it. She knew about the two-way mirror, how to conceal her theft. She knew our security operation and how to get around it. About the only thing she didn't know was the layout of United's floor plan. She apparently didn't plan on being chased."

Harv looked at his watch and mentally cursed this woman for ruining his Friday. The last thing he needed was to be thrust into the middle of a political dogfight among the top brass of his best client. He never liked Roger Cornish. He knew the man openly opposed ADI's move into the consumer marketplace. He was glad to see Chuck keep him in line, but he really wished Peter Burke was there. Peter was brilliant at corporate politics and at handling people like Cornish. *Peter would fry this guy's ass.*

"You notice anything peculiar about the contents of the purse?" Chuck leaned back in his chair.

"There's not much there," said Cobb.

"That's my point. Just four items. I don't know about you gentlemen, but if I turned my wife's handbag upside down on this desk, we'd be sifting through crap for two weeks—bobby pins, receipts, loose change, stamps, a wallet."

"That's significant," Cobb nodded his head, "no wallet with I.D."

"No wallet," Chuck continued, "just what you see here, a hamburger coupon, make-up, some chewing gum, and tissue paper with make-up stains."

"And, of course, our wave accelerator in its special sack," added Howard.

"That's all," said Chuck. "Harvey, you're sure this is everything? Nothing spilled out in the street or anything?"

"No Chuck. This is everything. I'm positive."

"This is not a normal purse." Chuck stared at the contents.

"It seems more like a prop than an actual housewife's purse," added Harv.

Cornish shook his head and snorted in disgust at Harv's comment.

"That's an excellent analogy, Harvey," said Weitz. "It *is* more like a prop. Like this woman was acting the role of a housewife involved in market research, and this purse was part of her costume. And we owe you a debt of gratitude for getting it back to us."

"That's right, son," added Cobb. "This means a hell of a lot to us."

When Chuck's secretary announced the arrival of the lab technicians, two gnome-like men entered the room, one with thick, horn-rimmed glasses and a blue suit, the other in a white lab coat. After introducing themselves, the one in the white coat put on white gloves and carefully placed each item from the purse in its own individual plastic bag. Each bag was sealed and tagged. Chuck initialed each tag, as did the gnome in the blue suit. He seemed to be the ranking technician and talked with Cobb and Weitz about the kinds of testing that would be done, what they might find, and how long each test would take.

"We're going to work around the clock all weekend on this," said the head gnome. "We'll have some initial findings for you Monday morning."

Chuck nodded and looked at Cobb. "I'll be in and out of the office all weekend. We'll keep you posted if there are any key developments before Monday."

Cobb got up, thanked Harv again, and left the room. Cornish followed, mumbling something to Cobb as they walked out the door. The only words Harv could make out were "jeopardize the entire." He didn't want to be there. He was tired. He looked at his watch and got up to leave but sat down reluctantly when Chuck put up his finger as if to say, "Wait just one more minute."

The Lab technicians left after a few final words with Chuck. The security chief thanked them, closed the door, and headed back to his desk.

"Long day, huh?" Chuck sighed and sat down. "Don't mind Roger. He's not a bad guy. He just thinks the sun rises and sets around the old defense contracting business."

"No, he doesn't bother me," Harv lied. "I've met him before. I just wish Peter had been here."

Chuck smiled. "Yes, that would have been an interesting conversation." He put the notes he'd taken into a manila folder. "Listen, Harvey, I just want to make sure we're squared away on this thing today. It's vital that everything remain totally secure."

"Chuck, believe me, nothing will leave this office."

"Good. At least until we get on top of things. Right now we've just got to climb on top of this situation and see what we're dealing with."

"Chuck, let me ask you a question . . . assuming all testing goes well, this oven is going to be out there in the marketplace eventually where anybody can buy it and tear the thing apart and get their hands on this wave accelerator. I assume it's patented." He paused. "So what's the fuss about?"

Chuck nodded his head. "It has nine patents, Harv, but in today's world a patent is only a way of slowing down the inevitable reverse engineering process by competition. There are pirates out there who will try to get their hands on other companies' creative technology, dissect it, figure out how a thing is made, tweak the process just enough to circumvent the patent laws and bring it to market themselves."

"Corporate espionage," said Harv.

"Absolutely. There are middle men and brokers who try to steal pre-production products and prototypes and sell them to established foreign manufacturers, mostly in China and Russia, and make a fortune."

"I had no idea," said Harv.

"It's all about timing and speed, Harvey. If a major competitive manufacturer can get their hands on a product and reverse engineer it before the original company can gain a foothold in the market, they'll reduce the price, spend a fortune on advertising, and establish themselves as the flagship brand in that market."

"So the original company is screwed."

"It becomes far more difficult. It can get brutal."

"I gotcha." Harv nodded. "Just to confirm—It's OK if I talk to Peter about this."

"That's fine. Peter might have some insights on this that could help," said Weitz. "In fact, I'm looking forward to talking with him myself. But that's all for now, just Peter."

"Absolutely. That's it."

Chuck smiled and looked satisfied, grabbing a pen and legal pad on his desk. "Harvey, before you go, I may have to get hold of you in the next few days. As this thing unfolds, I may need your input."

"My input?"

"Hell, at this point you know more about this crazy lady than anyone." He asked for Harv's cell phone number and wrote it down along with his address and office landline number. "I'm going to ask you to keep your phone with you and turned on for the next few days. Will you do that for me?"

"Sure, but you should know, I'm leaving for a short vacation next week."

"A vacation? What's that?"

Harv smiled. "You know. It's when you actually don't work."

"When you leaving?"

"Wednesday. I'll tie up a few lose ends Monday and Tuesday and leave Wednesday."

"Just do me a favor and keep your phone with you and turned on for the next three days, OK?"

"No problem." Harv got up to go.

Chuck raised a finger in the air. "Harvey, before you leave, let me ask you, do you mind if I have you checked out?"

"Checked out?"

"Nothing serious, just a security background check."

"No, I guess not. I think Peter ran some kind of check when I got my first assignment here."

"No, that's the standard thing we give all our consultants. I may have to share some security information with you. I'm talking about something a little more in-depth."

Harv shrugged and looked at his watch. "Sure, check away. But you know I'm going to be on vacation."

Chuck smiled and scribbled on his pad. "I know about vacations, Harvey." He looked up. "If I end up needing your help, believe me, I'll make it worth your while."

CHAPTER 4

Saturday morning a wet sponge sailed over the roof of Harv's old Chevy and hit him in the face.

"It's hopeless," came a young woman's voice from the other side. "You've got dirt over tar over rust."

"Hey, watch it." Harvey wiped his face with his sleeve. "There's a thing of tar remover in the trunk." Although his dented car was a slight embarrassment, it was one he could live with while fighting the cash flow challenges of his new business. He'd been thinking about replacing the thing more and more lately though, especially when client situations came up, like driving to Peter Burke's party.

"Ooh! We've gotta get that rust nice and clean. You really have such a knack for car maintenance."

"OK that deserves another shot." Harv aimed his hose at the brunette on the other side of the car.

He'd been going with Sheila Whitmore for almost five years. They met at Penn when he was getting his MBA and she was an undergraduate. Sheila had finely chiseled features and short, dark hair. Her body was pencil thin and perfect for modeling if she'd been slightly taller.

Sheila's stay at Harv's apartment Friday night had been a little awkward. Memories of ADI's mystery woman had thrashed around inside him, and it was hard not telling her, but he kept it to himself. He hadn't told anyone.

The alley behind Harv's first floor apartment on Marlborough Street was the most convenient place for residents to wash their cars. He lived in a restored town house in Boston's Back Bay area. The place backed up to another long row of old brick town houses running along Commonwealth Avenue where his friend, Buzz Riley, had a first floor apartment. A dash out the back door and Harv could be banging on Buzz's back door to mooch a beer in seconds.

"There. Spotless," said Buzz's girlfriend from the front seat. She wiped the last bit of Windex off the side window, opened the car door, and got out.

"Thanks, Jenny, I appreciate it."

"No problem." She stuffed a wad of used paper towels into a trash bag. "I like cleaning things when I get in a certain clean-up frame of mind. And when I'm alone and abandoned."

Harv looked over at Buzz's rear window. "How long has the genius been working on that thing?"

"Oh, since around five this morning." Jenny wiped a smudge off the windshield.

Buzz was an MIT graduate student who had developed a way of projecting electricity through the air. He had full access to the school's labs but preferred to experiment in the comfort of his apartment.

"Hey!" said Sheila. "You going to wax this thing or something?"

"Yeah, I guess it wouldn't hurt." Harv dried off the roof.

"No offense, Harv," said Jenny, "but I'd definitely wax it."

"Yeah, I know. I get the point."

Jenny smiled and walked over to the can of wax behind the car. "So, Harv, you're going to see Sheila's parents next week, right?"

"Next week?" Harv smiled. "Are you sure it's next week?"

Sheila gave him a punch in the arm. "You know perfectly well you're flying down to Philadelphia on Wednesday."

"I know, I know."

"And you're going to finally meet Mother."

"I can't wait."

"It'll be a nice long weekend. You can relax and recharge your batteries."

Harv loaded up his rag with wax. "I'm determined to relax, so hopefully your parents will understand. This is partly a vacation."

"Oh, you'll have plenty of time to relax. We have a huge old house. I've told you about it—out on the main line. You can wander around in it for days and not run into anyone."

"I just may do that."

"Harv's never met your parents?" Jenny applied wax to a sponge and rubbed it on the fender.

"He had lunch with Dad and me back at Penn." Sheila kicked soapsuds off her shoe. "He almost met Mother a year ago when she was visiting but had to cancel when a client needed him in Chicago." She glared over at Harv. "And then he almost met her six months ago when she was here but had to cancel again."

"You know both those excuses were totally legitimate." Harv rubbed wax on the car's hood. "When a client needs me I can't afford to say no."

"I know."

"And seriously, I want to keep things real simple. I just want to relax and unwind."

"You do look dreadful." Sheila smiled, putting her hand on his shoulder.

"No, he looks tired," said Jenny. "There's a difference. He's too good looking to actually look dreadful."

"Yeah! Now there's a woman who appreciates a good thing when she sees it," said Harv.

"I know a good thing when I see it." Sheila leaned into him, planting a kiss on his neck.

"You flying down together?"

"No, I'm going down Monday. Help Mother pull things together. Then I'll pick up Harv at the airport when he arrives Wednesday. I've got tons of vacation time coming. I'd better take it."

"Actually, mentally, I'm already starting to relax a little. All I really have to do is go to Peter's party tonight, press the flesh a little, wind up a few things at the office Monday and Tuesday, and then fly down to Philly Wednesday for a nice long weekend."

Harv and Jenny buffed off the wax, occasionally looking over to Buzz's open door where various banging sounds, grunts, and occasional expletives came tumbling out into the alley. They were used to his odd hours and bursts of experimentation in his apartment. No one really knew if the weapon concept he was working on would ever amount to anything. They just knew Buzz had to stay busy. He wasn't happy unless he was puttering with something.

"I think that just about does it." Harv buffed off the last bit of wax.

"There now doesn't that look better?" Jenny stood back and tilted her head, gazing at the car.

"I guess." Harv stepped back to get a better view.

"Hey! You know," said Sheila, "I saw a nice car with a For Sale sign near my apartment and—"

The explosion that ripped through Buzz's window popped and sizzled like fire works. Smoke billowed out into the alley as the frustrated inventor stuck his head out the door.

"Damn!" he said, shaking his head.

"You OK?" Jenny ran up to him.

"Damn, I almost had it."

Harv waved the smoke away and bent down to pick up a piece of glass from the ground. "What you have is two broken panes . . . again."

Buzz looked around. "Not bad though. More noise and smoke than any real concussion. And it never arced onto my wall." He smiled. "It stayed completely away from the wall this time."

They'd been through this before. Neighbors had complained to the landlord but Buzz had always been able to clean up his errant experiments quickly and fix any problems. Charred walls were covered with freshly hung, rearranged posters. Broken glass was replaced immediately. Buzz always managed to avoid eviction. The landlord lived an hour away and Buzz figured, in a worst-case scenario, he had just about that much time to make any needed repairs. They had it down to a science. Jenny ran inside while Harv threw the bigger pieces of broken glass into a trashcan.

"Harv, can you do me a small favor while I clean up here?"

"Yeah, I know. It looks like two pieces of eight-by-twelve window glass. They're running a tab for you at the hardware store."

"Thanks, man. I owe you."

"I know you do."

Harv drove his freshly cleaned car to the hardware store on Charles Street to get the glass. On returning, Sheila helped Jenny straighten up inside while Harv and Buzz replaced the windowpanes.

After celebrating a fifty-three minute repair job, Harv and Sheila walked over to the Charles River. June sunshine made the water glisten. White sails glided across the surface while several rowing shells cut through the water with oars stroking in unison.

"You know you really need to get a new car."

"Yeah, I guess."

"There's a beautiful white Audi parked on my street with a For Sale sign on it. You ought to take a look at it."

"Yeah, maybe I'll look at it when I get back."

They walked along the grassy riverbank holding hands, talking about cars and the upcoming trip to Philadelphia.

Their path took them back to Beacon Street and over to Newbury Street, past the art galleries and boutiques before they stopped at a little outdoor café for a bite to eat. Ferns hung down from the awning and the aroma of some pleasant seasoning wafted through the open window. After sitting down, Sheila ordered a broccoli quiche and a bottle of mineral water. Harv ordered a ham sandwich and a Miller draft. He eyed the list of mineral waters on the menu and shook his head.

They talked about Sheila's latest assignment at *Boston Today* where she worked as Assistant Fashion Editor. Soon after the meal arrived, Harv picked up her bottle of mineral water and looked at the label.

"Chateau Chardelais de Puess." He read the name printed in script over a castle. It was an exotic label with extensive design work, flags, heraldic shields, lion heads, and very small print. "This is French."

"The words are French. The product is Swiss actually." Sheila squirmed in her chair.

Harv took a drink from the bottle, swallowed slowly as if to savor it, then smiled saying nothing as he put the bottle down. Immediately, he reached for the glass of ice water the waiter had poured when they first sat down, took a long sip and paused. "Now there's some good water."

Sheila raised her eyebrows.

"Mmm! I wonder how much the waiter is charging us for this water." Harv took another long sip from the glass. "You know, it really doesn't matter how much he charges. It's going to be worth it. This water is so incredible."

Sheila gave a sarcastic smile. "You know Mother is really looking forward to meeting you."

"I met your dad. He seemed fine"

"Well, Mother and Dad are a little different."

"Different? How so?"

"Oh," Sheila paused and poked a fork into her quiche. "Just different. You'll see." She took a swallow of mineral water. "But that's the main reason you're coming down is to see Mother."

"Yes, I know. Somehow I think it's more for your mother to see me."

"Oh, don't be silly. Mother's an absolute dear. You'll love her. Besides Daddy already met you and adores you; so Mother will adore you too. And you'll adore her." She swirled her straw in the Chateau Chardelais de Puess. "After all, it's important, don't you think?"

"What's important?" Harv spoke through a mouthful of ham sandwich.

"To meet each other's family before we . . . you know. Before we get engaged or anything. After all, I've met your parents."

"That's because they live here in Boston. It was easy."

"And flying down to Philadelphia will be just as easy." She took a bite of quiche.

"I'm sure it will be."

CHAPTER 5

The Lexington village green looked like a carpet spread out under the ancient oaks hovering over the town. Harvey passed the minuteman statue and took his third left off Fieldstone Lane. It was seven o'clock and the sun had the warm glow it gets just before setting. The street gradually took on a mellow, established look as stone walls lined each side of the road, and driveways rambled back to stately homes.

At Oak Hill Drive, Harv turned left up Peter Burke's long driveway and headed toward the house. Driving slowly past the row of Mercedes, Jags, and BMW's, he was glad he'd taken the time to wash his dented Chevy.

"Excuse me sir." A uniformed security guard appeared next to Harv's open window. "May I help you?" His voice was well modulated and overly polite.

"I don't think so. Just looking for a parking place." Harv turned and headed back along another row of cars parked on the big side lawn.

"Excuse me sir." The attendant doggedly kept pace with the car. "I think you may have made a wrong turn."

"Ah, there's a place." Harv turned in beside a gray Lexus.

The guard came running up to him. "Look, pal, this

is a private affair. I'll give you thirty seconds to get yourself and this heap outa here." The well-modulated tone was gone.

Harv slowly got out of his car, shut the door and locked it. Then he turned around and leveled a gaze at the security guard. The man wore a tan uniform with knee-high leather boots, a brown cap, and a nametag over his left coat pocket that said: *A. Corvelli, Peterson Security.*

"You know, Corvelli," said Harvey, "Pinkerton's uniforms are a lot smarter looking."

"Listen wise guy—"

"You listen pal." Harvey stopped the guard with his mouth open. "First of all," Harv reached in his wallet and produced an ADI security card Peter had given him. "I'm a major consultant for ADI. I'm invited to this bash every year."

The guard looked at the card with Harv's photo, closed his mouth, and took a step backward.

"Secondly, I don't like you very much, Corvelli. You make a real shitty first impression. You're rude, you're superficial, and that uniform really sucks."

The guard lowered his voice. "Sir if you had told me you—"

"You didn't ask either did you."

"Well, I uh."

"Now, I'm going up to the party and I'll be talking with Mr. Burke about what an asshole you are, Corvelli."

"Sir, I'm really—"

"You picked a bad day to screw up, Corvelli." Harv

began walking up to the house. "I'm in a really crappy mood."

"Sir, I'm—"

"And another thing, Corvelli." Harv turned around facing the guard twenty feet away.

"Yes sir?"

"I don't want to see any dents in my car when I get back."

"Yes sir, uh, no sir."

Harv turned and walked up to the driveway. He wondered if he'd been too hard on the guy, but he was tired and didn't really give a damn at this point. Maybe he should get some of the dents removed. Maybe buy a new car. He'd think about that when he got back from Philadelphia.

The big white house stood proudly on top of a knoll overlooking a long horseshoe driveway. It looked serene under the canopy of poplars and oaks overhead. It was classic New England architecture with dark green shutters, a steeply-sloped roof, slate shingles, and dormers.

The low din of laughter and conversation danced down the lawn as Harv approached the house. People were sitting out on the front porch. For the first few minutes he didn't see anyone he knew well enough to talk to. He was too tired to initiate conversation with anyone he didn't know very well. He ran into two engineers he knew from the fiber optics division and engaged in a little idle talk on his way to the open bar in the living room. Reaching for an hors d'oeuvre on the passing tray, he heard his name called out and saw

Paul Sheridan, holding his drink in the air, winding past two guests.

"Harv, I've been looking for you."

"Hey, Paul, how you doing?" Harv patted Sheridan on the arm. "Peter's got you working pretty hard these days, I hear." Sheridan worked for Ted Bass and ultimately for Peter.

"Yeah, it's been unbelievable these past two weeks. How did that session go yesterday? I'm sorry I couldn't make it."

Harv had to assume Sheridan was ignorant of the mystery woman incident. In fact he had to assume everyone was ignorant of it except Peter and Howard. "It went fine," said Harv. "The new instruction manual worked like a charm."

"Thank God." Sheridan took a long tug on his martini.

They talked about the selection dial as Tom Keen walked up and joined them. Tom also worked for Bass in the Marketing Department but wasn't assigned to the Ultra 500 at this point. Harv knew him from previous assignments.

"Hey stranger," Keen said to Sheridan. "Hi, Harv." He paused and ordered a beer from the bartender. "Jesus, Harv, you look like hell."

"Thanks, Tom; it's a look I'm trying to cultivate."

"Well you've nailed it," said Keen.

"Actually, I do feel like hell. This bastard here is working me like a dog."

"Hey, misery loves company," said Sheridan. "If I'm going to be working my ass off, I don't want to be alone."

They talked shop until the voice of Peter Burke broke into the conversation.

"Now there's a mean-looking group." Peter walked up to them and smiled, putting his hands on the shoulders of Harv and Sheridan as they parted to make way for the man. Peter had a controlled warmth he could turn on and off at will. "How you doing, Harv?"

"Terrific," said Harvey. "I just got here."

"You look tired," said Peter. "You OK?"

"It's a look he's trying to cultivate." Keen took a swallow of beer.

Peter smiled. "No, I'm serious. You all right?"

"Yeah, I'm fine." Harv shrugged it off and changed the subject to the focus groups, which his host was happy to talk about.

Peter was not a tall man, about five feet nine inches with an average build. He had a self-assured, powerful presence, however, and penetrating, dark eyes that seemed to absorb everything.

"I hate to break up this bull session, guys," said Peter, "but, Harv, I need to talk to you a second." He patted Harv on the shoulder with a slight squeeze. That subtle squeeze, undetectable to the rest of the universe, spoke volumes. It told Harv that Peter knew about the mystery woman incident and wanted to talk about it. It said that no one else in the group knew, and that it was important to keep things quiet.

Harv extricated himself from the conversation and followed his host. They walked past the bar, through the central foyer, down a hall and into the den toward the back of the house. Burke closed the French doors behind them, cutting the party noises to a low gurgle.

The den was massive with wood paneling, leather sofas and chairs, pricey artwork, and an antique pool table. A moose head hung over the fireplace with a straw hat placed strategically on its head between the antlers. Framed photographs dotted the wall, showing Peter with various important people. Harvey assumed they were important. One was the governor; he did recognize him.

Peter poured brandy into two snifters, handed one to Harv, and immediately launched into a discussion of the mystery woman. Harv sat on the sofa while Peter sat in the big, stuffed chair in front of his desk. It was not as penetrating and serious a discussion as Chuck Weitz had conducted. In fact, Peter treated it fairly lightly. He asked a few questions Weitz hadn't, about the appearance of the woman, her voice, her movements. Like Chuck, he impressed on Harv the importance of keeping the matter totally secret. He also said how common this sort of thing was, especially when competing head-to-head with the Chinese and Russians.

Harv began to feel better about things. The brandy felt warm going down and helped him unwind. He told Peter about Bill Cobb and Roger Cornish at his meeting with Chuck and what Cornish had said about jeopardizing the ST-37 rocket system.

Peter took a sip of brandy and smiled. "That poor, misguided bastard." He shook his head. "The revenue potential alone makes it worth doing. Even if there were a security risk, which there isn't, the ST-37 is outdated technology as far as defense is concerned. And on the consumer side, the wave accelerator is useless without the security codes to activate it. Without those codes, the thing is nothing more than an expensive paper weight."

"I knew if you were there you'd be able to shut him up."

Peter smiled like a father hearing his son say something cute. "Don't worry. I'm on top of that situation. But thanks for bringing it to my attention. I think Roger and I are going to have a little one-on-one next week."

Peter talked about what a good job Harv was doing for ADI and how exhausted he looked. "You know, Harv, when I see you, I see myself when I was your age. You're a workaholic."

"No, I work hard but—"

"No *buts*. Believe me. I know the signs. Remember that Paco Gold project five years ago?"

"Yeah." Harv smiled, leaning his head back on the soft leather.

"You went to the wall on that for us and so did I."

The Paco Gold product they worked on together for Pan American Foods was a real dog. It was bad coffee, poorly processed with antiquated equipment. Harv was Account Executive at the advertising agency handling the account for Peter. When Pan American decided to unload the brand, they all put their heads together and came up with a marketing plan that made the product look terrific. They worked long hours for three months and finally unloaded the entire Paco Gold Division on an unsuspecting Mexican company for more than it was worth.

"It paid off," said Harv.

"Yeah, we were lucky. Some people will drink anything." Peter took a long sip of brandy. "Seriously, you know where I went after we signed that deal?"

"You went on some vacation or something didn't you?"

"It was a vacation all right. It was two months forced sabbatical under doctor's orders." Peter got up, walked behind his desk and took two cigars out of a wooden box. "I was suffering from extreme exhaustion the doctor said."

"Jeez, I didn't know."

"No one knew, except Nancy. I'm supposed to be mister iron-man, remember?"

"You do have that reputation."

"I know. And don't you go blowing the whistle on me either." Peter pointed at Harv with one of the cigars poised between his fingers. He retrieved a cigar cutter from the desk drawer, nipped off the ends of both cigars and gave one to Harv. Even though Harvey didn't smoke, he indulged in a good cigar about twice a year when the occasion called for it. Peter lit his cigar with a large silver lighter shaped like a horse head, which he then handed to Harv.

Harv lit up and took a slow draw. "Mmm, good cigar."

"Oughta be."

"Oh," Harv smiled, "one of Cuba's best?"

"Something like that."

Harv took a drag on his cigar, got up and walked over to one of the framed photographs on the wall. "You have a lot of cool stuff here." He looked carefully. "Here's a picture of you and the governor. Here's one of you and Nancy with that defense secretary guy who's on TV all the time."

"They bring back good memories."

Harv scanned the wall. "It looks like they all have you in them."

Burke smiled. "Now wait a minute. There's a picture over there without me in it." He pointed with the cigar between his fingers.

Harv walked over and looked. "Wow, a picture with you actually *not* in it. Very humble of you."

Peter laughed. "Actually, that's a very important photograph."

Harv looked at it again. "So, what's the story? It just looks like two guys standing on a lawn."

"That guy on the right is Vladimir Asakov, notorious arms and technology pirate. Deals with terrorists, rogue regimes; anyone who will pay his price." He paused, took a sip of brandy and shook his head. "The other gentleman is Stanley Coleman, Engineering chief for Altex International."

"Altex? The aeronautical engineering firm?"

"That's right. The FBI suspected he might be the guy leaking some serious stuff to the Russians but they could never catch him. This photo is the nail in the coffin that put Coleman away."

"But how did you get hold of it?"

"I saw this photo in a defense industry trade publication back when I was working in New York before I came here. The article talked about this new drone technology developed by ADI."

"Our ADI?"

"None other. It's our Hummingbird W-15 drone. It

can hover in mid-air. It's silent, and has a telephoto lens capable of taking incredible pictures from great distances. Amazing technology." Burke put down his cigar and looked at his watch. "When they approached me for this marketing gig two years later, I already had a positive impression of the company."

"I'd heard about the Hummingbird drone, but it was always so hush-hush and I've had practically zero contact with the defense side of the business."

"Drones, Harv. That's where it's at. With this technology, combined with existing satellite capabilities, the bad guys are scratching their heads." He looked at his watch again. "Listen, Harv, I've got to go, but seriously, I want you to take it easy for a while."

"I know. I'm taking some time off."

"When?"

"Next week, after I hand in that focus group report."

"Good, you deserve it." He paused and took another puff. "I need you rested and charged up."

"Wednesday I'm outa here."

"Hell, you look so tired, I'll bet Beth hasn't even made a pass at you tonight."

Beth Dreyfus was Peter's executive assistant. She was a single, liberated graduate of Bennington who made no secret of her attraction to Harv.

"Give her time," said Harv. "I haven't been here that long."

Burke smiled, put his cigar into a small guillotine on his desk and cut off the tip. "This is officially a non-smoking house, Harv, outside my office. I'm afraid we have to behead our cigars before rejoining the troops."

Harv put his cigar in the device and smashed off the tip. "More like a targeted circumcision."

Peter laughed. "Yes, I have a rabbi I rent this out to periodically."

Harv smiled and put the cigar in his inside jacket pocket. "I'll save this for later."

Burke gave Harv a warm pat on the back, and they both went out to mingle with the other guests.

After refilling his empty brandy snifter at the bar, Harv walked through the living room toward the pool area out back.

On the way, he met Ed Railsdorf, head of technical research and chief engineer of ADI's weapons division. Ed was convinced engineering was the backbone of the business and that engineers were smarter than the rest of the world. He resented marketing type people having any influence over his creative genius. Cobb had instructed Railsdorf to sit in on several marketing meetings and familiarize himself with the consumer marketplace, but it was an assignment Railsdorf detested, one in which he invested as little energy as possible.

"Hi, Ed," said Harv, unable to avoid the overweight engineer.

"Oh, hello . . . uh, yes Gallagher, right?"

Harv knew that Railsdorf knew his name, having met with him on several occasions. He was also aware of the man's negative attitude toward marketing in general and outside consultants in particular.

"Right, Harvey Gallagher." Harv extended his arm, forcing Railsdorf to switch his drink to his left hand

and shake hands. "We missed you at the focus group yesterday."

"Busy, busy," Railsdorf said, "can't be two places at once."

"You know, Ed, that is so true."

"Uh, excuse me." He looked past Harv to a group of people a few feet away. "I have to talk with someone over there."

"Oh, absolutely, Ed." Harv looked over at the group. "In fact they told me they wanted to talk to you."

Railsdorf looked surprised.

"Something about your fly being open."

The engineer quickly looked down, spilling his drink while Harv turned, took a swig of brandy, and walked through the open patio doors to the pool.

Outside, he met up with Ted Bass and Howard Cohen, who were talking about the focus groups and the selection dial. Their wives chatted quietly, holding plastic cocktail glasses with leaves sticking out of them.

"Still talking shop I see," said Harv walking up to them.

They greeted Harv, as did their wives whom he'd met several times before. The three men talked about the Ultra 500, all agreeing the focus groups went well. It was obvious from the conversation that Bass had not been told about the mystery woman and that Howard was keeping things under his hat. After a while, Harv noticed a buffet on the south side of the pool and realized he hadn't eaten dinner. Excusing himself, he wandered over to the food.

Several people were in the pool but most were still

in their party clothes just standing around enjoying the fresh air, balancing little plastic plates of food with their drinks. Men were decked out in their summer madras, or linen sports coats, the women in pastel party dresses. Harv wore a summer-weight navy blue blazer with a red paisley tie and tan pants.

Grabbing a plate at the buffet table, Harv noticed Beth Dreyfus standing at the other side of the pool in the skimpiest of bikinis. He tried not to stare, but she was virtually naked. He noticed the small swatch of red cloth that passed for a bathing suit bottom and the two strings tied at the hips. She had a great tan for so early in the season. Harv looked away. He didn't want to deal with Beth tonight. He tried talking with a couple he didn't know in front of the buffet table, but he was too late. The voice coming up behind him was unmistakable.

"Hello, Harv. I was hoping I'd see you here." Beth was a tall woman, about five feet eight, brownish hair with blond highlights, and she was brilliant.

Harv tried not to stare at her push up bikini top displaying her breasts.

"Hi, Beth. I'm not here for long," Harv said as she sidled up to him.

"No?"

"No I'm exhausted and feel like hell."

"You look pretty good to me." She leered over the top of her drink, tipping it slowly to her mouth.

Harv managed to keep the conversation mostly on business. He was used to her overt flirting, but it was always when she had more clothes on. Sometimes he wondered what she'd do if he ever flirted back. He didn't want to find out. She was potentially a loose cannon, and he didn't want to do anything to mess up his solid relationship with Peter and with ADI. He had to tread a fine line between keeping her at bay and not alienating her. It was additional stress he didn't need, particularly not tonight. But Beth seemed to be on her good behavior and talked with Harv about the focus groups and some of the other projects going on at work.

"So how's what's-her-face, that skinny thing you were going out with?"

"Sheila? You know Sheila; you just saw her three weeks ago."

"Yeah, whatever."

"We're almost engaged."

Harv's thigh began to vibrate. He hoped it wasn't a reaction to Beth's semi-naked body. "So I guess you're still going out—"

"Hold on; my phone's vibrating." He grabbed the phone in his pants pocket. On discovering it was Chuck Weitz, Harv put up his hand to beg off his conversation and walked around the corner of the pool to an unpopulated area.

"Chuck, how you doing?"

"I'm doing OK I think," said Chuck. "I'll be working all weekend on this little situation of ours. Listen, what's your schedule Monday?"

"Monday? I'm going into my office Monday morning, get this report typed up for you guys, then drop it off up in Marketing."

"Can you stop by my office when you're here?"

"Yeah, sure. Anything wrong?" Harv looked around.

"Something's come up about that mystery woman on Friday."

"You find out who she was?" Harv lowered his voice.

"I can't really talk about it on the phone, but you may be in a position to help us."

Harv glanced over his shoulder. "I was thinking something like early afternoon I'd be over there. What's a good time for you?"

"As soon as you can get here."

CHAPTER 6

Harv pulled into ADI's parking lot. The corporate headquarters were in a large, glass, four-story office building located in a park-like setting north of Boston. Mid-day sunshine glared off the big glass doors at the front entrance, and Harv noticed the odor of cleaning fluid as he walked over the newly-polished floor to the security desk.

"Hi, Mr. Gallagher, how are you today?"

"Hi, Jimmy." Harv greeted Jimmy Jarvis at the front desk and signed in. He'd gotten to know Jimmy fairly well while sitting in the reception area adjacent to the security desk whenever Peter, Ted or whoever he was visiting happened to be running late, which was most of the time.

"Peter Burke?" Jimmy asked.

"No, I'm seeing Chuck Weitz today." Harv signed his name in the visitor's register. "Good day for a jog, huh?"

"Got my two miles in this morning." Jimmy handed Harv a security badge and called Chuck's office. After a brief exchange, he nodded his head and hung up. "You can go right on down. No waiting today."

"Hey, at last I'm getting some respect around here."

Jimmy smiled as Harv pinned the badge on his breast pocket and headed for the elevators.

He pushed the button for the fourth floor. The focus group report was all freshly printed and he wanted to drop it off in Marketing before going down to see Chuck in the basement. It didn't matter whether Ted or Peter were there or not; their secretaries would make sure it got to the right hands. He gave the report to Bass's secretary and headed down to see Chuck.

The decor on the basement level had decidedly less teak and brass with more of an informal cement and chrome look.

There was no waiting in Chuck's anteroom. As soon as Harv was announced, Weitz came out of his office and greeted him with a warm handshake. "Come on with me." He motioned Harv toward the outer door.

"What do you have?"

"Well," Chuck moved out into the hallway, "I wanted to update you on that situation we discussed last week."

Following Chuck into the wide corridor, Harv surmised the security chief hadn't yet told his secretary about the mystery woman. "Is your office bugged or something?"

"No," Chuck smiled, "but I think it would be better talking down in the security lab. The reports are down there and some other things I want to show you."

Approaching the end of the hall, Weitz reached in his breast pocket and pulled out a small plastic card which he placed in a slot on the right side of the wall. Instantly, there was a humming sound, and two steel doors withdrew sideways into the wall, revealing an opening through which the two men passed. On the other side, Weitz put his card in another slot and the doors came together. He then escorted Harv down a corridor, lined with stainless steel skin, and turned left at an elevator staging area. Weitz pressed a button on the wall and spoke into a black microphone. "Chuck Weitz, three seven two."

"Jesus, pretty tight security," said Harv as the elevator doors opened.

"It's voice specific."

Harv joined Chuck in the elevator and watched the doors close behind him. "You mean if I said 'Chuck Weitz three seven two' into that microphone, it would know it?"

"If anyone ever tried to pass themselves off as me or anyone else, they'd be in some pretty steep shit."

The elevator started downward. "I thought we were already in the basement."

Weitz smiled as lights flashed over the door, and the slow decent continued. After thirty seconds it stopped, the doors opened, and the two men walked out into another steel and glass corridor. They rounded a corner and headed for a sign that said *Security Lab*. As Chuck inserted his card again, a red light turned on and the door opened.

It was a large room with bright walls of stainless steel and white paneling and had a suspended floor that vibrated when they walked. Around the perimeter, different workstations displayed high tech, exotic-looking projects. Tables were covered with wires, and gray, metal housings in peculiar shapes. Organized sets of tools and instruments were lined up on racks along the walls. Harv was struck by how incredibly neat and clean it all looked, almost like a hospital operating room. Colored tubes and wires shot out of the ceiling and led to different workstations. Bright purple tubes stood out against the white ceiling and stainless steel walls. Red and orange cables led from the walls to unrecognizable power tools, looking light years beyond anything Black and Decker had dreamed of. Yellow tubes went from each workstation up along the ceiling and exited the side walls.

"This place looks like it was designed by the combined efforts of Mr. Science and Salvador Dali."

Chuck laughed. "Just don't touch anything."

They walked over to a workstation that was messier than the others. Sitting on top were the mystery woman's purse and its contents, some computer reports, and several charts.

"You call anyone like the FBI?"

"They were here Saturday."

"Are they going to do anything?" Harv looked over the workstation and pulled up a stool.

"They're going to do some initial snooping around but there's only so much they can do now. As they pointed out, all we really have is a woman who tried to steal part of an ultrasound oven." He flipped through the computer reports. "I'm not sure they share my concern that it's perhaps much more than that."

"Like corporate espionage?"

Chuck smiled. "You're getting warm. Let's just say I don't get a real comfortable sense of focus and energy on their part. That's why you may be able to help us." Chuck put down the printouts, picked up the makeup, and looked directly at Harv. "Let me walk you through this."

"We can touch this stuff now?"

"Yes, everything's been dusted and analyzed. We ran the prints and got zip. But the other tests we did are kind of interesting." He tossed the plastic compact to Harv.

"Make-up," said Harv, catching it in both hands.

"Not just any make-up but if you look on the back, you see *The House of Fontaine*."

Harv turned it over, scrutinizing the small letters.

"Our FBI friends ran it through their computer and it's apparently a third-rate cosmetics outfit headquartered in Montreal, distributed throughout Canada and the northeastern U.S."

Harv opened the compact, sniffed the contents and placed it back on the table.

"We had our lab check out the powder. Apparently it's really crappy stuff, heavy and unrefined."

"So what does that mean?"

"I don't know yet. We called the technicians down at the FDA with the specs we turned up. They're really the ones who told us it was crap. They'll be talking with their Canadian counterparts to see if we can find out anything more. We're having the puff checked for skin flakes."

"So what else do we have?" Harv grabbed the coupon. "A hamburger coupon."

"Not just any hamburger coupon," added Chuck.

"Oh, that's right. Not just any coupon but a Burger World coupon. Good for one dollar off any Burger

World hamburger." He looked up. "What does that tell us?"

"I'll get into that later."

"Oh, and here we have a pack of chewing gum." Harv reached for the pack. "Let me guess. Not just any chewing gum but . . ." He carefully examined the small package. "Hell, this is just regular gum."

"That's right." Chuck smiled. "Just everyday Wrigley's Spearmint. Sold everywhere. No prints to speak of. No big deal."

"So where are we?"

"Well, with this stuff and the tissue paper," Weitz motioned to the Kleenex still inside a plastic bag, "all in all it doesn't look like much. We're having the Kleenex checked too for skin flakes, saliva and the like." He walked around to the other side of the workstation. "But there's more here than meets the eye." Chuck grabbed a large plastic map of the U.S. and placed it on an easel. "Walk through this with me for a minute. First of all, we know the House of Fontaine distributes its products in the U.S. only in the states of New York, New Jersey and the six New England states." He took a black marker, outlined the area mentioned, and drew large black lines through the balance of the country to block it out.

"Gee, this looks like set theory."

"Sort of." Chuck referred to one of his printouts and picked up the top sheet. "We also noted the location of each Burger World joint in our area." He grabbed a red marker and began placing dots in selected locations. "They're all over the country, as you know, but in our area there are twenty-three of them" He put the remaining red dots on the map while referring to the printout list in his other hand.

"Amazing," said Harv, sitting up straight. "So you think this woman lives in one of those twenty-three towns?"

"I'm not saying where she lives, but there's a high probability she's spent time in one of them."

"Chuck, let me ask you a question. Why are you going over all this stuff with me?"

Weitz lowered his arm and looked straight at Harv. "Because I'm going to ask you to do something in a few minutes and I don't think it makes sense to ask a person to do something unless they've been part of the decision making process that led to that request."

Harv nodded. "That's good. I like that. So how do you know which of these twenty-three towns we're after?"

Chuck picked up the purse. "You know, cloth is interesting stuff. It absorbs material from the air. It lets you know where it's been and where it hasn't been." He held up the purse and squished the material with his right hand. "We analyzed the fabric over at Arlington Labs."

"What did you find?"

"Well, first of all we didn't find a sufficiently high level of hydrocarbon deposits to indicate it had spent much time in any of the urban locations on our map." Chuck took the black marker and crossed out all the red dots in urban areas.

"You mean car emissions build up in cloth?"

"Car emissions, factory smoke, especially in cloth that doesn't get washed regularly like a purse."

"So, you've got five locations left."

"Well, we also found an extraordinary high level of salt in the fabric. You don't need to know the exact level but it was high. In fact the only way to get that high a level is to be right on salt water. It's in the air." He handed the purse to Harv. "Notice the metal loops holding the strap to the bag? See how they're partly corroded?"

"Son of a bitch." Harv examined the purse carefully.

"That's also the salt. Here, I'll let you solve the puzzle." He extended a big green marker to Harvey. "Come up here and circle the location yourself."

Taking the marker from Weitz, Harv walked up to the map. Four of the five remaining dots were inland, quite a distance from the ocean. There was one lone dot, however, on the coast of Maine right at the head of a cove winding in from Penobscot Bay. Harv put a green circle around the village of Black Hill Cove. "Damn, that's amazing. So you think the woman is from Black Hill Cove, Maine?"

"I'd bet she's spent some time there, or her purse has at least."

Harv walked back to his stool. "I am really impressed." He shook his head looking up at the map. "OK, what's the deal here? What are you going to ask me to do?"

"Didn't you say you were taking some kind of vacation next week?"

Harv nodded his head. "Yeah . . ."

"How would you feel about taking your vacation in Maine?"

"Maine?"

"Listen, I think there may be something heavy going on here, and I think Black Hill Cove may have a role it. But it's all speculation at this point. I need someone to go up there and snoop around a bit. Turn up something concrete."

"And you want me to go? This is my vacation don't forget."

"I don't want you to work. I want you to have fun, relax, enjoy yourself. Just keep your eyes and ears open."

"What about the FBI? Isn't that their job?"

"Frankly, Harv, they weren't as impressed with my little dog and pony show as you were. There are some flaws it. Hell, she could have gotten that coupon at the Burger World three blocks from here."

"But the hydrocarbon deposits."

"Exactly. It's not any one thing; it's the whole picture. It all seems to point to here." He tapped on the map where Harv had circled. "It could all be circumstantial but I don't think so. They said they might send an agent up there but they couldn't do it for a week. And frankly, as I said, they don't seem to think this is as serious as I do."

"Chuck, hold on." Harv put up his hand. "There's a basic issue here I don't seem to be getting across. I've made vacation plans for Philadelphia. I have a plane ticket."

"Philadelphia?" Chuck smiled. "Actually that's no problem. Any money you're out we'll reimburse you. Plus we'll pay for your stay in Maine."

"You'll pay my room and board?"

"That's right. And we'll pay your normal weekly consulting rate plus a bonus of twenty percent."

Harv rubbed his hand through his hair. "My weekly fee plus expenses, plus a bonus?"

"That's right."

Harv shook his head as the security chief's words gradually sank in. "Chuck, let me ask you something. Why me?"

Weitz leaned back on the workstation. "Two reasons, Harvey. First of all there's a security reason. You already know about it, and I don't want to open the loop up to anyone else at this point. Word of this on the street could send stock prices in the dumper. And secondly, the most important reason, you're the one who knows what she looks like. You know how she moves. That was quite an ordeal you had. You learn a lot about a person in a situation like that. Hell, you're the best person in the world to do this."

Chuck told him a reservation had been made at the Captain Hawkins House in Black Hill Cove, and they were expecting him Wednesday evening.

"And there's no hidden catch to this or anything?"

Weitz smiled. "No catch. Just keep your eye open for this woman, ask a few questions and see if anything unusual is going on. Reservation expires the following Thursday. That's eight days."

Harv looked at the map. "And that's it?"

"That and try to relax and get some rest."

Harv stood up and nodded his head. "Chuck, let me make a phone call and you've got yourself a deal."

CHAPTER 7

Katherine Vandenberg Whitmore slammed her fist on the counter. "Can't come? He can't see me?" She stared at her daughter. "What do you mean he can't come? I've made plans."

"Mother, if you'll just—"

"There's not going to be any wedding or any trust fund disbursements until I have met this young man and approve of him. I must say I'm not overly impressed at this stage."

Sheila put her salad on the kitchen table. "But Mother, Daddy already met Harvey and thought he was great."

"Your father," Mrs. Whitmore laughed. "You should see some of the people your father has taken a liking to. He talks to caddies out at the club as if they were his pals." She shook her head and began pacing back and forth. "Some of the people he has actually brought into this house . . ." She threw up her hands and walked briskly out of the room. From the parlor, she retrieved a decanter of sherry, brought it back to the kitchen, and emptied a good portion of it into a glass.

It's not that Sheila was a complete wimp. At twenty-eight years of age she knew she could date anyone she pleased. But her mother oversaw the management of the Vandenberg family trust, a huge portion of which was to be distributed to the children at various stages in their lives if, and only if, Mrs. Whitmore approved of their behavior and lifestyles. The major disbursement was earmarked for the two daughters' wedding days, and if Mrs. Whitmore didn't approve of the groom, there would be no cash. Sheila had been keenly aware of this fact since she was sixteen years old.

"The point is, Mother, I think he's really special, and I know you will too once you've gotten a chance to meet him." Sheila played with her salad.

Mrs. Whitmore took a drink and breathed in deeply. "It's not as if this was the first time this has happened." She took another drink. "I mean what possible reason can he have?"

"He's got some client emergency."

"He's what?"

"Some emergency came up at one of his clients and they're paying him a big bonus to help them with it. You should be impressed. His clients really need him."

Mrs. Whitmore grabbed a Hershey's Kiss from her purse, unwrapped it, and popped it in her mouth. "I just don't understand. I've never seen anything like it." A tendon in her neck flexed as she chewed her chocolate.

She was a large, full-figured woman with long, dark hair attractively streaked with gray. She had the presence and bearing of someone used to getting their way.

"And I'd like to know what, exactly, he does for a

living. What did you say, some kind of a consultant or something?"

"God, Mother do you listen? I've told you a hundred times he's a marketing consultant. And I've told you many times he's doing very well."

"Now there's another thing. You tell me he has no employer. What am I supposed to think? I mean if he were employed by some corporation, he'd have a title and a position and I'd know what to think about him. I mean he'd be the regional manager of this or the assistant manager of that. You know Todd Crumbly is an assistant supervisor down at the bank?"

"Mother, Harvey's the president for God's sake." Sheila banged her fork on the table. "He's the president of Gallagher Associates. Besides what difference does it make? He's happy. He's doing well."

Mrs. Whitmore looked at her daughter in disbelief. "Good Lord, where did you ever get ideas like that? Five years in Boston and your mind has turned to mush. Sheila, the young man's family isn't even in the Boston Social Register. I checked. He doesn't have—"

"Harvey's family doesn't care about social registers." Sheila raised her voice. "They don't care about job titles . . . Jesus, Mother."

"My God, girl, what do they care about? Don't they have any values at all?"

Sheila pushed her chair away from the table and stormed over to look out the window just as the telephone rang. Her mother picked it up, took off her earring, and began chatting away as if nothing had happened. Sheila could tell by her mother's tone of voice it was a social call from one of her lady friends.

The style and tone could shift from family mode to social and back to family in a heartbeat depending on the circumstances.

Mrs. Whitmore's social life was very important to her; maybe too important Sheila sometimes thought. It revolved around the country club, the Junior League, the William Penn Club in downtown Philadelphia and, most importantly, the Daughters of Gettysburg, the most coveted of all memberships. To be a member, a woman must have impeccable social credentials and be able to trace her ancestry back to a Union soldier who fought in the battle of Gettysburg. Over the years it had evolved into the most exclusive and highly prized club affiliation in all of Philadelphia.

Mrs. Whitmore inherited her membership from her mother who was able to trace her genealogy back to a distant grandfather several generations back—an alcoholic Union corporal shot for attempted desertion in the first twenty minutes of the famous battle. On the membership application, the historical documentation was edited to read: "Accidently shot by friendly fire doing rear reconnaissance for the Union faithful." The Daughters of Gettysburg, or DOG's as non-members called them, occupied themselves with two main activities: one, keeping others out and two, figuring out things to do in order to justify their existence. The organization was the centerpiece of Mrs. Whitmore's active social life, and over the years it took up a great deal of her time and energy.

The telephone call helped to cool things off a bit and the two women resumed talking in a more harmonious manner. They agreed that Harvey would come down after he got back.

When the phone rang a second time, the conversation had mellowed considerably. Mrs. Whitmore picked up the phone again, shaking her long hair away from her ear. "Hello." She resumed her perky telephone voice. "Yes dear."

From the way her mother said *dear*, Sheila could tell it was her father on the other end.

"Work late again?" She put her hand over the phone and spoke to Sheila. "It's your father . . . Yes, Alan, I know you have to set an example." She ran her fingers through her hair like a comb in an effort to spruce up a bit as if somehow her husband could see her. "By the way, dear, apparently we won't be having a house guest this week . . . That's right. We'll be going to the club Thursday night after all . . . Oh, I don't want to go into it now. We'll discuss it when you get home." She asked her husband to stop by the jewelry store downtown and pick up one of her bracelets that had been repaired, and after a few more pleasantries, handed the phone to Sheila.

"Hi, Daddy." Sheila never really talked much with her father, who was out of the house working most of the time. He was the one from whom she inherited the slight build and high metabolism. She had the attractive features of her mother but they were more finely chiseled and refined like her father's.

After handing the receiver back to her mother, Sheila walked out of the room and passed through the foyer leading to the front door. The double doors opened out onto steps going down to the sweeping front lawn. She walked over to the garden, sat down on the swing, and started swinging. Throwing her head back, she drank in the aroma of honeysuckles surrounding her.

"Sheila." Mrs. Whitmore's loud voice rippled across the lawn.

"Yes, Mother." Sheila kept swinging.

"I've made some calls and rearranged my plans so we can see this friend of yours the weekend after next."

"Oh, that's great, Mother."

"That should be enough advance notice for this Harvey person I should think."

"Great, Mother." She kicked the swing higher.

"Oh and another thing, dear." It was a different *dear* than the one used for Mr. Whitmore and quite distinct from the *dear* used with her friends. Sheila and her sister's *dears* were always more maternal and authoritative sounding.

"Yes, Mother."

"We're going to the Penn Club tomorrow night with Dorothy and Jeff. We'd love it if you'd join us."

"Oh great, Mother. That sounds like fun." It really didn't, but with Harv not there, she thought it would, at least, be something to break up the boredom.

Dorothy Biddles was Mrs. Whitmore's best friend. The two women had a relationship very much like Don Quixote and Sancho Panza, with Mrs. Whitmore being Don Quixote. They did everything together, sold cookbooks for the Junior League, played bridge, and dined at the William Penn club. Everything except participate in the hallowed activities of the Daughters of Gettysburg. Dorothy Biddles had outstanding social credentials and very much wanted to be a member, but when the issue of new members was addressed, her application was always rejected. Mrs. Whitmore would console her and talk her through the sad ordeal, coaching her, and promising to introduce Dorothy to more members.

As the dominant personality in the relationship, Mrs. Whitmore enjoyed her role as social Svengali to her appreciative best friend. Yet despite all her help and assistance, no offer of membership ever materialized. The members seemed to like Dorothy, but every even numbered year on the first day of July, when the secret voting box was passed around in the dark, somehow a single black marble found its way into the pile of white ones. No one in the club ever wondered if it came from the same source every vote. It could have come from a different member each time.

Although the blackball system was completely anonymous, Sheila suspected she knew the source of that solitary black marble. She knew how important her mother's relationship was with Dorothy Biddles. She knew how important the balance of that relationship was. She knew her mother liked things the way they were. Privately, in the dark recesses of her mind, she suspected that black marble came from her mother.

CHAPTER 8

Driving up Route 95, Harv started to relax. It was good to get away, and he liked a road trip now and then to clean the cobwebs out of his brain. The packet of information Chuck had given him included directions, and a confirmation for his reservation at the Captain Hawkins House in Black Hill Cove. He looked at the map, ran his finger up the west side of Penobscot Bay and found the little village of Black Hill Cove circled in red. Harv had forgotten how big the state of Maine was. On the map it looked bigger than the rest of New England combined.

The car raced northward as darkness crept in around it. In the twilight, Harv could see the trees gradually changing to tall firs and white birch. After considerable time and many turns onto smaller roads, Harv eventually saw the dark presence of a mountain straight ahead. With its peak standing out against the moonlit sky, Harv knew it had to be Black Hill.

On the map it looked as though Black Hill and its neighbor, Crotchet Mountain, formed a natural barrier, cutting off the village of Black Hill Cove from the rest of the state. The road wound its way around the mountain base and into town.

At ten o'clock he reached the Captain Hawkins

House, a three-story white colonial building in the center of town with a wooden sign out front. He wondered how the place could stay in business without some kind of neon sign. It had a stately appearance, gracious, old, and well maintained. He walked up to the front desk at the far end of the lobby, passing two highly detailed sailboat models displayed on the walls.

"Gallagher, I've got a reservation." Harvey ended the statement as though it were a question directed at the old woman walking up to the desk.

"Got a first name?"

"Yeah, Harvey. You have a lot of Gallaghers here tonight?"

"*E, F, G, G.*" She thumbed through her reservation file ignoring Harv's question. "Nope, no Gallagher, sorry. And we're full up."

"Listen, I'm tired. I just drove all the way from Boston. How about ADI Corporation? They're paying for it."

She gave Harv a stern look and fumbled through the cards again.

"Eah, we got an ADI for a mister H. Gallagher."

"Terrific, that's me."

"Got an ID?"

Harvey took out his wallet and thrust his driver's license down on the counter.

The woman carefully examined the license with its small picture of Harvey and looked up. "Don't look much like ya."

"I've gotten cuter."

She mumbled something and slowly copied the information from his license onto a registration card.

After what seemed an inordinate amount of time, she handed him back his license with the registration card to fill out. Finally, when everything was completed, she gave him a key. "Room seven, second floor, third door on the right," she said then immediately turned around and walked back to her knitting.

"Well thank you ever so much." Harv picked up his suitcase.

The room was spacious and clean. He unpacked, washed his face, and wandered downstairs to the restaurant area. The drive up was tiring and he needed to unwind. He ordered a Jack Daniels and took it over to a table in the corner. The room served as both a restaurant and lounge and had the appearance of a restored stable. On the far wall, five-foot tall dividers stood between the tables, the kind of partitions he'd seen between horse stalls, with brass trim and wooden spindles at the top.

After finishing his drink, Harv began to mellow out. He sat back, looking up through the dim lighting at the ancient support beams. When the waitress came up, he ordered a hamburger and potato salad.

"Did this place used to be a stable or something?" he asked.

"Still is sometimes." She smiled and turned to get his order. The spontaneous smile was a refreshing change from his dour reception checking in. It was a nice smile, a happy flash of white teeth and a glint in the eye. He realized he hadn't thought about ADI or Mrs. Whitmore for over two hours.

When the waitress returned with his food, he asked her what she meant about the place being a stable.

She laughed. "You'll have to disregard my sarcasm, I'm kind of tired tonight. I was just referring to some of the customers who drop in from time to time . . . present company excepted, of course."

"That's a relief." Harv asked her about the town, what there was to do, and she told him about the fishing and hiking activities and suggested he stop by the library to pick up some brochures which covered all the activities in the area, along with addresses, maps, and all the information he could want.

Sitting back in his seat, Harv watched her walking away. She had a well-proportioned figure, not pencil thin like Sheila's, but it was nice. He thought about the week ahead and decided to get his ADI snooping out of the way early so he could relax and enjoy the balance of his vacation. He thought about Sheila and about Mrs. Whitmore. He'd see her after he got back. Right now all he wanted to do was unwind.

While sitting back enjoying his mellow mood, Harv's tranquility was interrupted by sporadic outbursts of laughter and loud talking from the other side of the room. It wasn't constant but just cropped up every few minutes or so. He slowly realized the noise had been going on for quite some time and apparently wasn't going to stop. Irritated that his serenity had been shattered, he finished his drink, put some cash under his plate, and got up to leave.

While exiting, Harv took a wide walk along the far side of the room to check out the source of the noise. Around the corner of an oversized partition, in subdued light, three men talked with animated gestures. They were unshaven and looked like they hadn't bathed in a month. Harv tried to quickly categorize them but couldn't. They weren't bikers or punkers; they looked too bucolic and woodsy for that. Their appearance was strange but not contrived; they looked totally real. Two had long hair and soiled flannel shirts. The third and loudest of the group had a Mohawk haircut and a sleeveless, dirty T-shirt revealing a tattoo on his left arm.

Walking past the table, Harv was tempted to tell them to be quiet. In fact he couldn't understand why no one else had approached them. As he took in the full measure of the situation, however, his first instincts were modified. Something in their faces and their bearing looked like trouble, and Harv was just too tired.

"You got a problem pal?" Mohawk said as Harv turned his head away from the table and walked past. Something inside told him to ignore the question and keep walking. "Hey! I'm talkin' to you," came the voice again as Harv left the room, keeping his eyes straight ahead. Then a loud burst of laughter erupted back at the table.

Passing through the lobby, Harv had a sick feeling inside. Had he chickened out of something, or was he being prudent and mature? He'd never backed away from a fight in his life. Maybe it had something to do with the fact that he'd be sleeping upstairs in the same building, or maybe it had to do with the look of these guys. Perhaps he was just too tired to deal with it. He wasn't sure, but he didn't like it.

CHAPTER 9

The aroma of bacon wafted up from the kitchen and greeted Harvey the next morning. Through his window, he looked across the street and saw the cove glistening like cut glass.

After eating, he checked out the town. The Captain Hawkins House opened out onto Main Street in the village center, and a dock area with several fishing boats stood across the street. Buildings were mostly painted white with black or dark green shutters. Harv decided to follow his waitress's advice and go to the library first. He could pick up some brochures on fishing and see what other activities were available. Plus he could get some general information on the town for ADI, something tangible he could give Chuck to prove he was actually snooping around.

While walking, he noticed there was something different about the place. He wondered where the billboards and parking lots were. The buildings looked like restored older structures with traditional architecture. No steel and glass boxes. Even the Burger World outlet was in a mellowed, established building with a slanted roof and dormers. Harv figured it must be one of their smaller operations. Probably a local franchise.

Perched on a grassy knoll to his right, the library stood next to the town hall. Unlike most of the other buildings, which were wood frame, it was an old brick structure. Inside, wooden beams crisscrossed the ceiling. Harv found the main desk and a small information section off to the side with a display of brochures. He selected one on fishing locations and another on boat rentals. He also got a small map of the area and a community profile with financial and statistical data along with a listing of all major businesses in the area.

Leaning against the reference desk, Harv looked over the information, noting places he could rent a small outboard fishing boat. One was directly opposite the Captain Hawkins House. The community profile he got for Chuck looked good. The facts and statistics about the town might provide some insights.

"May I help you?" A woman's voice interrupted him, an older woman with glasses attached to a silver chain around her neck.

"Oh, no thank you," said Harv. "I'm just looking over these brochures."

"Well they're free as the sign says." She put on her glasses. "If there's anything else you need, let me know." She smiled and shuffled off, looking disappointed she couldn't help.

"Uh, excuse me," Harv called out quietly. "There is one thing you may be able to help me with." He noticed the woman's face light up as she turned around. "Do you have any information on where I can maybe do some hiking, you know, hiking trails or something?"

"I know they do a lot of it around here," she said, walking back to the information area. "We don't have anything in the rack?" She put on her glasses again and ran her finger over the display of brochures.

"I didn't see anything."

"You might want to try the real estate office," she said, still looking through the brochures. "They tend to have a lot more of these things, what with all the Summer rental people going in and out of there."

"Thanks, which real estate office?"

She smiled. "There's only one; Cove Realty, opposite the firehouse on Main Street. You can't miss it."

Harv thanked her and wandered back outside. The morning sun seemed brighter than he remembered. Shafts of light splashed against the buildings on Main Street. He enjoyed the luxury of facing a huge block of unstructured time in front of him, no deadlines, no crises. In the hardware store he struck up a conversation with a man in the fishing tackle area who had a wealth of information on lures and where to fish.

"Striped bass, mackerel and pollock are what you're gonna see mostly out there," the man said.

Harv thanked him and promised to return.

Walking along Main Street, Harv kept an eye out for his mystery woman. Now that he was away from the city in this little town, the stress of his focus group experience seemed far removed. He wondered what he'd do if he saw her. What if she saw him first? He hadn't thought of that.

He decided to go into the drug store and buy a pair of sunglasses. A little caution never hurt anything; plus, he needed a pair. After browsing a while, he also bought a khaki rain hat with the brim bent down. He'd seen several men wearing them and felt it would help him blend in while also hiding his identity a bit. The woman had gotten a pretty good look at him while being chased. He decided to err on the side of caution.

With the brim of his new hat pulled down over his forehead, Harv looked out along Main Street from behind his new sunglasses, feeling completely secure. He continued down the street and stopped in a gun store just for the fun of it. He thought again what he might do if he saw the mystery woman. Probably follow her from a distance to see what she was up to and then call Chuck. He wasn't about to get into another confrontation. That definitely was not part of the deal.

He passed a fire station with a red hook and ladder out front being washed by two firemen. Remembering the reference librarian, he looked across the street and saw Cove Realty. A sign hung over the porch of a white two-story building, which obviously used to be a private home. He decided to continue his walk down the east side of Main Street and drop into the real estate office on his way back along the other side. He stopped into a general store with antique floorboards about a foot wide and old-fashioned penny candy displayed in glass jars. After buying some postcards, he browsed around then headed across the street.

Cove Realty was set back from the sidewalk about fifteen feet with a small yard area in front. It was a freestanding old house, well landscaped, standing out nicely from the connected stores and shops on either side. Harv walked up the front steps and entered a newly-decorated office with two desks off to the left, a waiting area on the right, and a wide hallway leading to several closed doors toward the back of the building. One of the desks was empty while the front desk was occupied by a well-dressed, middle-aged woman talking to a young couple. She talked primarily with the husband, something about a water heater, how to turn the heater on. The wife was busy coping with two young boys pulling on her arm.

"I'll be with you in just a minute," the real estate woman said to Harv.

"That's fine. I'll just wait over here." He walked over to the waiting area and looked at some of the listings posted on the bulletin board. The woman was interrupted by several telephone calls. There was no question it was a busy place. But then, thought Harv, it should be if it was the only real estate office in town. That seemed a little strange. Even the smallest of towns usually had more than one real estate firm. He continued gazing at the listings on the wall and looked up when a man came out one of the doors in the back hallway. Originally heading for the rear desk, the man noticed Harv and walked over to him.

"Hello, I'm Steve Smith. Can I help you?" He extended his hand with a warm smile. There was no Maine accent here. The man was about six feet tall, somewhere in his forties, brown hair cut trim. He wore a pinstriped, button-down shirt with sleeves rolled up, a rep tie, and tasseled cordovan loafers. Not at all what Harv might have expected.

"Uh, hi," said Harv, shaking the man's hand, "Harvey Gallagher. I'm visiting for a few days and just wanted to inquire about summer rentals." He didn't want to just ask for brochures as a stranger off the street. If he passed himself off as a potential customer, he'd have a lot better chance of getting what he wanted. Besides he kind of liked the little town and was genuinely interested in finding out what a rental might go for.

"Sure," said Smith, "nice to meet you." He looked over at the real estate woman discussing water heaters. "Ruth should be through in a second. She'll be glad to help you."

"Thanks. Uh, while I'm waiting, do you by any chance have any brochures showing the different activities in the area?"

"Absolutely. Just help yourself." He motioned to the display with his hand. "Ruth will be with you in a second." He smiled and returned to his original destination. Rummaging through the second desk, he retrieved some papers, walked back into the hallway, and disappeared behind the same door from which he'd come.

Harv looked over the brochures and thought about how polished and urbane Smith seemed. He was definitely incongruous with the rest of the population, but Harv figured it wouldn't be the first time a burned out urbanite had packed it in for a simpler life in the country. It was happening more and more these days. He looked at the brochures and was impressed by the selection. He took one on hiking trails and a fishing pamphlet which the library didn't have.

The walls were decorated with pictures of houses, along with an impressive array of framed certificates including: Maine Board of Realtors, Stephen L. Smith, Broker's License; Ruth M. Hutchins, Real Estate License; Blanche A. Crenshaw, Real Estate License; Stephen A. Smith, Alumni of the Year award.

When the water heater crisis was over, Ruth Hutchins introduced herself to Harvey and offered him a chair next to her desk. He felt a little uncomfortable going through this charade after he already had the brochures. But he really did want to know what rental rates might be in case he ever came back, plus he was mildly curious about this little monopoly, run by a yuppie refugee from Brooks Brothers.

Ruth Hutchins asked Harv his price range, the type of house he wanted, and when he wanted it. He said he preferred a two-bedroom with a water view if possible. After flipping through a big loose-leaf book, she wrote five entries down on a piece of paper and gave them to Harv.

He got up and noted their location on a big wall map. "I'm surprised none in Black Hill Cove have water view. You have nothing to rent with a water view?

"There's one on your list with a great water view," she said.

Harv looked at his list and then at the map. "But it's in Corvellisville. You have nothing in Black Hill Cove with a view of the bay?"

"No I'm afraid not." She closed her book and a small red flag went up in Harv's head. It wasn't what she said; it was more how she said it. There was a finality to it, no explanation, just, "No I'm afraid not."

Harv's curiosity was piqued as he smiled and decided to take another approach. "Well this place in Corvellisville certainly does look good. I'll check my schedule and get back to you about maybe taking a look at it."

Her face warmed up and she smiled, saying she'd

be glad to show him the place and any other property on the list.

"Oh, by the way," said Harv, "I'd like to talk to you about houses for sale too."

"Well, that's a completely different book." She smiled again and flipped the page of her legal pad to take more notes.

"Any houses for sale with a water view?"

"Not in Black Hill Cove, not with a water view."

Smith walked up from behind. "We'd go broke if the only property we could sell or rent is what's here in town." He'd come back to rummage through the second desk and had apparently overheard the conversation.

"Oh, hello." Harv was startled as he looked up.

"It's just that Black Hill Cove is such a small town and properties like that are hard to come by," said Smith. "They tend to get passed down from generation to generation and if they get rented, they get rented out to friends and family. They don't need us." He smiled. "We have several listings up in Corvellisville and Barnwell."

Harv didn't want to get into an argument and just nodded his head. It was clear this pair of property pushers was not going to find anything in Black Hill Cove on the water. He feigned interest in two rentals on his list and let the conversation take its natural course toward a conclusion.

Walking back toward the inn, Harv looked at his watch and noted he'd been in the real estate office almost an hour. It was quarter to noon and his stomach agreed it was definitely time for lunch. He didn't browse in any shops on the west side of the street, partly because he was hungry and partly because he was preoccupied. Something at that real estate office was not quite right, but he couldn't put his finger on it. A guy like Smith running a real estate firm in a small Maine village. Maybe he had family money and just decided to leave behind the more urbane culture from which he'd sprung and run his own little business in Maine—a monopoly. That was a little strange, no competition. And no listings with a water view.

The dining room at the Hawkins house didn't seem too full. After taking a booth by the wall, Harv looked over his brochures.

"So, the food couldn't be that bad." The young woman's voice penetrated his thoughts.

He looked up, noticing the same waitress he had last night.

"I see you decided to return," she said.

"Well, since I'm staying here, I figure I owe the place some loyalty."

She smiled, handed him a menu, and bounced away. She had a sassy walk, Harv thought. Unlike Sheila's smooth, controlled gate, this was more youthful, more exuberant, although she seemed to be about Sheila's age.

When she returned, Harv ordered a turkey club sandwich. He thanked her for referring him to the library and told her how helpful her suggestion had been.

"I know most of the people at the library," she said.

"Do you know anything about the boat rental place across the street here?"

She looked around and quietly recommended another one just outside of town. "It has lower rates and newer motors," she said.

Harv was impressed at how friendly she was, but when he mentioned his visit to Cove Realty, she turned off like a light switch. The pleasant, open face turned hard and business-like.

"OK," she said. "So will that be all? Just the club sandwich?"

"Yes, that and some iced tea." He handed back the menu, looking straight into her face, wondering what exactly caused the change.

It had to have something to do with Cove Realty. He thought it over while waiting for his meal. As soon as he'd mentioned the name and that he'd been there, she turned icy. There was something there.

When she returned with his food, Harv tried to open her up with a little conversation. When that failed, he went for broke. "Let me ask you something." He caught her just before she left. "I may be going way out on a limb here but when I was in Cove Realty, I got some strange vibes. Is it just me or is that place a little weird?"

She looked at him and smiled ever so slightly. "Let's just say you're pretty observant for a foreigner."

"A foreigner? Have you seen my hat?" He reached for his newly-purchased rain hat on the seat next to him and put it on.

The light reappeared in her eyes and a flash of white teeth peeked out behind a smile. "Oh yes," she said, "that's just so Maine."

"In this thing, I could enter the state without a passport."

"Just make sure you've had all your shots." She turned and headed back to the kitchen.

So that was it. There was something about Cove Realty that pushed her buttons. He didn't want to probe now. He knew he wouldn't get anywhere if he did. He'd weasel it out of her over the next few days. Even if it had no importance for Chuck, he was curious to know what the story was.

The food wasn't bad, and lunch passed uneventfully until Harv was just about finished. Taking his last few bites, he heard a familiar loud voice coming from the other side of the room. From his booth, he couldn't really see any of the other patrons except those directly across the room. The partitions were too high. He finished eating and put enough money on the table to cover his meal and a generous tip. As he headed for the exit, his worst suspicions were confirmed. The lowlifes were back, just two of them this time, Mohawk and a bearded gorilla.

Something churned inside him. He had mixed feelings about avoiding an altercation the night before. Although it was probably the prudent thing to do, something in it smacked of running away, and that bothered him. He had always confronted things head-on, and last night's incident had festered inside him. This time he had to walk right past the two cretins to exit the dining room, and somehow he was looking forward to it.

"Well what do ya know." The one with a Mohawk haircut looked up at Harvey. "If it ain't Joe College from last night." He had the word *Blade* tattooed on his left arm.

"That's right. I'm Joe College and you must be Blade Bushwacker." Harv said, pointing to the tattoo. "Nice to meet you, Blade."

As Harv continued to walk past them, both men got up. Blade threw his napkin down on the table and stepped out into the aisle. "A real wise ass huh? I don't like your attitude."

Harv continued to walk. The one with the beard, stepped out into the aisle, causing people at nearby tables to move away.

Harvey turned around and faced both men. They looked young. "Thanks for sharing that with us Blaze." He deliberately mis-spoke the name. "If you have any other likes or dislikes you'd like to share, just write them down on a piece of paper and talk them over with your parole officer."

"Oh, you're dead meat." Blade took two steps toward Harv and uncorked a roundhouse swing with his right. Harv ducked and countered with a wicked upper cut to the young man's midsection. Blade bent over, groaning as Beard Face whipped out a knife and headed for Harvey.

Harv grabbed a bottle of beer from a nearby table and tossed it to him. "Here, catch."

In the split second it took Fuzzy to look at the bottle and decide if he was going to catch it, Harv's right foot shot across the front of his body catching his hairy assailant's kneecap. He knew if he hit it just right, he could pop it over, tear the cartilage, and cause excruciating pain.

Harv's heel hit the knee just as Beard Face caught the bottle with his empty hand. It wasn't a perfect kick; the kneecap wasn't bulging out the side, but it was deft enough to make his attacker drop both bottle and knife, grab his knee, and scream with pain.

Blade straightened up and landed a glancing blow to Harv's head, sending him spinning into a table. Beard Face hopped around on one foot and grabbed hold of Harv's arms, pinning them behind him while Blade reached back to deliver another blow. Harv twisted to free himself while looking up to avoid the expected fist. Suddenly he saw broken glass and liquid spray out from behind Blade's head. The youth's eyes rolled up. His fist stopped its journey toward Harv's face, and he slumped to the floor. In the space previously occupied by Blade before he was rendered unconscious, Harv now saw his waitress clutching the neck of a broken beer bottle, her eyes full of fire, her face covered with beer.

"Thanks," said Harv as he grabbed the hairy one's wrist, twisting it up and away. Harv spun around, maintaining a firm hold on his opponent's wrist. The wounded attacker hopped on his one good leg as the twisting arm moved his body backwards and to his left. He was too off- balance to muster any kind of offensive strike. Harv jacked the arm up higher, twisting it to its maximum while his assailant groaned, hopping on one foot. As Beard Face reached up to free the grip, Harv kicked his one good leg out from under him, sending him sprawling to the floor on beer and broken glass.

Harv stood there a second but neither attacker was going anywhere.

"You OK?" asked the waitress.

"Yeah. I guess I owe you a beer." Harv stepped over broken glass toward the door.

At that moment, the old woman who had checked Harv in the night before walked briskly over to him. She did not look happy. "OK, you, out." She pointed her gnarled finger at Harv. "I want you out o' this place." She apologized to one of the nearby patrons, asking if everything was OK.

"Me?" said Harv.

"Yes, you."

"But I was assaulted. I'm a guest here. I was attacked in your inn."

"You ain't a guest here no more," the old woman said.

"These Neanderthals attacked him," said the waitress, pointing at the two floored lowlifes.

"That don't matter. Trouble is trouble. I want 'em all outa here."

"But that's—"

"Don't worry about it." Harvey stepped over broken glass on his way out. The waitress followed him out to the foyer as two busboys helped the groggy and bleeding attackers up from the floor and out the side door.

"Hey, thanks for helping out in there."

"That's OK." She grabbed a napkin from a freshly folded stack on the front desk and wiped beer from her face and arm. "I enjoyed it. But I feel terrible about you getting kicked out." She shook her head. "Martha can be such a complete bitch."

"Yeah, she's a sweetheart." Harv touched the side of his head where he caught Blade's initial blow.

"Way to go, Carrie." A passing customer gave the waitress a pat on the back.

She nodded and exchanged a few words.

"Well, at least now I know who I'm thanking for saving me in there," said Harv. "Thank you, Carrie."

She redirected a strand of hair over her forehead. "You're welcome, Mister Out-of-Town Hat Person."

"You figured out my code name. Don't tell anyone. It's not widely known."

She smiled. "Your secret's safe with me. What name do you use for everyday public consumption?"

"Today, I'm going by the name, Harvey Gallagher."

She wiped the last bit of beer from her cheek. "Well, Harvey Gallagher, what are you going to do now?" She folded the napkin, put it in her pocket, and walked with him over to the bottom of the stairs.

"I'm sure there are other inns or motels around. Got any recommendations?"

"Actually, I do." In a subdued voice she told Harv her family owned the best place in the entire area. She said she couldn't go into it now but she'd be off in twenty minutes and would tell him all about it. "You know the Blue Whale?"

"The Blue Whale. Is that your family's place?"

"No, no." She smiled and looked around. "It's a sandwich shop right across from the library. Meet me there in twenty minutes." She turned back toward the dining room.

"The Blue Whale." Harv repeated.

"Right. You can't miss it."

Walking up the stairs, Harv chuckled to himself, thinking over what had just happened. Here he was, Mister Straight Arrow, respected school leader in high school and college, rising young marketing consultant, getting thrown out of a hotel for brawling. Buzz would die laughing. He was always telling Harv to loosen up and be more spontaneous.

He hadn't really unpacked, so it took no time at all to get organized. Sheila would be horrified he thought, smiling to himself. She just wouldn't believe it. He thought about Chuck and how to tell him. He'd just tell him he found a better place; after all it was his vacation.

The Blue Whale, like the rest of the town, had an authentic Americana look to it. Over the doorway, an iron bracket stuck straight out with two hooks holding a wooden sign with the profile of a blue whale. Not just the species blue whale but a whale painted blue. The building was set back, leaving extra room for little round tables near the sidewalk. A blue awning hung out front covering most of the tables. Those not covered had umbrellas, giving the place an outdoor café kind of look.

Inside, Harv reviewed the offerings displayed on the menu. Having just eaten, he wasn't hungry but wanted to scope the place out for future meals. He was delighted to discover this establishment was *Home of the Whaleburger.* He'd never heard of a Whaleburger but it was nice to know this was its home, a bit of gastronomic trivia he was sure to use the next time he wanted to impress a client with his worldly acumen. On further review, he was happy to learn the

Whaleburger was *A Whale of a Deal*. He ordered an iced tea and took it to an outside table.

The people passing by seemed to be mostly locals, but then he wondered how many of them had purchased clever disguises like he did to blend in. He readjusted his hat and put on the sunglasses.

The first sighting of Carrie occurred when he noticed someone waving at him out of the corner of his eye. He recognized the bouncy walk, but her hair looked different, hanging loose around her head.

"I recognized the hat," she said, walking up to him.

Harv smiled and pushed a chair out with his foot under the table.

"So, I see you found the place OK."

"I did but it was a challenge. Let me ask you something—how do people know where to go around here without big neon signs to guide them?"

Carrie laughed and ordered a BLT and Coke from a passing waiter. They talked for a while, and Harv felt comfortable with her. He found out her last name was Nickerson. They talked about the fight, and Harv thanked her again for the beer bottle number she played on Mohawk's skull.

"Don't thank me. You just gave me a good excuse. I should thank you."

"Glad to oblige."

She sat back in her chair and smiled.

"Those guys don't look like the Black Hill Cove type," said Harv.

"They're not, really." Carrie paused while the waiter brought her order.

She told Harv they lived about forty miles away in

a little logging community. "It's well inland, tucked in the valley between Black Hill and Crotchet Mountain." She took a bite of her sandwich. "The place is so isolated and small it has no formal name on any map. Most people refer to it as Glen Hollow and call its residents Holler Rats." She took another bite, sat back, and looked around until she was finished chewing. "They're strange people . . . clannish. Lived near the poverty level in the same spot for generations. Nice folks generally, but over the years a few occasionally came into town and caused trouble. Nothing the police couldn't handle easily. But the last two years, with Blade and his pals, it's gotten worse."

"So that's really Mohawk's name, Blade?"

"That's what people call him." She paused to take a long sip of Coke and shook her head. "They hassle tourists. Summer business is way down."

Harv smiled and stirred his iced tea. "Sounds like a nice little enclave of in-breeders."

"Don't laugh."

He decided not to ask about Cove Realty. He'd have plenty of time for that. The subject had turned her off once and right now he needed somewhere to stay. "OK, so now that I'm out on the street, tell me about this terrific place you have for me."

She told Harv about her family's old inn outside of town on a point of land sticking out into Penobscot Bay. "The Nickersons have owned that property for two generations. My grandfather bought it when it was a private estate. After raising his family, he put on an addition and turned it into an inn. The Seaview's been a fixture around here for years." She smiled.

Harv liked her smile—the pleasing proportion of her features. She was tan and healthy looking.

"Our guests come back year after year, even generation to generation. It's got tennis courts, a private boat dock, a spectacular view of the bay. We're outside of town." She raised her eyebrows. "And we have acres of private woods all around."

"Sounds a little pricey compared to the Captain Hawkins House."

"Oh, it is. It's a whole different ball game. But I think we can work something out."

"Like what exactly?"

"Well, like the same rate as the Hawkins House."

"You can do that?"

"We've done things like that before." She stopped to wipe her mouth with her napkin. "Business is down this summer. And a paying guest at a lower rate is better than no guest. Vacant rooms don't make us money."

"So how come you're working for the competition?"

"I always come up from Portland in summer to help run the Seaview. A friend at the Hawkins House had a family crisis a few days ago and needed to take a week off, so I agreed to fill in."

Harv nodded and drained his iced tea. "So what do you do in Portland?"

"I'm a teacher. Working on my master's degree nights."

Harv leaned back in his chair. They talked easily as Carrie pointed out some of the local characters walking past. Harv told her about his consulting practice and that he was on vacation to recharge his batteries for a while.

"I noticed the Captain Hawkins House seemed to be doing OK," said Harv. "At least they were full last night."

"It's completely different. They're an in-town hotel. They get more of the day-trippers, the transients, the one and two-nighters. Our guests stay for weeks at a time. And the Hawkins House, in fact, *is* down in business. The whole town is. They used to be full almost every night in season; now they'll just be full once or twice a week."

"And you're sure you can get me the same rate for room and board at your place?"

Carrie tossed her head back and smiled. "Relax, I told you we need the business, and when I tell Mom and Uncle Bart about the raw deal you got at the Hawkins House, you'll be all set."

CHAPTER 10

Harvey followed the yellow Volkswagen along Cove Road south of town. Carrie was a fast driver, and periodically the yellow blur would disappear behind a sharp curve then reappear as the road straightened out. On the right, deep woods lead to Black Hill, looming high overhead. To the left, blue water caught the sunlight.

After fifteen minutes, the water disappeared. Finally Carrie turned left into a long driveway heading into the woods, and Harv saw a wooden sign saying *Seaview Inn*. As the trees cleared, the inn came into view, overlooking green lawns and a sweeping view of the bay. Carrie followed the driveway past the near side of the inn and parked.

The first thing Harv noticed after exiting his car was the cool sensation of fresh salt air. "This is spectacular." He took a deep breath.

"We kind of like it."

Harv got his suitcase, put it down next to his car, and walked out onto the lawn to take in the view. It was a prime piece of property sticking well out into the bay. The inn faced east, overlooking a vast expanse of water. The village itself was well off to the left at the head of a cove, winding in from the bay. Straight ahead, the lawn sloped down to a boat dock and two tennis courts. To the right, as the shoreline curved around the inn's far side, the ground rose to a rocky outcropping covered with bushes.

"Not too shabby," said Harv. He took in another deep breath and turned back to the inn.

The structure was a three story Victorian. Wooden shingles, turned silver by salt air, covered the exterior, and gray shutters framed each window. Dormers and gables jutted out in all directions. Interior chimneys poked up at different heights, and a tower bulged out of the far front corner, rising upward past the third floor.

"You say your grandfather put on just one addition?"

"It was a big addition."

They walked up the front stairs to the porch.

"Follow me." Carrie walked across the porch into the lobby.

Harvey wandered in after her, looking up at the beamed ceiling in the open atrium foyer. The aroma of baking bread wafted through the air. Stone walls soared up to the rafters.

"I'll find Mom, and we'll get you checked in." Carrie turned and smiled. "You can hang out here a second. I'll be right back."

Harv nodded as Carrie walked past the oversized fireplace into an adjoining room that looked like the dining area. He turned and gazed up at the canti-levered interior veranda overlooking the lobby. Its dark walnut molding stood out against the lighter stone wall.

Harv brought his suitcase over to one of the big

couches and looked around. Freshly cut flower arrangements caught his eye. He leaned against the back of the couch as two guests in tennis gear walked by.

While tucking in his shirt more securely, he heard a familiar voice and looked up to see Carrie walking toward him with a pleasant-looking, middle-aged woman. She was about the same height as Carrie, five feet six or seven, blond, hair cut short, speckled with gray—a handsome woman.

"Marge Nickerson," she said, extending her right hand, "welcome." She had a warm smile and joked about Carrie stealing customers from the Captain Hawkins House. Mrs. Nickerson had the same sparkling blue eyes as her daughter and made Harv feel instantly at ease. He was concerned the price issue might be a problem but any thoughts he might have had along those lines were immediately dispelled. "Carrie told me how dreadfully you were treated at the Captain Hawkins House." She shook her head. "On behalf of the town, let me apologize. It wasn't always like this."

She told Harvey the pricing arrangement he had with Carrie was fine, and they all walked over to the front desk to sign him in. Instead of going behind the desk, she turned the guest book around and stood in front along with Harv and Carrie.

Harv was impressed by the craftsmanship of the dark wooden check-in desk and the ornately carved dark wall paneling behind it with alphabetical slots for guests' mail.

"Sally generally does this," said Mrs. Nickerson,

writing in the oversized pages. "We've got her doing double duty this summer." She smiled. "Right now she's out in the kitchen peeling potatoes."

His room on the third floor overlooked the bay. To his left, he could see the cove opening in the distance. Behind it, the twin peaks of Black Hill and Crotchet Mountain cut the place off from the rest of the world. From his vantage point, he got a sense of the thick woods surrounding him. The room had a small fireplace, a couch and sitting area, and a queen-sized bed. He wondered if the furnishings were genuine antiques; they looked expensive.

Harv unpacked and flopped down on his bed. He yawned and thought about the week ahead, his plans to do a little fishing, a little hiking, definitely unwind. Reading through the Seaview brochure, he noticed the inn stayed open in winter for skiing on Crotchet Mountain. The picture on the front didn't do the place justice. He looked at the pricing schedule and smiled.

He spent the afternoon walking through the surrounding woods, breathing clean air, and enjoying the scenery. Harv realized that all the paths were on Seaview property, but he had to concentrate on his bearings to keep from getting lost. By keeping the bay within sight at all times, he knew he could always find his way back.

On returning for dinner, Harv took a side path inland which seemed to head directly toward the inn. After a short while, in a clearing up ahead, he saw a small, white building and a man apparently painting it. Closer inspection showed it to be a storage shed, and as Harv approached, the man looked up and stopped painting.

"You a new guest here?" The man smiled. "I don't believe we've met. I'm Bart Nickerson." He seemed to be in his fifties, had gray hair, an athletic build, and a friendly face.

"Harvey Gallagher." Harv extended his hand, and Nickerson smiled again, holding up his right hand, showing the wet paint on his fingers. "Beautiful place you've got here," said Harv.

"Yeah, it keeps us out of trouble." The man wiped his brush on a rag. "Tell your friends. We could use the business this summer." He was wearing Bermuda shorts, tennis shoes with no socks, and a green polo shirt stained with white paint.

"Yeah, Carrie told me things are a little slow these days."

"Slow all over." He dipped his brush in water and wiped it on the rag again. "You know Carrie?"

"Well we only just met. I was staying at the Captain Hawkins House and she kind of told me about this place."

The man joked about stealing customers from the competition, and Harv told him how he was asked to leave. "I got into a little scuffle with some strange-looking guys over there—sort of backwoods biker types."

"Ah, say no more." He shook his head. "Weird hair cuts, ear rings?"

"Tattoos." Harv said nodding. "Don't believe in shaving."

"Except their heads."

Harv laughed. "You got it."

"I'm sorry about that, son." Nickerson looked genuinely concerned. "You all right? Those guys can be rough." He took the rag and wiped off his hands, apparently through with his shed painting for the day.

"Oh yeah. I'm fine." He paused a second. "Thanks to your niece."

"Carrie? My Carrie?"

"Yeah, one of them was about to plant his fist down my throat when Carrie bashed him in the head with a beer bottle."

The man's eyes lit up. His head went back, and a laugh rolled out. "Our Carrie clobbered one of those clowns with a beer bottle?" He could barely contain his glee. "By God, I always said that girl was a pistol. A real pistol that one." He put the lid back on the paint can and stowed it inside the door, smiling and chuckling to himself. "I tell you, Harry—"

"Uh, it's Harvey, sir."

"Right, Harvey." Nickerson kept the paintbrush and began walking back toward the inn. "I tell you, Harvey, it's about time someone stood up to those scum bags." He shook his brush for emphasis, getting out the last of the paint.

"Yeah, that's what Carrie said." Harv walked along side of him. "I guess they're kind of a nuisance around here."

The man shook his head. "Only recently son. Don't get me started. It didn't used to be like this."

It was clear Nickerson could provide a lot of information for Chuck, but Harv didn't want to press him right away. He had established a good rapport and didn't want to spook the guy by appearing too interested. The conversation drifted into other areas as they approached the inn and walked up the porch stairs.

"Have a nice stay now, son. I'm sure you'll like our guests better than those at the Hawkins House." Nickerson smiled and turned off to the left toward the dining room.

Harv washed for dinner and walked over to his window again to take in the view. He breathed deeply and got a good whiff of salt air. Somehow the tangy, clean oxygen made him sleepier and hungrier than he was in the city.

Going down stairs to the first level, Harv felt the massive piece of wood the Nickersons called a bannister. It was almost seven inches wide and five inches thick—smooth, polished mahogany that felt like it would support an elephant. Deep inside he wanted to slide down the thing but quickly thought better of it.

In the dining room, about nine tables were set up and covered with white tablecloths. The aroma of roasting beef greeted him. He liked it. A handful of waiters and waitresses scurried across the room, some pouring water, others setting tables. He wandered out on the covered porch and saw a few more tables set up out there. A middle-aged woman leaned against the railing. Bending forward with her eyes closed, she pressed her face out toward the water and breathed deeply. Harv continued walking as the porch wrapped around the corner and extended along the far side of the inn.

"Are you going to be eating out here, sir?" asked the waiter.

Harv looked over at the young man, standing by the end table. "You know, that sounds like a great idea." He scanned the water view and sat down.

His waiter was a clean-cut young man who said his name was Scott. He wore a white dinner jacket, black bow tie, and looked very young. Harv ordered the prime rib dinner.

The guests tended to be mostly middle-aged couples and families. Nickerson was nowhere to be seen. Harv assumed Carrie was at the Captain Hawkins House doing her evening shift. Mrs. Nickerson made an appearance, going from table to table, talking with the guests like old friends. Several called her Marge.

Harv was surprised how few bugs there were on the screenless porch. He figured the location had a lot to do with it. The point of land sticking out into the bay caught the sea breezes, which apparently blew steadily enough to keep mosquitoes and gnats away. That and a few bug lamps helped make dinner pass comfortably.

After eating, Harv got up to walk off his meal along the bay. Several guests were playing croquet on a flat portion of the lawn. He walked to the right this time, to the southeast, but couldn't keep close to the water. As he passed the boat dock, the ground rose and the shoreline was covered with large rocks and bushes, making passage impossible. He turned inland, walking to the top of the rise and around the far side of the inn. The ground flattened out, and off to his left, he could see the bay again.

Harv walked for about a mile. Soon he noticed how quickly the light was fading and decided to turn back toward the inn. He thought maybe he'd read out on the porch a while and then turn in early. He was tired. Harv followed the path, watched a sailboat glide past, and took a deep breath. For the first time in years he was beginning to relax.

CHAPTER 11

"Chuck, Harvey." At 10:45 Friday morning, Harv got Chuck on the phone.

"Well, the happy wanderer. How the hell you doing?" asked Chuck.

Harv leaned back on the sofa in the parlor. "Oh not too bad. I think I could get used to this."

"You find anything?"

"I'm not sure."

"Not sure? What does that mean, exactly?"

"Well, I don't know." Harv sat alone in the big parlor, where the landline allowed him to talk with a good connection. He just punched in his room number, and the charge was put on his bill. Putting private phones in each bedroom was a concession to modern civilization the Seaview was unwilling to make, and Harv wasn't sure about the connection he'd get with his cell phone. "There's nothing specific I can really hang my hat on. I haven't seen our friend." He went on to tell Chuck about Cove Realty, Smith, and his experience trying to rent or purchase property with a water view.

"Strange perhaps," said Chuck, "but not overwhelming."

"It's just a bunch of little things. None of it probably

has any relevance to ADI. But you wanted me to keep my eyes open."

"No, you're doing great. You're doing exactly what I asked you to do. You can never tell what might be relevant. What else you have?"

"Well, I ran across some guys up here who are sort of wild. I don't know how to describe them. I may have discovered an entirely new sociological subspecies, like really grubby backwoods types with a little punk biker thrown in on the side . . . very strange." Harv stopped talking as Mr. Nickerson entered the room. He wandered over to the magazine rack, picked up a copy of *Field and Stream* and slowly walked out.

"Harv, what's going on?" asked Chuck. "You conk out on me?"

"No," said Harv quietly as Nickerson left, "someone came into the room."

"So what about these backwoods yokels?"

"Well, they act like they expect people to be afraid of them. They bully people, hassle tourists. Hell, two of 'em tried to push me around."

"Are you OK?"

"Oh, yeah, thanks to a little help from my current landlord."

"Current landlord?"

"Yeah, I'm not exactly welcome at the Captain Hawkins House anymore." Harv told Chuck about the scuffle with Mohawk and Fuzzy Face, and about his waitress with the beer bottle. He was glad Chuck seemed only interested in his safety and didn't address the maturity level and judgment exhibited by his well-paid consultant getting into a brawl.

"So where are you now?"

"At the Seaview Inn, the place my waitress referred me to just outside of town. Here, let me give you the number."

As Harvey reached for a brochure with the inn's phone number on it, Nickerson came walking back into the room. He returned the *Field and Stream* and picked up a copy of *Yankee* magazine, thumbed through it, and slowly walked out. Harv gave Chuck the telephone number and pointed out he was getting the exact same rate as the Captain Hawkins House. They talked another five minutes, and Chuck told him to keep up the good work before ending the call.

"Turnin' into a great day," said Nickerson, ambling back into the room. He walked over to his pipe rack, grabbed a briar and sat down across from Harvey. "Should be good for fishin'." He hammered the pipe against his palm.

"Uh, yes. Maybe I'll do that this afternoon." He asked Nickerson about using the boats at the dock and the best places in the bay for fishing.

"Our guests can use those three boats any time they want. We leave the keys in during the day and take 'em out at night." Nickerson answered politely but clearly had something else on his mind. "Listen, son. I don't mean to pry, but I couldn't help hear you talkin' to someone about the strange goin's on in this town."

"Well, I . . ."

"Hey, don't worry. I know there are strange things happenin' here." He dipped the pipe into his tobacco pouch and filled the bowl with his thumb. "Problem is, no one's got the backbone to stop it. Or get to the bottom of it."

"Well, sir." Harv smiled. "I have to admit I was talking to someone about the observations I've made up here."

"I knew it." Nickerson's face lit up. "I knew my complaints to the state police would bring someone here. Ed Bradford send you?"

"No," Harv put up his hand and shook his head, "believe me; I'm not with the state police."

"The Feds huh? That's even better." Nickerson held a lit match to his pipe and puffed.

"No, Mr. Nickerson, honest, I'm not with the FBI, the CIA or anything like that. Really, I'm basically on vacation just checking out a few things for one of my clients."

"Clients huh?"

"Yes sir. I'm a marketing consultant. One of my clients is involved with a security situation. They just want me to keep my eyes open while I'm on vacation. That's all really."

"Corporate security stuff in Black Hill Cove huh?" Nickerson sat back and stared through the smoke.

"Sounds pretty far-fetched, I guess."

"Not necessarily." Nickerson took the pipe out of his mouth. "Anything illegal, strange or weird, I can believe it. There's somethin' different and unnatural goin' on here, and it may as well be the stuff you're talkin' about as anything else."

"Do me a favor, Mr. Nickerson. Please don't tell anyone I'm looking around or checking things out up here."

Nickerson sat up straight and put his hands on his knees. "Son, I don't think you've got the picture here. I'm on your side. I couldn't be more tickled you're up here snoopin' around. I started askin' questions and got nowhere." He paused as one of the guests walked into the parlor.

"Listen, Henry—"

"It's Harvey, sir. But most people call me Harv. It's easier."

"Ah, I like that." Nickerson looked over at the bald man leafing through the newspaper and lowered his voice. "Listen, Harv, why don't we go sit down in my private office?" He looked over at the man again. "I don't feel too comfortable talkin' about this here. You know what I mean?"

Harv agreed and followed Nickerson out of the room, through the front foyer, and up the main stairway to the third floor. Instead of turning right toward Harv's room, Nickerson turned left and walked all the way to the end of the hall to a non-descript door on the right-hand wall. He unlocked it, turned on the light, and locked the door behind them after entering.

Harv looked at the cleaning supplies, vacuum cleaners and brooms. "Interesting office décor."

Nickerson laughed. "I get inspired by the whole cleaning idea." He walked to the back of the closet, unlocked another door, and lead Harv to a short staircase at the top of which he opened another door, entered another room, and turned on the light.

Harv followed his host into a big circular room. Light spilled in through a curving bank of windows overlooking the water. Harv figured this must be the tower portion of the inn. He could picture the curved tower bulging out of the far front corner. From the raised, circular ceiling hung two big chandeliers made of old wagon wheels with lamps at the end of every other spoke. Corkboard and bookshelves covered the opposite wall facing the woods. Large maps and aerial photographs were pinned to the bulletin board. In front of the windowless wall stood a large wooden desk with two computer screens, books, manuals, and manila folders stacked neatly on top. Below the windows, another bookcase held still more books, and Harv saw plenty of couches, chairs, tables, and lamps scattered around to give the place a comfortable feeling. Next to the desk an old table had a shortwave radio on it.

"Does the Pentagon know about this place?" Harv walked into the center of the room.

"No, we keep it pretty much a secret."

"It looks like the command center for a military operation." Harv went to the windows and peered out at the treetops and the bay. "This is amazing."

Nickerson laughed, walked over to the desk, and sat down.

Harv looked up and down the bay through the windows. He walked to one of the two couches beneath the windows as if preparing to sit down then walked over toward Nickerson and sat in a straight-back chair in front of the desk. "This place is incredible. How the hell did you get this desk up here?"

"Took it apart, brought it up in sections, then rebuilt it."

"Couches?"

"Same."

They talked about the town and some of the strange things that have been happening in recent years. Harv was glad to see how open and forthcoming Nickerson was and asked him when the strange events started.

Nickerson reached over, grabbed a match and relit his pipe. He leaned back in his chair, put both feet up on the desk, and took a long puff. "About two and a half years ago one of our real estate companies got bought out by a New York fella. Not our biggest real estate firm but the second biggest. There were only three of 'em."

"Cove Realty?"

Nickerson looked surprised. "You're on the right track. They bought out Pierce Realty and changed the name to *Cove*. How'd you know?"

"Lucky guess. It's a long story."

Nickerson took two quick puffs. "Six months later he buys out Mavis Johnson's little operation and instantly Cove becomes the only real estate business in town."

"Yeah the lady at the library told me they were the only one in town."

"That's when the trouble started. This New York guy, name of Smith, this guy started puttin' pressure on some of us to sell our places to Cove."

"To sell the Seaview?"

Nickerson held up his hand. "I'm gettin' to that. Started with Will Stewart. Had a beautiful home on the water." He motioned to his left with his pipe. "He and Doris lived there for years. Raised their kids there." He took a long puff and blew the smoke out slowly. "Anyway they start gettin' offers from Cove to buy their place. They refused, and every time they refused, Cove would come back with a higher offer."

"I assume you and Stewart are friends; he told you all this?"

"Hell, we're practically neighbors. They're good friends." He shook his head slowly, stood up and walked over to the window. "Then the intimidation started. Swastikas painted on the side of their house. Holler rats knockin' on their door, threatenin' violence if they didn't sell." He turned, walked back to the desk, and sat down.

"Any holler rats I might know?"

"Yeah it was the two you tangled with."

"Mohawk and Fuzzy Face?"

"That's the two. Most all the trouble can be traced to them. The Mohawk guy is Maurice Ouellette and the bearded fella is Carl Chavone."

Harv laughed. "Maurice?"

"That's him."

"Does he go by the name *Blade*?"

"Yup. He's kinda the leader."

"So what happened?"

"It got worse. Busted into their house; started pushin' Will and Doris around. They're older. It's not like they could fight back." He shook his head. "Then they killed their cat."

"Killed their cat?"

"Left Tiger lyin' dead on their front porch with a note to sell their house—beautiful Maine Coon. Huge cat."

"Holy crap."

"That was the last straw. They sold the place and moved to Corvellisville. Got a great price for it but, God, I hated to see 'em cave. They were really scared though. Afraid to press charges. Just up and moved. Wouldn't talk about it afterwards. The weird thing is the Stewarts have been gone for two years and the house was never put on the market. It's been vacant all this time."

"Why in hell did Cove want the place? It's completely vacant?"

"I went over and looked in the windows. Not a stitch of furniture in the place."

"That is weird. And you said they've been after the Seaview?"

"After Stewart moved, they came after us. Jim was here then, Carrie's dad. Died of a heart attack last year."

"I'm sorry. Carrie didn't tell me." Harv could see there was still a lot of emotion there.

Nickerson told Harv how his older brother, Jim, was more the businessman and a natural to take over the family inn. "I had set up shop in Portland. He'd come down, spend a few days now and then. Helped me get my helicopter transport business off the ground." His eyes looked somber as he paused to relight his pipe. "Then, of course, when he needed some extra help up here, I'd come up and help out." He told Harv he'd been operating his business for fifteen years and had been thinking of selling it when Jim died. "It was only natural for me to come up here and help out the family. Got a good price for my business." He took a deep breath. "And Barbara loves it up here."

Harv learned that Barbara was his wife for thirty

five years and asked if Jim's death was caused by the holler rats.

"It was a heart attack, pure and simple." Nickerson's eyes looked sad again. "Got it haulin' wood, which he shouldn't of been doin'. Got all kinds of help he's payin' good money to." He sat forward resting his elbows on the desk. "But there's no question this thing had him under a lot of stress. Nearly got run off the road once. Jim didn't scare easy. Everyone in the family thinks it was a combination of the two. But there's no question in my mind if it wasn't for the pressure to sell this place, Jim would still be alive today."

"Run off the road sounds pretty serious."

"Yeah, they've calmed down a bit lately. The physical intimidation stuff didn't work on Jim. He was one tough cookie; let me tell ya."

Harv smiled. "Neither Fuzzy face or this Maurice guy are particularly big when you get right down to it."

"No, just ugly and mean."

Harv laughed. "Hell, Carrie and I put 'em both on the floor."

Nickerson's eyes lit up. "That's right; I forgot about that. Jim could of taken both if he had to. I probably could too."

"You look in great shape. I have no doubt you could."

Nickerson nodded his head and sat back in his chair. "That's probably why they changed tactics with us. Now they put on demonstrations on our front lawn here, tryin' to turn off our guests so business'll go down."

"What kind of demonstrations?"

"Oh, you name it, unfair labor practices. Actually

we treat our employees like family. And then there's discrimination against minority religions. That's a big one with them. Anything to cause a ruckus and disturb our guests."

*   *   *

After following Nickerson out of the tower room, Harv took a boat out into the bay and called Chuck.

"Didn't I just talk with you this morning?" Chuck laughed.

"Hey, I'm sitting in a boat out in the middle of Penobscot Bay, calling on my phone. You should be paying me extra for this." Harv told him about Nickerson overhearing his telephone call, about the tower room, and all he'd learned about Cove Realty.

"You didn't mention ADI to this guy did you?"

"No, just that I'm keeping my eyes open on a security matter for a client. That was it."

"That's fine . . . You trust him?"

Harv said he did trust Nickerson and asked if he could tell him a little more about exactly what he was looking for in Black Hill Cove. "The guy's a storehouse of information, and I just think if I could be a little more specific with him, it would help him focus on things that might be relevant to you."

"Everything's relevant to me at this point."

"I think he could be a big help."

"Let me check him out," said Chuck. "He could be a shell shocked lunatic or a highly credible source. I'll let you know tomorrow."

CHAPTER 12

Elsa Ouellette hummed quietly, milling around her kitchen with an oversized spoon, occasionally stirring venison stew on the stove. The small two-story house was surrounded by dense woods, and out front three motorcycles cooled their engines. On the pine needles and bark that passed for a front lawn, a statue of the Virgin Mary stood with her arms extended over four ceramic lambs.

The house was one of the few two-story structures in all of Glen Hollow. And, despite the fact that half the front porch had fallen down, the place was considered relatively upscale for this little enclave. The hollow was not a real incorporated town, certainly no place the census bureau knew about. Nestled in the remote cleavage between Black Hill and Crotchet Mountain, it was too isolated for most people to even find. Aside from a smattering of small houses, there wasn't much to the place. At the community's center, a solitary gas pump stood on one side of the road and an old wooden saw mill on the other. Past the sawmill stood seven other buildings and a wooden church, unpainted and gray. It had no steeple, but a log cross on the roof showed it to be a house of worship.

This was the domain of Elsa Ouellette, minister and spiritual leader of her people.

"Claude, where's that son of yours?" She always referred to their two children as her husband's whenever they had been behaving badly, and for the past fifteen years their twenty-one-year-old son, Maurice, had behaved very badly. "Tell him supper's in five minutes." She was a tall, angular woman with straight, black hair, high cheekbones and sunken cheeks.

"What's that Mother? I'm out on the porch." Claude Ouellette sat in an old, stuffed chair on the part of the porch that hadn't collapsed. He sat with his left leg propped up over the right, exposing his wooden leg—a peg leg necessitated by a logging accident twenty years ago when a tree fell on him.

Elsa leaned her head out the kitchen doorway into the living room to increase her decibel level. "I said supper's nearly ready. Get Maurice and find out if those no good friends of his is stayin' or not. Leslie, come set the table." She paused and stuck her head out the door again. "And stop whittlin' on that leg of yours. It'll break again and then where'll ya be."

Outside, Claude slowly rubbed his fingers over the freshly exposed wood on his leg where he'd recently been carving. Embellishing his wooden peg with relief carvings was one of his quiet pleasures in life. He'd already used up the entire surface area of two pegs that were displayed in his bedroom like artwork. One, carved with religious themes, was rubbed with pine tar to create a dark relief impression. It was kept for church and other formal occasions. The other peg was just left to weather naturally. It had broken where he'd carved away too much wood near the lower tip, and Claude had fallen and broken his wrist. Now the glued and repaired leg was never worn but hung on the wall of his bedroom solely for its artistic value.

"I hear you Mother. No need to shout." His eyes squinted as he bore down on the knife with exacting precision. The top part of the peg had been decorated with a family of beavers circling the circumference. Claude was now busy on a moose whose antlers were particularly difficult.

"Leslie," Elsa screamed at the top of her lungs.

"Yes, Ma." A voice came from the other room as a teenage girl slouched through the living room into the kitchen. Leslie Ouellette was seventeen, wore a stained dress, had stringy, brown hair, and was pregnant.

Loud male laughter bellowed down the stairway from above. It was more sinister than happy. Soon heavy feet pounded the staircase like cattle coming to a watering hole. The laughter turned to serious whispering and low mumbling as Maurice Ouellette, Carl Chavone, and Craig Porter entered the large kitchen.

"You boys stayin' for supper? 'Cause if you ain't, I want you out o' here." Mrs. Ouellette spoke without looking up from her stove.

"They're stayin' Ma," said Maurice. "What are we haven' anyway?" He swung his leg over the back of a chair and sat down at the long table.

"Never mind what we're havin'. Just thank the Holy Mother we have enough to eat regular and share," she looked at the two guests, "no matter who we share it with."

"It smells real good, Mrs. Ouellette," said Craig

Porter. The three young men smiled at each other as Carl Chavone stifled a snicker through his full beard. Elsa ignored the attempted civility and went on serving dinner.

Like many Glen Hollow residents, the Ouellettes were descended from a band of French Canadian religious zealots who had wandered south from Quebec in the 1700's. Having somehow picked up the English tongue from neighboring Anglican influences, the group acquired religious practices so deviant and unnatural, it was driven out of Canada by the intolerant French Catholic majority. Half starved, the zealots wandered through Maine and were guided to the little hollow by local Indians. Two years earlier a band of dysfunctional Puritans had wandered north from Massachusetts and been brought to the same place. The Puritans had been kicked out of every town they'd inhabited because of their radical religious beliefs. Through the years the two groups intermarried and adopted each other's customs, becoming one people. Cut off from the rest of civilization, the two groups' mores and religious doctrines combined into a twisted subculture allowed to evolve in its own way.

Claude got up from his seat on the porch, dusted off the wood chips from his lap, and joined the others. With Elsa sitting at the end of the table near the stove, everyone helped themselves from large serving bowls passed around the table. "Here's a little somethin' I carved for ya, pet." Mr. Ouellette handed Leslie a little carved wooden animal.

"Gee thanks, Pa." She reached over and took her father's gift.

"Thought it might make a nice toy for the young'n when he arrives."

Elsa Ouellette cringed. Her unmarried daughter's pregnancy was a major embarrassment, particularly in light of her position as minister at Glen Hollow's church. She never liked discussing the situation in front of others, although everyone in the hollow knew about it. It was hard to hide. Over the last few months Leslie's belly had blossomed forth like a ripe watermelon. She had done her penance required by the church, the daily chanting, the public confession of sin at high mass, but that didn't mitigate the embarrassment.

"What the hell's that, some kind of dog?" Blade nodded toward the carved figure.

"It's whatever Claude Junior wants it to be," Mr. Ouellette said, "just a little toy animal is all."

"Could be Claudine too, Pa," said Leslie.

"I don't know," said Claude. "From the way you're stickin' out, I think it's gonna be a big, strappin' boy."

"So how's the house comin', son?" Elsa interrupted her husband.

"Yeah, when you movin' out?" Leslie asked with her mouth full.

"It's comin' along. We just gotta get that timber for the roof."

"I'm startin' one too," Chavone chimed in.

"Saints alive," Mrs. Ouellette shook her head, "you boys is all doin' good these days. Town work didn't used to pay half so good."

"It sure didn't." Claude reached for some stew. "When I was startin' out, there was only loggin' and workin' at the saw mill. It took years to save up for a car or motorcycle. "

"Well ya just gotta know the right people," said Blade.

Mr. Ouellette stopped chewing momentarily and looked at his son's head. "You get some kind o' bump on the noggin there, boy?"

Blade reached up and lightly touched the sore spot. Although the bump had gone down some, the effects of Carrie's beer bottle were still evident on his shaved skull. "Just bumped my head on somethin' the other day. That's all."

Carl Chavone instinctively looked at the bandage on his left hand where he'd fallen on broken glass. It had required five stitches at the free clinic in Mapleton. He wiped some food off his beard with the back of his right hand and continued eating.

"You boys best be careful of too much of a good thing. You hear me?" Elsa's voice began to take on a preaching tone. "Money, too much of it, is the root of all evil."

The three young men looked up at each other, smiling. Blade rolled his eyes.

"The root of all evil I tell ya, and I see it already in you three."

"Ain't nothin' wrong with money, lady," Chavone said without looking up.

Mrs. Ouellette raised her eyebrows. "Listen to me, son. It's not money that's evil; it's what money does to people that's evil." Elsa glanced at the young men. "Look at you three. I see the work of evil already movin' in your lives and you don't even know it."

"Hey," said Blade, "that's enough o' that crap."

"Look at you." Elsa rose to her feet. "Shavin' your head, lookin' like some fool Indian. And Craig Porter, I've known you since you was born. What are ya doin' with paper clips poked through your ears?"

"That's it, Ma," yelled Blade, banging his fist into the table. "Sit down and shut up."

Elsa grabbed a spoon and shook it to emphasize her words. "Listen to that back talk. It's gettin' worse I tell ya."

"This ain't no church sermon, Mother," said Claude in a controlled voice. "Let's everyone just calm down."

Elsa turned away from the table, grabbed a dirty pan from the stove, and put it loudly in the sink. With an amused smile on his face, Chavone looked across the table at Blade, who shook his head in disgust. After an awkward silence and a lot of loud cleaning noises from the sink, Elsa took a deep breath. "When I see evil, I have to tell it." Her preaching voice was gone. "I have to say it. That's my job. That's what I do."

"We know, Mother," Claude reached for a platter of potatoes, "and you done a good job of it too."

"Because that's the only way you can fight it." Elsa's voice stayed calm as she turned back to the table. "You have to first see it." She paused. "And I see it. If you're not careful, the Antimadonna will come into your lives to make way for her accursed son, the devil himself." Her voice began to preach again. "And when the Antichrist controls your life . . . it's over. It's hellfire and damnation."

As the strident voice returned, Claude got up from the table and walked over to his wife.

"It's hellfire and damnation," she continued as Claude put his arm around her.

"It's OK, Mother," he said softly. "It's OK."

Elsa took a deep breath. "Well, I just don't like what I'm seein' lately."

"I know, Mother." Claude helped his wife back into her chair. "I know. And you told 'em."

The atmosphere at the table gradually became more relaxed. Although the conversation was somewhat forced, supper passed uneventfully. When it was over, Elsa kicked everyone but Leslie out of the kitchen and began cleaning up. Claude returned to the front porch. The three young men headed for the living room.

Blade noticed his sister's carved wooden toy lying on the counter near the door. She'd carefully removed it from the table before clearing dishes at supper's end. After Chavone and Porter passed through the doorway, Blade looked up and saw his mother and Leslie busily working at the sink with their backs to him. Quickly, he reached for the toy and pressed its rear leg hard into the countertop. His thumbnail turned white as the pressure increased, snapping off the little leg. No one heard. Blade looked up and smiled as the two women kept banging away at the sink. He joined his two friends in the living room where they talked for a short while before they walked out the front door, got on their motorcycles, and rode away.

CHAPTER 13

Saturday morning Harv got up early to go fishing. He took his gear down to the dock and headed out over the misty water toward a spot Nickerson had showed him down the west coast of the bay. After no luck with the bone-colored popper lure, he changed to a paddle tail swim shad and caught a striped bass, which he brought back to the kitchen. Mrs. Nickerson put it in the refrigerator and said she'd tell the chef to cook it up special that night with a white wine sauce. Following a quick trip into town for lunch and a few errands, his phone rang just as he was pulling into the Seaview's driveway.

"Just wanted to let you know about this guy Nickerson," came the familiar, deep voice over the phone.

"He check out OK?" Harv walked out onto the big front lawn.

"Harv, you can tell that gentleman just about everything you know," said Weitz.

"So he checked out then."

"The man's a retired captain in the Marines. He flew helicopter gunships. It's a tough gig, believe me. He was awarded a purple heart and a silver star. Impeccable record."

"I told you." Harv looked around the open lawn.

"Started his own helicopter charter service in Portland. Contract work for the military mostly, some geological survey work, aerial photography, some private sector stuff. Impeccable record, credit rating."

"He's a good guy, believe me."

"The only thing you can't talk about with him is the product itself, the technology. No mention of wave accelerator technology used in an oven. That's a definite no, no. Got it?"

"Got it."

"You can just say it's an oven we're working on and this woman attempted to steal a part of it. End of story."

"That's cool." Harv lowered his voice as two guests walked by.

"I'd be particularly interested in Nickerson's thoughts about that compact we recovered. The make-up in the purse. If you can trace it to a specific store this woman might frequent, you can focus on that location and increase your chances of finding something."

"Absolutely. He'll be a good guy to just talk with to see if there's any relationship at all between the strange things he's mentioned and your security leak."

"The odds of two strange scenarios like these going on independently in the same little town are kind of remote."

"Yeah, I guess."

"My gut tells me they're related somehow." Chuck impressed on Harv the importance of continued secrecy. "Tell Nickerson not to talk about this with a living soul. You hear me?"

"I hear you."

"Tell him to treat it just like a top secret mission in the Marines, to be discussed only with his contact, which is you. He'll understand."

Harv asked if anything had been found yet on Smith, and Chuck said it hadn't. Harv also asked Weitz to run a check on Carrie and Marge Nickerson just in case.

Chuck agreed that would probably be a good idea and promised to get back as quickly as possible. "Until you get clearance from me though, Nickerson and I are the only people you're to talk to about this. No one else."

"I haven't told a soul, Chuck."

"That means no one, Harvey. Not Peter. Not Bass. No one knows what you're doing up there but me. And soon Nickerson."

"Not Cobb?"

"Cobb doesn't even know. Not yet. Just me. I told you I suspect an inside security leak. That means especially people at ADI are not to know. You got me?"

"I got you. Believe me, I haven't told anyone."

"In this kind of situation you have to be really careful who knows what. You got kind of snookered into this thing. You were there. You saw the theft. You saw the woman and chased her. You're the only one who can I.D. her. I'm kind of stuck with you."

"Gee, thanks."

"Nothing personal."

"No, I hear what you're saying."

"But as this thing unravels, Harvey, you've got to stick with your story. You're on vacation. No one knows anything different."

"I hear you."

"If I seem to be preaching, it's because things are getting a little dicey around here, and secrecy is getting more important than ever."

"Dicey?"

"Well, yes, it's getting kind of interesting." He paused a moment. "Roger Cornish and your friend Peter had a little set-to in my office yesterday."

When Harv asked what happened, Chuck said he couldn't tell him. "Just suffice it to say things are getting real nervous around here as you might imagine."

After hanging up, Harv called Sheila.

"God, I'm glad you called." Her voice sounded tense.

"Well good. Your mother take the news OK?"

"She's getting over it. She was obviously disappointed."

Harv sat down on a bench overlooking the water. "I promise you this is a very big deal. It's top secret, so I can't talk about it, but it's huge. And they're paying me a big bonus."

"I know, you told me."

He told Sheila about the Seaview Inn and about how he was asked to leave the Captain Hawkins House. It made her laugh.

"I'm so glad you called. I was about to call you. We kind of rescheduled your visit."

"Rescheduled to when?"

"You going to be free the weekend after next?

"Let me think. I'll be coming home next Thursday. That will lead to next weekend. We're not talking that weekend but the weekend after that. Yes, that sounds good."

They talked about the new date and the logistics of Harv flying down.

"So it's set, finally." She didn't pose it as a question.

"Absolutely."

"Great, we'll set it up. There'll be tons to do."

"I'm looking forward to it, really."

They talked a little longer until Harv saw Nickerson heading out toward the storage shed.

He wound down his conversation and took off after his host. He told him about his conversation with Chuck. He didn't tell him ADI had him checked out but simply said he'd gotten permission from Chuck to open up about what had happened and why he was there. Nickerson put his big tool chest down and sat on it while Harv told him about the mystery woman, about chasing her through the testing lab, and recovering her purse.

Nickerson focused his attention and hung on every word.

Harv looked around and told his host about the contents of the purse and how Chuck had zeroed in on Black Hill Cove.

The innkeeper's eyes lit up. He smiled and nodded his head. When Harv told him to regard it as a top secret matter just like in the marines, Nickerson agreed.

"I want you to know, son, I appreciate your tellin' me this. I take top secret matters very seriously. You tell me it's top secret and that's the way it'll be." He went on to tell Harv about his experience with high security missions in the military. "I do recommend though, at some point you open up the loop to include Ned Crowley and Marge."

"Who's Ned Crowley?"

"Chief of police. He's got a deputy named Anderson, but you don't want to open this up too much. Ned's the one you want. He's totally up to speed on the holler rat situation. Sent Ouellette to juvie a few times. We've all been involved in this thing for a few years now. Believe me, he could provide some real help, Carrie too."

Harv agreed that was a good idea. He didn't tell him Marge and Carrie were already being checked out. They talked about Cove Realty and Smith. Nickerson said they suspected Smith was the one pulling the strings behind the holler rats and the violence. He said Crowley had seen Smith talking with Blade on two separate occasions. "Ned and I came close to buggin' Smith's phone line about a year ago."

"Now that'd really be cool, if you could bug his phone." Harv sat down on a tree stump. "So, why didn't you do it?"

"Got too complicated on the legal end. Crowley wanted to make it happen more than anyone. Pressed his contacts as hard as he could to do it legally. Ya know, court order and all. We just couldn't get enough probable cause."

"Yes, bugging someone's phone is probably best if done legally."

"Unfortunately yes. Crowley was only willing to bend so far."

Harv nodded his head. "So he's willing to bend."

"Absolutely. He even considered doin' an end run

with Will Stewart's nephew. Tom was a trainee with the phone company a few years ago. Learnin' how to be a repair guy. You know, up on the poles, fixin' lines. Just a trainee. Hated the work and left to be a commercial fisherman. The thing is, though, he hates Smith for what happened to his uncle. Crowley and I were hopin' Tom could figure out a way to bug Smith's line on a, you know, freelance basis. He wanted to do it but wasn't sure how to do it."

Harv smiled, grabbed the handsaw and sawed off the end of a new board where Nickerson had marked. "I've got a question for you. This is totally hypothetical, but suppose I could produce someone who was relatively casual about his interpretation of our legal code. An outsider. Someone who knows every conceivable way there is to tap a phone line and could do it so there'd be no possible way it could get back to Smith?"

The twinkle slowly came back into Nickerson's eyes. "I don't know where you're goin' with this, son, but if you could produce a person like that, I'd be happy as hell."

Harv told him about Buzz and how he thought his friend was the most technically gifted person he'd ever known. "We were in high school together." Harv smiled. "He was always tinkering with things and inventing weird contraptions."

"I like the sound of it."

"He used to be kind of wild and got into trouble occasionally for hacking into the school's computer system and leaving strange messages for the teachers, and hot wiring peoples' cars and leaving them on their neighbors' lawns."

"Sounds like an interesting fella."

"He's calmed down since then, of course. He's getting his doctorate at MIT right now. Doing some kind of advanced directed study work. I have no idea whether he'd be willing to come up here and do it or not."

Nickerson sat up straight and put his hands on his knees. "Well it sure in hell wouldn't hurt to ask him."

"If this guy, Crowley, this local police chief is willing to bend a little, as you say, I could maybe see this happening."

"I'm sure he would."

"I'd like him to be totally on board with what we're doing. If we do it."

"Harvey, I've known Ned for a long time. We've been through a lot together. I know how hard he tried to make that other wire tap happen. I know he'd be on board."

"Here's the key question though. If my friend is able to come up here, can you put him up for free? I see you have a few vacant rooms."

"Son, if he's willing to make room in his schedule to come up here, and if he's half as smart and crafty as you say he is, I'll gladly put him up here for free. You tell him that."

"That's all I wanted to hear."

CHAPTER 14

After failing to reach Buzz Saturday afternoon and evening, Harv walked into the empty parlor Sunday morning, punched in his room number on the phone, and tried again. He knew how Buzz ignored his landline and turned off his cell phone when he was involved in a project. On the fourth ring, Harv heard the familiar recording asking him to leave a message at the tone.

"Hey, Buzz, Harv. Pick up the phone. I'm not going to leave a message . . . I know you're there." Harv looked at his watch. "I know. I'll sing your favorite song. That'll wake you up." Harv looked around and, in his most off-key voice, began to sing. "A Louie, Louaye. Oh Baby, we gotta go now. Yeah, yeah, yeah, yeah. A Louie, Louaye." Harv heard a dragging and banging sound over the receiver.

"This better be important, Gallagher." Buzz's voice was groggy.

"That's an awfully negative way to answer the telephone, especially on such a bright, happy morning."

Buzz breathed heavily, adding a slight groan at the end. "Christ, Gallagher, what the hell are you doing calling at five in the morning?"

"Eight forty three to be exact."

"Do you know what a pain in the ass you are?"

"Yes, but a loveable pain."

Buzz took another deep breath. "Gallagher, I'm not a happy camper right now. You're about two seconds from getting hung up on."

"Listen, this is important. I need your help."

"The only way I'd listen to anyone needing my help right now is if they were female, beautiful, and naked."

"How'd you guess? Maxine is shy. She wanted me to call you on her behalf. It's somewhat awkward for her. You know, being naked and all."

"Gallagher!"

"Hey, this could actually be fun and it's kind of important. Want me to call back later?"

"No." Buzz yawned. "I'm awake now. What the hell is it?"

Harv first swore his friend to secrecy, then he told Buzz about his corporate sleuthing, about Cove Realty, and his desire to bug Smith's phone. He mentioned Nickerson and Crowley and their past attempts to bug the line. "Plus, Nickerson has offered to put you up at no charge. This inn is incredible."

"Bugging a phone, huh?" Buzz's voice sounded amused. "I thought you were going to Philadelphia."

Harv glanced around quickly. "One of my clients redirected my vacation to Maine. They're paying my way as long as I do a little snooping."

"Gee, that sounds terrible."

"I told you it could be fun. When's the last time you pulled off one of your wild-assed stunts and really nailed someone?" Harv looked up as Nickerson walked into the parlor and locked the big door behind him.

"Wouldn't it be great to bring that contraption of yours up here and field test it in the wide open spaces instead of demolishing your apartment?"

"Hey, this is a highly sophisticated weapon capable of throwing an electrical charge with pin point accuracy up to seven hundred feet."

"You say that, but do you really know what the hell it can do?" Harv nodded hello as Nickerson sat down opposite him. "Maybe it could do eight hundred feet."

"Actually a little field testing would be good right now," said Buzz. "I've stopped it from arcing you know."

"Great!"

"I'm serious. Last night it shot straight across the living room, past the radiator and the water pipe, clear to the kitchen."

"I'd hate to see what your kitchen looks like right now. Bring your thing up here and let's see what it can do outside."

Buzz said nothing for a second. "What's in this for me?"

"You mean besides the tremendous field testing opportunities?"

"Yeah, besides that."

"I'll tell you what. My client is paying me a fee to do this. If you come up here, I'll split my fee with you for the days you're here."

"Half your fee?"

"Half my weekly consulting fee." He listened to silence on the other end of the phone. "Plus, as I told you, free room and board at the most incredible old inn you've ever seen." He looked over at Nickerson and put his hand over the receiver. "You did say free right?"

Nickerson nodded.

The line was quiet again. "Does this mean there's not really any Maxine?"

Harv smiled. "You'll never know unless you come up here."

"Jesus, Gallagher." He paused a second. "Listen, before we go any further, let me ask you something. Is this a landline you want to bug or a cell phone?"

"A landline. I've been in this guy's office. It's hard to get a good mobile connection in the center of town."

"Do you know this guy's current number? I mean the exact line you want to bug?"

"It's unlisted. We've got his number from last year, but he may have changed it. That's not going to be a problem is it?"

"No, that's fine. I just want to know what I'm dealing with here. I mean, if I were to do this." He took a long breath. "Another thing, how many phones do you have at that inn? I mean how many separate landlines with their own numbers?"

Harv told him there were two landlines, a main line for the inn and a separate one for Nickerson's office in the tower room. He confirmed with Nickerson that the parlor phone worked off the main Seaview line.

"Landlines are perfect," said Buzz. "One will have to be dedicated to the tap."

Harv looked over at Nickerson. "We can dedicate your office phone to the tap, right?"

Nickerson nodded. "Absolutely."

"Yes it can be totally dedicated," said Harv.

Buzz was quiet. "I take it this is going to be done alfresco."

"Alfresco? You mean outdoors?

"Let's just say *outside* rather than *outdoors*. As in outside the suggested guidelines of our legal system. It's my own special, euphemistic term."

"Alfresco is the only way this is going to happen. That's why we need you. You're the king of creative, outside-the-box thinking. You are Mister Alfresco himself."

"That's a lot to ask, you know."

"I know, Buzz, but let's face reality here. You're one of the only people on the planet who could do this with the sophistication and stealth required to pull it off with total impunity."

"That's probably true."

"This would be a piece of cake for you. It would be like first grade finger painting for you."

"I aced first grade finger painting."

"I'm sure you did. And if you're concerned about the alfresco thing, my innkeeper here assures me the local police chief will be totally on board with the program. It'll still be alfresco, but this guy is very flexible."

"Really."

"He's been trying to bug this guy's phone for a long time. Just couldn't get it done the traditional way. He'll be available for any tacit support or looking the other way that might be required." He looked over at Nickerson who nodded in agreement.

"We've also got a guy who used to be a telephone lineman and is highly motivated to help out."

No one spoke for a second. "I'll tell you what I'll do.

I'll come up, get the lay of the land, talk to this phone guy, and then let you know if it's doable."

"You're doing a noble thing." Harv smiled, giving Nickerson a thumbs up.

"Yeah, I'm a saint. I'm going to have to make a few calls and get out of a meeting."

Harv and Nickerson spent the next ten minutes passing the phone back and forth, each talking with Buzz, discussing the kinds of tools Nickerson had and what Buzz was going to bring up.

After Nickerson gave Buzz directions to the inn, Harv immediately called Chuck Weitz and asked him to check out Crowley. There was no way he would ever tell him about the illegal wire tap. He'd stop the cash flow and call Harv home in a heartbeat. And without a discussion of the wire tap, there was no point in telling him about Buzz. He knew his friend was an unconventional, lateral-thinking kind of guy, and Chuck would insist on a security check. A check that would certainly look less than ideal, particularly in Buzz's youth. Harv wanted Buzz as his own secret draft choice. He was beginning to really like this town. He hated what Smith was doing and was totally sympathetic to the Nickersons. He knew Buzz could make things happen.

"Give me a couple of days to check out Crowley," said Weitz. "I'm sure everything will be fine. By the way, Marge Nickerson and Carrie Nickerson both checked out fine. It's Smith I'm worried about."

"He's dirty right?"

"Well, he's got a spotty track record. He was a defendant in a real estate fraud case in Connecticut.

Settled out of court. Problems with the Better Business Bureau. A lot of things." Chuck told Harv to be careful of Smith and said he'd continue to check him out.

After dinner that evening, Harv and Nickerson were drinking coffee out on the porch when Carrie showed up. After talking briefly with two of the guests, she walked over to Harv's table. She looked happy.

"After lunch tomorrow, I'll be free from the Hawkins House." She grabbed a chair and sat down. "I never knew a week could pass so slowly."

Nickerson and Harv quietly told her their plans to bug Smith's phone. Harv told her everything he'd told Nickerson, why he was in Black Hill Cove, about the mystery woman, and about Buzz coming up the next day.

Carrie smiled. Her eyes lit up. "This is exactly what we need." She looked around and lowered her voice. "This is incredible."

Nickerson told her about being sworn to secrecy and that she was not to discuss the situation with anyone outside their little group.

"Hey, mum's the word." Carrie gave Harv a light-hearted shove on his arm. "I knew there was something different about you."

CHAPTER 15

Harv got a call from Buzz at 2:30 Monday afternoon.

"So where the hell are you?" Harv looked at his watch.

"I'm at a gas station south of town and I'm tired."

Harv knew the Seaview was not easy to find and was more than happy to go retrieve his wandering friend.

While in town, they walked past the Cove Realty office to check it out. Buzz noticed the telephone wires running up the side of the building and paid particular attention to the outside relay box just underneath the window.

"I'm glad it's landlines." Buzz nodded his head and walked back toward his car. "I much prefer doing this with landlines. I mean, if I were to do it."

"I told you on the phone. I've been in the office. I've seen them conduct business. They all use landlines."

"Good," said Buzz. "I just needed to see for myself. Now how about leading me to this inn of yours."

Buzz followed Harv out of town, along the bay, and up the long driveway before pulling to a stop next to the Seaview. His Jeep Cherokee had 140 thousand miles on it and made that quiet humming sound all well-maintained cars have.

Buzz stepped out, stretched, and took a long look around. "Jesus, Gallagher, you weren't kidding, were you."

"Not bad huh?" Harv walked over from his parked Chevrolet.

"I usually discount your marketing jive by about fifty percent but this . . ." He looked out over the bay. "This is outstanding."

Buzz was two inches shorter than Harvey, at about five eleven, and had a slight build. He had dark, medium-length hair, brushed over to the side, and an oval face with smiling eyes.

"We've gotta get you looking more relaxed." Harv opened up the back of the Cherokee and began unloading supplies.

"Hey, this is relaxed." Buzz wore long, khaki pants, ripped in the knee, brown shoes, and a pinstriped, long-sleeved shirt with the sleeves rolled up. Along with his white skin, the ensemble gave Buzz the clear look of an urban transplant.

By contrast, Harv had a good base tan started. He wore tennis shorts, jogging shoes with no socks, and a teal green polo shirt.

It took a while to unload the equipment, including a battery pack, two outlet boards, two sets of head phones, a digital recorder, and a load of couplers, wires, and other paraphernalia.

Nickerson came down the porch steps and walked over to help.

"We knocked over an electronics store on the way," said Harv as the innkeeper approached.

Buzz put a coil of wire down on the lawn and shook

Nickerson's hand. They talked briefly about the ride up, and the innkeeper told Buzz how glad he was to meet him.

The next item out of the car was Buzz's experimental weapon, which he carried up to the tower room with Harv leading the way. Nickerson had moved a few chairs to make extra room for the equipment. With Buzz gasping for breath, they spent the next half hour toting the remaining gear up the stairs. On the final trip, Harv saw Buzz and Nickerson bending over the prototype weapon.

"The idea of throwing an electrical charge with any kind of accuracy has been the hardest thing for people to accept." Buzz talked to Nickerson while picking up the plastic housing of the device. "Electricity traveling through any kind of open environment will arc randomly onto the first grounding substance it can find."

Nickerson nodded his head with interest as Buzz opened up the housing and pointed into the guts of the weapon.

"You know, you don't have to listen to him if you don't want to." Harv put the digital recorder down on the floor.

"No, this is fascinating, Harv," Nickerson looked up, "really."

Buzz ignored Harv and continued. "Working with light photons on a subatomic level, I developed a way of ionizing the air molecules along a preselected vector, thereby providing an excellent conductive medium for electricity."

"Subatomic huh?"

"Absolutely. And here's the kicker. I've incorporated

into it a laser capability that can be adjusted to various power levels. It can do some serious damage."

"I can personally attest to that. You should see his living room," Said Harv. He'd heard all the talk before but was glad to see the thing finally brought out into the open air for some real long-range testing. Having written the business plan for Buzz's new company, he had a vested interest in the weapon's success. Buzz paid Harv in promissory stock certificates and they were piling up. He figured if the thing ever did take off, he'd make a bundle.

With the gear neatly stowed, Buzz packed away his weapon and sat down on the couch. "I assume you want to get started on this little project as soon as possible," he said, looking at Nickerson.

"I'm ready, son, any time you are."

"The sooner the better," said Harv.

Buzz looked at his watch. "I can tell you the first thing we need to do is call your telephone lineman friend."

"Tom Stewart." Nickerson told him he'd called Tom the day before and let him know Buzz was coming up.

Stewart arrived at the inn with an armload of charts and telephone equipment. He even had a big Men Working sign. "My wife yells at me for never throwing anything out," he said. "Sometimes it pays off." He and Buzz smoothed out the master blueprint of the area's phone lines and zeroed in on the relay box at the corner of Maple Crest Drive and Arlington Street. "That's the box Chief Crowley and I focused on last time we talked about this." Stewart pointed at the blueprint. "I even climbed the pole to look at it. I just wasn't sure how to run a jumper line or how to tap into Smith's phone without him findin' out."

Buzz smiled. "You have the ANAC code, Tom?"

Stewart's eyes widened. "Yes, but how do you know about ANAC codes?"

"Don't ask; he can be scary sometimes." Harv looked at Buzz. "What the hell is an ANAC code?"

Buzz explained that the ANAC code was a special number repairmen call to determine the specific phone number they're tapped into.

Stewart nodded. "Believe me, when faced with nothing but wires, it's the only way we can verify we're working on the correct line."

Buzz walked over to Stewart's pile of gear and picked up a handset with wires coming out of it. "Can I borrow this for a day? I'm going to make a little trip into town tonight to find out exactly what number we want to tap."

Stewart agreed and listened closely while Buzz explained to him how to create a line splitter with a supplementary bridge link between Smith's line and Nickerson's office line so that Smith's phone would operate normally and not be affected. "You think you can do that up there on that pole?" said Buzz.

Stewart smiled. "Absolutely. Do you have a battery-powered soldering iron?"

Buzz walked over to his equipment area, retrieved the requested item, and handed it to Stewart. "I think this is doable, people."

"Tom, I want to tell you how thankful we are to have your help here," said Nickerson.

"I swore I'd never climb another pole again," said

Stewart, "but to nail Smith, I'm actually lookin' forward to it."

They talked further and decided to meet at the target location the next day at noon. "That's the only time Crowley can get off," said Nickerson. "And we definitely want his cruiser parked at the foot of that pole to give cover to our little operation."

After dinner Buzz set up the big answering machine in the tower room. "There won't be any outgoing message," he said, "but it'll record all incoming calls, blink when there's a call recorded, and relay all dialogue to the back-up recorder."

When the alarm rang at 3:00 A.M., both Buzz and Harv got up and quietly drove into town. The village had few lights at night, and the side alley between Cove Realty and the flower shop next door was completely dark. They parked in the shadows along Main Street and slipped beneath Smith's window. While Harv held a small flashlight, Buzz unscrewed the cap from the terminal box on the side of the building, attached Stewart's special hand set to the two phone lines inside the box, punched up the ANAC code, and wrote down both numbers.

"I recognize the first one. It's Cove Realty's main number." Harv looked at the paper where Buzz had written the numbers. "The other one's obviously the one we want."

"Your deductive powers can be truly awesome at times, Gallagher." Buzz packed up his gear and walked back to the car.

Harv quietly closed his car door, turned on the ignition, and headed back to the inn.

*   *   *

Tom Stewart was bent over, strapping on his leg gaffs when Harv and Buzz arrived at the telephone pole on Tuesday. He'd already set up the Men Working sign in a prominent position and parked well away from the pole. Crowley turned the corner on Arlington and cruised in nice and close.

Buzz walked up and gave Tom a pat on the back. "I can see you're anxious to get this done." He smiled. "You remember what we talked about yesterday?"

Stewart assured him he remembered and strapped on his tool belt. "I can't believe how tight this thing is," he said. "I have to move it out two notches. Must have gained more weight than I thought."

They talked about the tools Tom would need as he loaded up his belt. Then he grabbed the big body belt that goes around the pole. "This baby is key," he said. "It lets you lean back so the gaffs go into the poll at the right angle. If you don't lean back, you fall."

"That's never good," said Buzz.

"No, it isn't." Stewart looped the body belt around the pole and headed up. "Every instinct is to cling close to the pole, but you have to lean back. That's what I hated about this job. That's why I quit after six months."

"Listen, Tom," said Crowley, "whatever you do up there, I'm gonna need you to undo when this thing's over."

Stewart assured him he would as he slowly made his way up the pole. It took him about ten minutes to

find the correct phone lines and perform the procedure Buzz had showed him.

When he got down, Buzz walked over and shook
his hand. "See, that wasn't so hard."

"I'm sure I did it right," said Stewart.

"I'm sure you did." Buzz picked up the leg gaffs
Tom had removed. "You mind if I give these a try?"

"You want to climb the pole?" said Harv.

"Just a little. I just want to see what it's like."

Stewart assured him it was OK and helped Buzz
put on the gear. Then Buzz grabbed the big body belt,
walked over to the pole and started climbing. He was
about five feet off the ground when his leg gaff slipped,
and he grabbed the pole.

"Damn!" he yelled and quickly looked at his right
hand.

"It's not easy is it?" said Stewart.

"No, it's not easy," said Buzz, "and I got a damn
splinter."

"Come on down, Tarzan," said Harv. "Remember
what Clint Eastwood said: 'A man's got to know his
limitations.' "

Twenty minutes later, Buzz looked at the splinter
in his finger and walked upstairs to the tower room.
Harv and Nickerson watched as he hooked up the
digital recorder to the listening system. After five
minutes he turned off the soldering iron, turned on
the answering machine, and smiled. "Time to do a
little listening, people."

*   *   *

That evening they all sat around the dinner table out on the porch. Marge and Carrie joined the group as they finished off desert at the corner table.

Bart Nickerson put his napkin on the table and leaned back in his chair. "So tell me, Harv, what are some of these wild pranks our resident inventor used to pull off in his youth?"

"God, Gallagher, you've been dredging up my past again."

Harv smiled. "Gee, I don't know; there are so many."

"Ooh! Tell us," said Carrie.

"Gallagher, these people hardly know me; now you're going to puncture my carefully contrived professional image."

"I think my favorite is the Peter Pan incident," said Harv.

"Oh, God." Buzz shook his head.

"Tell us about Peter Pan." Carrie smiled.

Harv cradled his coffee cup in both hands and leaned back. "It was in junior year of high school." He sipped his coffee. "Buzz had a little run-in with the president of the senior class. He was a pompous, self-important guy who kissed up to all the teachers."

"Gallagher, I don't—"

"Unfortunately he had the poor judgment to lecture Buzz in front of his friends about his bad attitude, need for more school spirit, more respect for the school, and more conformity to school standards."

Marge Nickerson smiled. "Buzz, I'm just so shocked to hear about your bad attitude."

"Needless to say, Buzz was not amused. The following month, when the guy won the lead role as Peter

Pan in the annual senior class play, Buzz decided to modify the automated crane that operated the thin wire, hoisting Pan in the air to make him fly."

"This sounds good," said Nickerson.

"On the day of the opening performance, while three other guys and I stood guard, Buzz overrode the manual controls on the crane, keying the system to a remote control he'd brought in from home." Harv looked over at Buzz who just sat shaking his head. "During the performance that night, Buzz and I and our dates . . ." He looked at Buzz. "There were about ten of us weren't there?"

"It's your story, Gallagher. I'm certainly not going to help you with it."

"A bunch of us were up there in the front row of the balcony while Buzz operated the remote control, sending the unfortunate actor skyward at completely inappropriate times in the production."

Carrie burst out laughing.

"When Pan was supposed to be flying, Buzz sent him crashing into the orchestra."

Marge choked on a sip of coffee she'd taken and buried her face in her napkin.

"Buzz worked the control to make Pan display these weird up and down movements and forced collisions with props and other actors."

"Stop, I can't stand it." Carrie shook her head.

Nickerson threw his head back laughing.

"Somehow the performance muddled through to its ultimate conclusion. The audience was in hysterics."

"Poor guy, just needs an outlet for his creative genius," said Nickerson.

"Thank you," said Buzz. "At least someone here understands me." He picked at the splinter in his finger.

"What have you done to yourself there?" Marge asked.

"Just a splinter I picked up on the telephone pole."

Marge reached over and gently grabbed his hand to get a better look. "Ooh, that looks nasty."

"Yeah, I'm thinking of billing Harv for hazardous duty pay."

"Let me get my needle and tweezers. I'll have that out in no time." She got up from the table and walked inside as Buzz plunged his finger into his icy gin and tonic.

"Needle?" said Buzz.

Carrie smiled. "Oh, Mom's great. You should see some of the quilts she's made. She's got the fastest needle this side of Kennebunkport."

Buzz stirred his drink with his finger. "Fast is nice." He looked over at Carrie. "How about painless?"

"No, just fast."

CHAPTER 16

Wednesday morning at 9:00, two calls, with no particular relevance, showed up on the system. At 10:30, after Carrie checked the system at her assigned time slot, she assembled the troops and played the latest recording:

["Hey, it's me."

"What the hell do you want, Blade?" It was clearly Smith's voice.

"You owe me money."

"I owe you money for what?"

"That busted shutter over at Stewarts. I fixed it like you told me. Had to borrow a ladder. Buy paint."

"OK, OK, I'll check it out."

"I figure you owe me about a hundred bucks."

"I said I'll check it out."

"You're always checkin' things out. Don't you trust me?"

"Trust but verify, Blade. Trust but verify."

"I want that money."

"I'll check it out. Tomorrow or the next day. I'll check it out."]

Carrie turned off the machine

"This ties Smith to Ouellette," said Harv.

"Something we already know," said Buzz, "but it's comforting to have solid proof."

"At least he's keeping the place up." Carrie poured herself more coffee.

*   *   *

Wednesday afternoon was a complete bust. All calls were personal or focused on the ongoing business of Cove Realty.

After checking the system, Harv and Buzz drove over to the Stewart Place. A red and white sign on the front lawn said *Private Property—Keep out.*

"I can't wrap my head around Smith's relationship with this house." Buzz followed Harv past the sign across the front lawn.

"I know," said Harv. "He had to buy it. Put incredible pressure on Stewart to acquire it. Never tries to flip it. Keeps it empty and tries to keep people way from it. It makes no sense."

They walked around to the back and took in the view over Penobscot Bay. It was a different orientation from that of the Seaview. While Nickerson's place looked straight out across the water, the Stewart house and property took in some of the coastline of the west bay.

"There's the Seaview." Buzz pointed to the familiar inn, sitting on a promontory looking out over the water.

"Ah," said Harv, "my home away from home."

Buzz peeked in a window and shook his head. "Totally empty."

Harv looked at his watch. "We better not stay too long. Smith said he was going to check out Ouellette's handiwork. I don't want him to see us snooping around."

As they continued their walk around the other side of the house, Buzz pointed at a window on the first floor. "I'll bet that's the shutter Ouellette repaired."

Harv looked up and noted one shutter painted a different shade of green from all the others. He laughed. "I'm shocked."

"I know," said Buzz. "I thought holler rats were known for their highly developed aesthetic sensibilities."

*   *   *

Following an afternoon with no relevant calls, Harv, Buzz, Carrie, and Nickerson sat in the tower room nursing cocktails and cracked crab. Buzz was on his second refill.

"By the way, folks," said Harv, "my ADI budget ends tomorrow. It was for eight days. I came up last Wednesday and tomorrow's Thursday."

"The hell with your budget," said Nickerson. "We won't charge you."

"You can't leave now," said Carrie.

"You guys are already putting Buzz up for free," said Harv.

"That's our decision," said Nickerson, "and I'm

decidin' that you're not goin' home tomorrow. End of discussion."

Harv smiled. "At least let me call Chuck tomorrow and see if I can get the budget extended."

"You can give it a try," Nickerson said, "but if he doesn't cooperate, I'm gonna to have Crowley impound your car so you can't leave. I trust my gut, and my gut tells me there's somethin' here."

Harv got up and looked out the window. "Let me ask you something, Mr. Nickerson."

"*Bart*; please call me *Bart*. We're all in this together. We're a team."

Harv laughed. "It's a deal."

"You da man, Bart." Buzz raised his single malt scotch in the air and took a swig.

Carrie smiled and took a sip of her gin and tonic.

"Let me ask you, Bart," said Harv. "Do any of those aerial photos on the wall up there show this place? The Seaview?"

"Absolutely, both do from different altitudes." Nickerson got up and walked up to the photos. "Why do you ask?"

"I'm not sure yet." Harv looked closely at one of the photographs. "Can you point out the Seaview for me on this Photo?"

Nickerson moved closer and pointed to a spot on the image taken at the lower altitude.

Harv looked closely and moved his finger slowly along the picture. "And this, I'm guessing, is the Stewart place?"

Nickerson looked. "Damn. Right on the money. Good guess for an out-of-towner."

Harv told them how he and Buzz had gone over to Stewart's house to look around. "We were impressed at the great view he had."

"Yes, they've got a great view," said Carrie, "but we have a better one."

"He's got a great view of the water and he has a great view of this place," said Harv.

No one spoke for a second.

"You da man, Harv." Buzz raised his glass and took a swallow of scotch.

"Look at the curve of the coast here. Stewart's property doesn't face directly out over the bay. It's angled at this location to face down the coastline and directly at the Seaview."

Nickerson and Carrie looked closely at the photo.

"And, as I look at this picture and the other one with the wider view, I don't see any other properties nearby with such a great view of this place."

Carrie walked over and looked out the window. "I always knew we could see the Stewart house, but I never thought about or cared about the idea that they could see us."

"I'm beginning to see Smith's odd real estate behavior in a whole new light," said Harv.

"Absolutely." Buzz stood up and leaned on his chair. "He didn't want Stewart's place to rent out or resell and flip, or to live in, or for any other normal reason. He wanted that property because it's unique, because it has a spectacular view of the Seaview, and he mothballed it because he doesn't want anyone else to have a spectacular view of the Seaview." He raised his glass, took another sip, and sat down. "I rest my case."

"Oh, my God," said Carrie. "That's it. But what does it mean? What's this guy up to?"

"We know he wants the Seaview," said Nickerson.

"And his plans involve something he doesn't want anyone else to see," said Harv. "Beyond that, I have no clue."

Carrie walked over and looked out the window again.

*   *   *

Harv called Chuck Thursday morning and told him about their conversation in the tower room.

"Things are falling into place, Chuck. I know my time is up today but there's no way I can leave now."

"So you're seeing some progress?"

"Absolutely. We're starting to put things together. I just need a few more days."

"Anything you can tell me about?"

"Right now it's all speculative. Fresh observations here, weird behavior over there. We're starting to piece it together, but I don't want to say anything and end up looking foolish. I'd rather come to you with real solid information."

"I'll tell you what. I can give you to Sunday. You leave this Sunday. I can't stretch the budget any more than that."

"I sense there's something here, Chuck."

"I think you're right, but Sunday is it. Whatever you have by then, bring it to me next week and we'll compare notes and see where we are . . . Monday morning first thing in my office." He told Harv the security check on Crowley worked out fine then mentioned he was late for a meeting and had to go.

No relevant phone calls came in Thursday morning and afternoon. At 4:00 Harv joined several other guests in a volleyball game down by the tennis courts. At 4:15, Carrie came running and called for Harv.

"Buzz says bingo." She had a big grin on her face as Harv walked over.

"Bingo?"

"Bingo, as in eureka, as in pay dirt."

The other guests continued their volleyball as Harv looked up at the tower room to see Buzz waving out the open window. After collecting Nickerson, they bounded up the inn's stairs.

"Just wait." Buzz adjusted the recorder. "I think this is going to be self-explanatory." After everyone sat down, he pushed the Play button.

["Hello," said Smith, answering on the first ring.

"Hey, this is Nick," came a new voice with a slight New York accent.

"Hey, how's it going?" said Smith. There was a short pause and Smith continued. "So tell me. Can your man make the deal?"

"Yeah, he can put it together but it's got to be extremely low profile. He's not setting foot in Boston or in ADI. He knows about Zhang."

"Don't worry, all our deals are going to be up here from now on," said Smith, "Total control, complete safety."

"Damn well better be. Dead bodies aren't good for business." There was another pause. "He wants a general introductory meeting. Kick the tires sort of thing. Face to face. Talk money, logistics."

"I thought you said he was ready to deal?"

"He is. Nobody's just going to make this kind of deal cold, Smith. He needs to know who he's dealing with, feel comfortable with you. The oriental mind, you're going to have to get used to it."

"I told you the Shamosho are sourcing for the same client didn't I?"

"Yes. You told me that when you told me they were the ones who knocked off Zhang."

"The point is if they get their hands on this little contraption first, we can kiss this deal goodbye."

"Don't worry. I'll bring him up. He'll meet with you. He'll like you. You'll talk details. In a few days, you'll close the deal. Just make sure you can really get your hands on that thing when we need it."

"Hey, listen, everyone feels bad about what happened in Boston. I told you that." Smith sounded irritated. "That was a freak one-in-a-million situation. Believe me, we can get our hands on it when we need it. When can you bring him up here?"

"This Saturday night would be the soonest. That OK with you?"

"Of course it's OK with me. The sooner the better."

"Your place again?"

"Yeah, my house."

"It'll be nice when you finally get hold of that inn. We can put everyone up in style with room to spare."

"Soon, Nick, soon. It's only a matter of time."

"Your man from ADI going to be there, I assume?"

"Yeah, he'll be there."

"We'll get there after dark. Nine o'clock or so."

"Fine, we'll see you then."

They said goodbye and the line clicked silent.]

"The man from ADI," Harv threw a dart into the board from his sitting position in the chair.

"I kind of thought you'd like that part." Buzz smiled with a self-satisfied look.

"That contraption they're referring to has got to be that thing you recovered, right?" said Carrie.

"The wave accelerator. I'd bet on it." Harv got up from his chair and began pacing.

"It's a good fit." Buzz reset the recorder. "They couldn't get their hands on it because of some freak problem in Boston. That sounds like you, Gallagher."

Harv smiled, grabbed the remaining darts, and began throwing them at the target.

Nickerson struck a match to light his pipe but quickly shook it out when he realized the tobacco was still smoldering.

Carrie walked over to the window and looked out. "What's this Shamosho thing they were talking about?"

"I have no clue," Harv threw another dart hard into the target, "except the fact they knocked off some guy named Zhang."

"That makes me a little nervous," said Buzz.

Nickerson walked over to the map and looked closely. "Sounds like they want to use the Seaview as a place to conduct some kind of illegal activity."

"A veritable bed and breakfast for bad guys," said Buzz.

Carrie began searching the back-up file for the recent conversation in order to transcribe it. "This man Nick," she said, "he's obviously some kind of middle man or broker or something."

"Sounds like it." Harv threw another dart. "All I know is that someone from ADI is going to be at Smith's house this Saturday night." He took out his phone, headed for the door and paused.

"You thinking of calling Chuck?" asked Buzz.

Harv put the phone back in his pocket, turned, and walked back to the center of the room. "I don't think so. I can't tell him about the meeting because he'd want to know how we know about it, and I'm certainly not going to tell him. And beyond that, I know he'd never approve of what I want to do now."

CHAPTER 17

Friday morning Nickerson called Ned Crowley and asked him to come over. He was about the same height as Nickerson with thinning brown hair and a weathered face. Harv could tell that he and Nickerson were old friends by the easy way they acted around each other. He knew Crowley was aware of the wire tap and was willing to look the other way. That fact alone made him one of the good guys.

Up in the tower room Buzz played the most relevant recordings for Crowley, who commented, "even though we can't use this stuff in a court of law, we can use it ourselves to nab these guys."

"I want to find out who that ADI man is tomorrow night," said Harv.

"It's a once-in-a-lifetime chance." Nickerson packed fresh tobacco into his pipe. "When are we ever gonna be in a position like this again?"

After some words of caution, Crowley finally agreed with Nickerson that it was a good way to "kill the beast by cuttin' off its head."

"Hey, wait a minute." Buzz held up his hand. "I hate to be negative here, but I definitely heard the word *dead* in that last cut." He walked over, picked up the transcript, and ran his finger down the page. "Yes, here it is 'dead bodies aren't good for business.' Now that's a phrase that gives me a little concern."

"There's no need for anyone but me to be involved," said Harv. "I know a lot of ADI people. There's a decent chance I might know this guy or have seen him and can give Chuck a description that can help. But this only needs to involve me."

"Count me in." Carrie put a mark on the wall map where Smith's house was located.

"I'm definitely in." Nickerson ignited his pipe.

"Hey, I'm not saying I don't want to be involved." Buzz reset the recorder. "I'm just saying this could be dangerous."

"I know there's some danger," said Harv, "but I think we can come up with a plan that'll tell us what we want to know and still be safe."

"Let's rule out sneaking up and spying on them," said Carrie.

"Good idea." Crowley walked over and picked up the transcript.

Harv grabbed the darts and started throwing. "The goal is to get me into that house so I can see who's there."

No one spoke for a good period of time.

"What you need," said Crowley, "is a pretext for bein' there."

"A pretext." Nickerson took a puff on his pipe. "That's exactly what we need. We need a good pretext."

"You mean if we could find a good reason for going up to Smith's house and barging in, we might be able to pull it off." Harv slung a dart into the target.

"If you had a good enough reason and the right cover," said Crowley.

Harv resumed throwing darts, while Buzz got up and poured himself more coffee.

"Life or death," Carrie said, staring out across the bay.

"What do you mean?" said Buzz.

"Life or death." She turned back toward the room. "The only pretext that would justify going up to Smith's house, the only one they could possibly buy, would be if it were a matter of life and death."

"I like it." Crowley looked up from reading the transcript.

They kicked the idea around. After several trial balloons and a lot of input from Crowley, they came up with a plan everyone liked.

"If you guys can pull off an average acting job," said Buzz, "I think this thing will work."

"It'll get us in that meeting." Harv nodded and threw another dart.

"Carrie, you sure they won't recognize you?" asked Buzz.

"I've only seen Smith from a distance. And those sales ladies I'll be talking to, I've never seen." Carrie walked over to the mirror and ran her hand through her hair. "A wig, some different make-up, no one will know me."

Crowley drove into town to get a bee sting anti-toxin kit from Norton's Pharmacy. It was going to be Carrie's key prop and had to look legitimate. Since Crowley was close friends with Bill Norton, getting the real thing was easy. All Crowley needed to do was tell Norton it was for a good cause and Bill knew what he meant. Norton typed up a nice official-looking prescription label with the name *Emily Thompson*, and placed it on the small, plastic box, holding an epinephrine injector pen.

Carrie called Cove Realty and, posing as Emily Thompson, made an appointment with Blanche Crenshaw for three o'clock Saturday afternoon. She wanted to make sure she was going to be in the office late enough in the day so no one would discover her planted anti-toxin box before close of business.

Harv, Buzz, and Nickerson drove past Smith's house on Ledge Road just to get the lay of the land. Nickerson already knew the location but felt it was important everyone get comfortable with the general terrain in daylight. They saw a parking area at the top of the driveway and talked about how critical it was to drive up quietly and park as far away from the house as possible to reduce noise.

"It's important," said Nickerson, "that the first time they know we're here is when we're practically inside."

* * *

Saturday morning Carrie visited one of her old friends from high school and borrowed her wig. She combed it out until it looked perfect and got her costume in order. At 2:45 that afternoon she entered the tower room in full regalia as Emily Thompson, the bee sting anti-toxin kit tucked snugly in her purse.

Harv looked at Carrie.

"You look . . ." Buzz starred at her.

"You look like a movie star," said Nickerson.

"You look . . . different," said Harv.

Carrie threw her head back and laughed. "It's the makeup. I usually don't wear much, so when I pile it on like this, it makes me look different."

"She looks like . . . who is it?" said Buzz. "Jennifer Lawrence, Rita Hayworth; somebody."

Harv looked and said nothing.

*   *   *

For the next three hours Carrie saw more houses than she cared to count, three in Black Hill Cove and two in Corvellisville. As planned, she made a point of rummaging through her purse several times for makeup and candy in order to remove her anti-toxin kit for public viewing. When she first arrived at the office, it tumbled out onto Blanche Crenshaw's desk. Carrie quickly retrieved it, mentioning what it was, and that she was allergic to bees. At the end of the day, just before planting it in the lady's room, she was sitting next to Crenshaw's desk when Smith himself walked up on his way home. He introduced himself to *Emily* and confirmed with Blanche that she was going to be working Sunday. Carrie capitalized on the situation by looking through her purse for her keys, removing the kit, and placing it on the desk right under Smith's nose.

At 6:30, Carrie drove up the Seaview's long driveway and waved to Harv and Buzz on the tennis court. She collected Nickerson, and all four walked up to the tower room.

"Well, it's in there." Carrie took off her wig and shook her hair.

"You sure she didn't find it after you left?" asked Buzz.

"No, I stayed to the very last minute. She had the lock-up keys in her hand and was about to throw me out." Carrie took out a tissue, wiped off some makeup, and flopped down on the couch. "You know, she's really a nice lady. I don't think she has a clue what Smith's really up to."

* * *

The ride over to Smith's house that night went quickly. Buzz drove his Cherokee because it was the quietest vehicle they had. Harv sat in the back seat. His watch read 9:53. He figured anyone they wanted to see should have already arrived. The Cherokee drove south of town and took a right on Ledge Road. After two miles, Smith's driveway appeared on the left. It was hard to spot at night; everything looked different.

Light poured out from the white cape atop the sloping drive. Skylights adorned the roof and a sun deck ran along the near side. The four-wheel drive crept up the paved driveway to a wide turn-around area out front. Buzz kept as far away from the house as possible. A white, barn-like garage stood off to the right. Between it and the house, pulled up into the shadows, four cars sat silently. A black Mercedes with New York plates was the most visible.

Buzz turned the car around and parked heading out the driveway. "OK thespians," he said as Harv and Nickerson got out and pressed the car doors closed.

The smell of pine needles pierced the night air. Stepping over the front walk, they headed toward Smith's back door where there appeared to be some illumination. The front door was dark.

"Don't sneak," whispered Nickerson when he saw Harv trying to scope out the cars back in the shadows. "Remember, we're here to save a life. We're on a noble mission."

Harv nodded and took a deep breath as they continued toward the house. He was conscious of the loud racket made by insects in the surrounding woods. Rounding the side of the house, he saw that the sun deck turned the corner and ran all along the back. Its short stairway was midway, directly across from the back door. On ascending the deck's three stairs, Harv was relieved to see the back door was left open with the screen door offering an unobstructed view of Smith's kitchen.

Nickerson knocked on the door.

"What the hell?" Smith boomed from inside. His voice sounded tense. Clearly he did not expect anyone else.

Nickerson had the screen door half open when Smith entered the kitchen.

"What the—"

"Sorry to disturb you, Steve," said Nickerson, entering the kitchen, "but we got a medical emergency down at the inn."

"You too?" Smith looked at Harv, entering behind Nickerson. "Jesus Christ, you just come walking into—"

"It's a life and death situation, Mr. Smith." Harv

closed the door behind him. "I'm just trying to help out Mr. Nickerson any way I can."

"All right. What the hell's going on?" Smith glanced quickly over his shoulder toward a louvered door behind him.

"We got a guest allergic to bees," said Nickerson. "Been goin' out lookin' at houses with your gal down at the office—Blanche Crenshaw."

"Yeah, so what's the emergency?" Smith did not look happy.

"She just got stung by a bee 'bout a half hour ago and can't find her anti-toxin kit anywhere, and last time she remembers seein' it was at your office today."

No one spoke for a second.

"Your number's not listed," continued Nickerson, "We didn't know what else to do."

"We hoped you could let us into the office to see if she left it there," said Harv.

"The hospital's quite a ways and she might not make it," added Nickerson.

Smith took a deep breath and looked at the door behind him again. "OK, OK, I'll give Blanche a call. She can meet you there." He walked over toward the wall telephone while Harv stepped around him closer to the louvered door. He could hear the low gurgling of male conversation. Nickerson paced back and forth on Smith's other side, distracting attention from Harv. The instant Smith turned and faced the wall to dial, Harv opened the door and walked in.

"Sorry to disturb you people," he said to the four surprised men. Indeed, the level of shock, astonishment, and rage in the room could have set off a small bomb. A tanned, patrician man in a blue blazer was seated on the couch. An oriental man with glasses sat across from him. The third, sitting on a straight back chair, was blond, muscular, probably mid-thirties, and rose to his feet as Harv entered the room. To the blond man's right, in a large wingback chair sat Peter Burke.

The usually collected exterior of ADI's senior vice president melted as Harv stood looking at him. The implications of Peter being at this meeting pierced his brain like an ice pick.

"Peter?" Harv's eyes widened. He tried to organize his thoughts.

Burke reached out and grabbed Blondie with his right arm, stopping the man from accosting Harv.

"We've got a medical emergency down at the inn," Harv looked at the other men. "I apologize for the interruption."

The tendons popped out on Burke's neck as he pulled his angry colleague back toward his chair. "Well I'll be damned," said Peter. "I can't get away from you anywhere." He smiled, stepping between Blondie and Harv. The two shook hands as Smith entered from the kitchen.

"Hey! Nobody told you to go barging in—"

"Relax, Steve," said Peter, holding up his hand, "I guess there's some kind of emergency."

"Just wanted to apologize to your friends."

"Terrific. Now if you'll just wait in the kitchen, I'll finish calling Blanche."

"That's OK, I know this guy," said Peter. "I'll make sure he doesn't steal anything."

"You know this guy?" Smith's annoyance turned to

panic. Harv heard the man in the blue blazer groan quietly.

"Yeah, he's always barging into meetings down at ADI. We've learned to live with it." Peter smiled and gave Harv a light punch on the arm.

Smith swore and returned to the kitchen.

"Talk about small world," said Peter.

"Yeah," Harv forced a smile, "so you on vacation here or what?"

The other men looked at each other.

"Sort of a working vacation," said Peter. "Nancy and I've been coming here for years. Thought we'd invest in some real estate."

"Oh yeah. I guess that's always a good investment."

"Hopefully," said Peter. "Steve's an old friend. He's putting together a real estate trust thing with some associates here." He nodded toward the other three men, who just sat there looking tense.

"OK." Smith rushed back into the living room. "Blanche is on her way to open up the office. She'll, no doubt, be waiting for you when you get there."

"Oh great." Harv was glad to get the hell out of there. "We may have saved a life tonight."

"Yeah, terrific," said Smith, motioning Harv toward the door.

"I apologize again, gentlemen."

"Listen, Harv," Peter held up his hand as if he'd just gotten an idea, "Give me a call when you get back to Boston. When you getting back? Monday?"

"Yeah, I've got a Monday morning meeting."

"I'll be in the office all day Monday. Why don't you

drop in and see me. We've got another project I've been meaning to talk to you about. Could be a biggie."

"Great," Harv tried to generate his sincerest smile, "I'll do it." He didn't feel comfortable agreeing to see Peter. He was dazed, and that's all he could think of saying at the moment.

No one spoke inside the car as it left the driveway. When Harv told them who he was talking to in the living room, there was more silence.

"Your friend has got to be dirty," said Buzz, pressing down on the accelerator.

Harv was quiet.

"You know him long?" asked Nickerson from the back seat.

"Yeah," Harv stared blankly ahead, "for quite a while."

The lights in Cove Realty's office were on, and Blanche Crenshaw's gray Acura was parked out front. She'd checked the lady's room and had the anti-toxin kit in hand when Nickerson entered the office. After a polite exchange of 'thank you' and 'best wishes for Mrs. Thompson's recovery,' he returned to the car and sped off toward the Seaview.

"You recognize any of those guys in there, Bart?" asked Buzz.

"No. I was tryin' to keep Smith distracted in the kitchen so Harv could do his thing."

Buzz turned on to Cove Road. "How about you, Harv? You recognize any of the others?"

"No. Just the one."

Buzz checked his speedometer. "You going to be OK, sport?"

Harv stared out the window. "Yeah . . . I'll be OK."

CHAPTER 18

Harv left for Boston Sunday afternoon still dazed, as if some other body was driving the car, and he was just tagging along, not really plugged in.

He'd spent the morning emotionally numb, slowly packing up his things, wondering if he should call Chuck, but decided this was definitely the kind of information that had to be delivered face-to-face.

Buzz had accepted Nickerson's invitation to stay up in Maine for a few extra days to test his invention. They'd marked off some experimental sites where Buzz could test its range and accuracy.

The Saturday afternoon traffic was not as bad as Harv had feared, and the Chevy raced south to Boston.

Peter Burke is the mole, Harv said to himself again. His mind had been going over the same thing for the past fifteen hours. *How could Peter not be the mole?*

He tried to construct a scenario that would accommodate the overheard telephone conversation, the security problem at ADI, and Peter being at Smith's house—a scenario that would accommodate those facts and still paint Peter as a good guy. He couldn't do it.

*   *   *

At 9:30 Monday morning Harv bounded up ADI's entrance stairs two at a time. Instead of Jimmy Jarvis, another security guard was manning the desk. Harv signed in, trying not to look tense. After receiving his security badge, he went quickly over to the visitors' phone to call Chuck.

"Shirley, this is Harvey Gallagher. I'm here to see Chuck."

Weitz's secretary told him her boss was still at a meeting but was expected back any minute. Her voice was calm and relaxed, devoid of any urgency or excitement. He'd rather have been greeted with more enthusiasm, although he understood she was completely out of the loop and had no idea what he was about to unload on Chuck.

"Shirley." Harv looked around the waiting area quickly. "This is important. Can I wait down in Chuck's outer office?" The last thing Harv needed was to have Peter find him waiting in the visitors' area for Chuck.

"You're in a big hurry today I see."

"Yeah, I guess I am; it's really important, Shirley."

"OK," she said. "come on down."

Harv took a chair across from Shirley's desk in the reception area outside Chuck's office. He removed the short outline he'd prepared from his briefcase and read it for the fifth time. It did an excellent job of laying out the facts heard in the key telephone conversation they recorded. There's no way he was going to let Chuck know about the wiretap, so they created a false narrative about a friend of Crowley's overhearing a conversation at a coffee shop between Smith and another man, an out-of-towner. According to their narrative, the friend knew Crowley suspected Smith of wrongdoing and would love to put him away. He purposely sat down in the next booth and wrote down what he'd heard on a napkin. Harv's little paper was an outline of those notes. It was purposely sketchy. After all, one doesn't overhear everything when eaves-dropping. Just the basic facts. A few key words. They wanted Weitz to have all the pertinent information without letting him know about the wiretap.

They knew Weitz would not be like Crowley and look the other way. Indeed, they knew they'd be in serious trouble if he knew the truth. Crowley had been totally on board with the false narrative they created. Harv hoped Weitz would be so shocked and absorbed in the Peter Burke issue, he would not look a gift-horse in the mouth or do much questioning about the outline.

Shirley typed and answered the phone while Harv looked at his watch and put the outline back in his briefcase.

"No, Mr. Burke, he's still not back. I have your other message for him to call you." Shirley's words ripped through Harvey. "Yes, sir, top priority. I understand. Certainly. As soon as he gets back."

Harv sat up straight. "That was Mr. Burke? Peter Burke?"

"Uh, yes," Shirley seemed a little put off, "although that's really Mr. Weitz's business."

"I'm sorry, Shirley. I'm not prying, I'm really not." Harv sat back, then sat straight up again. He looked at his watch.

When Chuck turned the corner into his reception

area, Harv stood up and thrust out his hand. "Chuck, it's good to see you."

"Well," Chuck smiled and shook Harv's hand, "the happy wanderer returns. I guess we've got a lot to talk about." He motioned to his office.

"More than you realize."

"Uh, before you talk to Mr. Gallagher, Chuck, Peter Burke has called several times." Shirley stood up and handed her boss the messages. "He wants you to call him. Says it's top priority." She looked at Harvey.

Weitz nodded. "Let me just take care of this, Harv."

"Chuck, listen to me." Harv grabbed Weitz's arm. "If it turns out that I'm wrong and that what I'm about to do is inappropriate, I want you to feel free to fire me as a consultant and never hire me again. But, Chuck, trust me. Right now the most important thing you can do is come into your office with me, close the door, and listen to what I have to say."

Weitz paused and looked straight at Harv.

Harv looked back.

"Hold my calls, Shirley. Tell them I'm still in a meeting." He extended his arm, motioning Harv into his office. After closing the door behind them, he walked over to his desk and sat down. "OK, Harv, shoot. What do you have for me?"

Harv told him about the overheard conversation, about Smith's meeting Saturday night and finding Peter Burke at the meeting. He handed him the notes and explained the false narrative they'd created.

Chuck's facial expression changed. He looked dead serious—almost angry. He examined the notes and was silent. Harv's stomach churned as Weitz stared and read for what seemed an hour.

"And Peter Burke was at that meeting." Chuck's eyebrows went up. "Our Peter Burke?"

He bought it. "Yes, I'm sure it's just a coincidence and he's just gotten involved with some bad real estate people or something."

Chuck stared at the notes. "Crowley's friend has great hearing." He shook his head and looked out into space. "You know I wish you'd called and told me you were going to crash Smith's party."

"You'd have told me not to go, right?"

"I don't know." He looked straight at Harv. "Probably. You put yourself in more danger than you realize."

"And if I hadn't gone, we'd be completely ignorant about who the ADI man is in those notes. And the opportunity would be gone forever."

Chuck held up the outline. "I'm keeping this." It was a statement, not a question.

"It's yours," said Harv as Weitz gazed at the notes again.

"This name, *Zhang*, we're investigating that incident right now. The guy was passing himself off as a Shanghai manufacturer and was found floating in the Charles River with some ADI papers in his pocket three weeks ago. We suspected a Shamosho hit," he looked at the transcript again, "and this confirms it."

"What's the Shamosho?"

Chuck looked up from his reading and paused a moment. "You don't want to know."

"I don't?"

"They're like middle men, Harv. Brokers of stolen

technology to any company willing to pay their price. And they're dangerous as hell. They get hold of pre-production secret technology, sell it to foreign manufacturers, and make a fortune. Look, Harv, when you start messing around in corporate espionage, you tend to run into some pretty bad dudes. There are some things we definitely have to check out before I can open up on this as much as I'd like." He paused for a second, looking very serious. "Believe me, I'll tell you everything you need to know as soon as I can."

Harv looked at his watch as Chuck read the document again and tapped his pen slowly on his desk. "The words 'Your man from ADI', that's what gets me. Smith's coffee companion says 'Your man from ADI.' Then bam! There's Peter at the scene, a man from ADI." He paused a moment. "It's too tight."

Harv's fingernail dug into his wooden pencil. He took a quick breath. "You mean you didn't send Peter up there to scout around or go undercover or anything?"

Chuck stared at Harv for a second. "No."

Harv changed positions in his chair and glanced at his watch. "Oh, I almost forgot. When I saw Peter, he told me to stop in and see him today. He said he had a new project for me which could be really big."

"That it?"

"Yeah, that's all. Just that it could be a really big project."

"And he just called me with a top priority message; I think I can guess what it's going to be about."

They both stared at each other for a moment.

"Harv, I want you to listen to me. I know what you're

thinking, and you know what I'm thinking. First of all, I need your word that nothing you and I have talked about will ever leave this office."

"You got it."

"Secondly, either Peter is involved in this thing, or there may be some explanation and he isn't involved. I've been doing this for a lot of years now, and my instincts are pretty good." Chuck forced a joyless, businesslike smile. "I'm going to discount the possibility that you're lying to me."

"Gee thanks."

"If Peter's somehow involved in this, you've got to be very careful. He knows what you're probably thinking. If he's dirty, you've blown his cover and he's going to do whatever it takes to protect himself. I don't want to scare you, Harv, but there may be some shit hitting the fan around here and you're a prime target."

Harv's thumbnail scratched more paint off his yellow pencil, making a long groove in the wood.

"Frankly, I'd like to see you lay low for a while. Somewhere away from ADI, away from Boston, someplace where you'll be safe but I can still get hold of you."

"I've got some clients I could call on this week. Out of town clients. I'd be on the road." He paused. "Oh, damn, I've got to be in Philadelphia this weekend. I almost forgot."

"Philadelphia's out of town. That qualifies."

"No, it's just that I almost forgot. I definitely have to be in Philadelphia this weekend."

"OK, it's still out of town. That's good. That's a good start. But I think two weeks out of town is better.

Don't forget, we're paying all expenses. The farther away the better."

Harv took a deep breath. "God, what a pain in the ass this is."

"I know. All I'm asking is two weeks out of town to keep you safe, and then I think we can start getting back to normal."

"You're still paying my weekly fee, right?"

"Plus the bonus. Plus expenses; so keep your receipts."

Harv nodded his head. "I've got some prospects I've been trying to crack in California. I could fly from Philadelphia to LA and make sales calls for a week."

"Sounds good. Keep your phone on so I can check up on you. I want you to call me once a day to check in." Weitz leaned forward on his elbows, looking very serious. "Harv, Peter Burke is one of the smartest, wiliest men I know. I've seen him maneuver around this company like a brain surgeon with a platinum scalpel. He's well connected. He's wealthy. He's the kind of man you don't want as an enemy. If he's involved, and frankly it looks like he might be, you're a direct threat to him."

Harv wiped his wet palm on his pant leg and brushed away the little yellow paint chips his thumb had scratched off his pencil. "Chuck, you know what he's going to say when you call him don't you."

"I've got a pretty good idea. What do you think he's going to say?"

"I think he's going to bad-mouth me somehow, even implicate me in this thing or discredit me."

"Not a bad guess." Chuck leaned back, looking

straight at Harv. "If he's dirty, he knows you can finger him, so his first step would be to somehow discredit you. I'm expecting it. I'll be real interested in seeing what he does. If this top priority message of his trashes you somehow, I'm going to interpret it as very possibly the predictable smoke screen of a guilty man."

Harv nodded. "What happens if he does implicate me and it turns out to be his word against mine? As you said, he's well connected. I'm a damn outsider."

Chuck's serious expression warmed up a bit. "If he does, Harv, I'll certainly have to check out whatever he brings up. But I'll tell you this—I'm good at what I do. I have real good instincts, and I'm good at separating fact from fiction." He looked at his watch, got up from his desk, and walked around to the front. "Harv, if you're clean and you shoot straight with me, you'll have nothing to worry about from me. Right now it's Peter I'm concerned with, and I want you to get the hell out of town."

Harv sat in silence.

"Listen, Harv, there's one last thing before you take off."

"What's that?"

"How good an actor are you?"

"Actor? Why?" Harv closed his briefcase and got up from his chair.

"Peter asked you to come see him right?"

"Yeah."

"It was to see him in person today, not just to call him?"

"Yeah, he wanted me to stop in and see him today. Why?"

"What did you say when he asked you?"

"I said I'd do it. But I'm not going to. Not now. What are you getting at?"

Chuck rubbed his hands together and sat on the arm of the big couch by the door. "Well, if he's dirty, this would be a very predictable ploy. He probably wants to read you to see if you think he's involved, or if you bought into his story about real estate investing."

"So what does that have to do with acting?"

"Listen, a lot will depend on how you behave. If you think he's guilty, you'll avoid him and run like hell."

"That's exactly what I intend to do. That's what you told me to do."

"If you can pull it off, I think it'll help your cause by dropping in and seeing him here at ADI before you leave. He can't hurt you here."

"Are you kidding?" Harv stared at Chuck and paced across the floor. "I can't. I can't do that."

"If you were convinced in your gut that he was Mister Clean, involved only in some innocent real estate deal in Maine and had a big, profitable assignment for you, what would you do?"

"I'd be in his office in a flash."

"That's right and he knows it. He's already testing you and you don't realize it yet." Chuck smiled, watching Harv pace around the room. "Even if you're only an average actor, the fact that you went to see him will say a lot. If you can pull it off, you'll buy yourself some breathing room."

Harv looked at his watch, then at Chuck, and continued pacing.

"Peter's already started to play his hand," said

Chuck. "I'll be interested in seeing how he plans to lay down his cards."

"I don't know, Chuck," Harv shook his head.

"Hey, all I can do is make recommendations here." Chuck walked up and put his hand on Harv's shoulder. "If you can't do it, that's OK. I'm just saying it would be a good idea."

CHAPTER 19

Harv went up to the fourth floor and down the familiar glass and teak corridor to Peter's office. He didn't want to be there. In fact it's the last place on earth he wanted to be, but Chuck's argument made sense. Showing up might buy Harv some breathing room. If he could just get through a quick meeting with Peter without blowing it, then he could get the hell out of there and let things shake themselves out.

He recalled the first time he'd walked that corridor. The world looked a lot different then. He was calling on an old friend, a mentor who had meant a lot to his career in the past, someone who was potentially a great client for his new business. The place looked bright and shiny then, very impressive. Now he was nervous as hell. The modern decor now looked garish and cold. The flowers looked plastic and he noticed a stain on the carpet.

"Hi, Harv," Peter's secretary called out as he approached, "you here to see the man?"

"Absolutely. How've you been?" Harv tried to look as relaxed and normal as possible.

"I've been great." Lois smiled. "Hang on. Let me tell Peter you're here. He said he was expecting you sometime today." She buzzed Peter and, after a short conversation, told Harv he'd be right out.

Harv tried to relax as he sat down in the waiting area. He rubbed the palms of his hands against his pants and picked up a magazine but put it down quickly because his hands were sweating. After chatting with Lois, he waited some more. Part of him expected Peter to come out immediately. After all, wasn't he dying to find out what Harv was thinking? But then Peter was the master of perception. Harv always had to wait a bit in the past. If everything was supposed to be normal, why shouldn't he wait now?

The complexity and brilliance of Peter's mind flashed into Harv's consciousness. He didn't know if he could pull this off. He told himself to relax, that this was like any other meeting with Peter. *Don't let him read you. Just be cool.* He looked up to see if Lois could perceive his stress, but she was busy typing. He looked down at the coffee table and picked up another magazine.

"Coffee?" asked Lois.

"Huh? Uh, no thanks." Harv threw the magazine back down on the table. "I've already had three cups this morning. I'm trying to cut down."

"I know what you mean." Lois resumed her work.

Harv began to hope this delay was legitimate and not just a typical Peter Burke contrivance. Maybe the guy got involved in a corporate crisis and would have to postpone the meeting. Suddenly Harv saw a way out of this thing. He'd tell Lois he was in a hurry, and maybe he could reschedule the meeting. He looked at his watch. Seven minutes had passed. It seemed like twenty. Seven minutes wasn't long enough to justify a postponement. He decided to wait for fifteen minutes. Then he'd do it. Then he'd be out of there. At least he'd have shown up.

He picked up another magazine and tried turning pages without shaking the paper. He looked at his watch. Eight minutes. His stomach was a knot. He turned more pages. He skimmed an article but couldn't concentrate. When the minute hand hit fourteen minutes, he put his third magazine down and stretched. Fourteen minutes was close enough. As he sat up in his chair to talk to Lois, however, Peter Burke emerged from his office.

"Hi, Harv," Peter said, then turned to Lois, put a folder on her desk, and asked her to do something.

Harv stood up and said hello as Peter turned and shook his hand. Harv knew his hand must have felt warm and sweaty but Peter smiled and seemed perfectly normal.

"You made it back in one piece I see."

"I can't say I'm all that thrilled to be back," Harv followed Peter into his office, "but all good things must end."

Peter's office looked the same, but it didn't feel the same. The antique gumball machine no longer looked irreverent and funky. It came across now as phony and contrived.

"Sit down, Harv, I just have to make one call then we can chat." Peter sat down behind his big mahogany desk and picked up the phone.

Harv took a seat, wondering what Peter meant by "then we can chat." It sounded like he had a definite agenda. Was he going to mention the Maine thing? It had to come up somehow. Then he realized, of course there was an agenda, talking about the new assignment. That was the agenda. Harv tried not to over-analyze the situation, but it was difficult. He knew Peter well enough to understand that whatever public agenda was transpiring, the man always had his own personal, hidden agenda, churning in the background. Harv had to watch for it. He had to stay on top of things.

He sat back and looked around the office. The pictures of famous people and successful advertising campaigns somehow looked less impressive. Rather than casual displays of marketing experience, they came across as badges of self-promotion. The expensive artwork looked ostentatious now.

"Glad you stopped by, Harv." Peter put down the phone.

"You said the magic words, Peter, 'big assignment.' I'm like Pavlov's dog. Show me money and I salivate." Harv recoiled at his own words. *God, too tacky. Don't overdo it.*

Peter smiled. "Just don't go drooling on my furniture."

They both laughed. Maybe the Pavlov's dog crack wasn't too tacky after all, Harv thought. It got things focused on something other than Maine. Harv seized the opening.

"So what's this new project that's going to make us all stinking rich?"

Peter sat back and told Harv all about the new venture, a new microchip breakthrough that would take cellular communication to another level. It would allow for total personal communication through an enhanced wristwatch. The everyday timepiece could double as a smartphone.

"I know Apple has the jump on this," said Burke, "but our concept will be more reliable and more powerful." They talked about how the system would work and what market research would be needed.

Harv paused to wipe the sweat from his palms and hoped Peter didn't notice. Somehow the fact that Burke hadn't yet mentioned Maine was significant. He was probably uncomfortable about it and wanted to take a reading of Harv to see how best to play it. Peter was always careful, always calculating. But if he was uncomfortable, that fact alone meant something. Harv's mind raced. Why would Peter feel uncomfortable unless he was guilty? If he'd been up in Maine at Smith's house for some benign purpose, he would have said something first thing. Something like "small world," or "what the hell were you doing in my vacation spot?" Peter's super calculating, cerebral nature was his undoing. His need to calculate, to plan, to be cautious overshadowed the spontaneity and naturalness of simple truth.

Harv tried to focus on taking notes and listening to Peter, but his mind kept racing with thoughts of guile, deceit, and hidden agendas. There was still a chance Peter was innocent, but in his heart, Harv knew he wasn't. It was like filling in the lines of a connect-the-dots drawing, showing Peter as the mole. Some of the dots were still untouched, but one could look at the page and anticipate how new lines would fall. Peter's handling of the Maine incident simply allowed Harv to fill in more lines.

He looked across the desk at Peter and listened to the details of what was almost certainly a bogus ruse of an assignment. Apple had this market cold. It was a fool's errand to try and catch up. He felt strange sitting there, watching someone he once admired lie through his teeth.

"We're going to need market projections, consumer perceptions, probably focus groups, and an initial marketing plan," said Peter.

Harv continued taking notes and asking questions. He did his best to play the part. When the conversation reached its conclusion, he asked a few final questions and got up to leave.

"Say, did that woman make it OK?" Peter stood up and walked around the desk to stand by Harv.

"Woman?" Harv paused for a moment. "What woman?"

"In Maine."

Harv's mind drew a blank for a second. "Oh, the bee sting." His face flushed as he realized he'd better keep his own ruses straight while trying to see through Peter's. "Uh, yeah, she made it OK. It was close but she recovered pretty quickly."

Peter smiled. "Good, so you found what you were looking for?"

Harv's face flushed again. For the first time in the meeting he felt off balance. "Looking for?"

"Yes, looking for." Peter stared intently at Harvey. No one spoke.

Looking for what? He wondered if Peter knew they had gone to Smith's house looking for information.

"The bee sting anti toxin kit you were looking for," said Peter finally. "I assume you found it at the office."

"Oh, yeah." Harv took a breath and smiled. "It was there. The real estate lady had found it before we got there." He started walking toward the door. He wanted to leave. "We brought it back to the inn and the woman recovered pretty quickly." Harv felt violated. Chuck was right. Peter was a smooth surgeon probing with a scalpel. He worded his questions perfectly. He probed at the right time in the right place. Harv knew his facade had been compromised, but hoped it wasn't shattered.

"That's good." Peter followed Harv toward the door. "People with bad allergies like that have got to be careful."

"That's true. She shouldn't have let that kit out of her sight." Harv felt he was just bobbing and weaving. He sensed Peter was dancing around, looking for another opportunity to probe. He had to take himself out of the cross hairs and seize the initiative. "So how did that real estate thing go? You close the deal?"

Burke's facial expression changed. "Not yet. There are still some legal technicalities to overcome but I'm optimistic. I can't believe you picked the same little town for your vacation."

"Small world I guess." Harv forced a smile, wishing he was somewhere else.

"It sure as hell is. But I suppose there are only so many places people can go. You're bound to bump into someone you already know at some point."

"Yeah, I guess so." Harv took another step toward the door. "Listen, if your deal up there is half as successful as all your other projects, let me in on it OK?" He tried to look natural and sincere.

Peter smiled. "We'll see." He patted Harv on the shoulder. "We'll see."

While opening the office door, Peter stopped suddenly and closed it again. "Hey, I almost forgot. I want you to have some working capital up front on this one." He turned and walked back toward his desk. "I've got a signed purchase order here and the necessary clearance documents in this secure envelope." He opened the top desk drawer and pulled out a large, white envelope with orange tape sealing the flap and the words *Top Security ADI Corporation* printed on both sides.

When Peter handed the envelope to him, Harv examined it carefully. "This sure is official looking."

"It's just routine for security projects like this one. I want you to take it to Michael Plitski over in Special Projects Payroll. He's in the east wing." Peter opened the office door again. "Take it to him on your way out, and he'll get the bureaucratic paperwork out of the way so we can get a retainer out to you as soon as we get your proposal and cost estimate. Assuming it's reasonable." He smiled.

"That'll really be a help." Harv walked out into the foyer.

Peter guided him past Lois's desk out to the far side of the Marketing Department toward the main corridor.

"I'll get a proposal out to you in two weeks." Harv

opened his briefcase and inserted the envelope. "So where exactly is this guy's office anyway?"

"Go to the east wing, third floor, office number fifty-seven. And remember, that orange seal has got to be unbroken." Peter smiled. "Those are the rules."

"I hear you." Harv said goodbye and headed to the main corridor toward the elevators. Walking briskly, he had the same mixed feeling of relief and worry he used to have after a final exam when he wasn't sure how well he'd done but was glad to have it over with. He didn't know whether Peter had seen through him or not, but he was glad the meeting was behind him. He figured he'd drop off the envelope, get the hell out of there, and call Chuck from his apartment.

Harv had to ask directions through the maze of ADI hallways. He'd heard people speak of the east wing, but his visits had all focused on the west wing where the executive offices were.

After walking what seemed to be several miles of hallways, he entered the east wing, and found the right area. It was a suite of related offices like Harv had seen in the west wing, but the ambience was different. It was noisy, packed with support people, assistants, and secretaries, walking around in all directions. He found the head guy doing paperwork behind a brass nameplate reading *Michael L. Plitski*.

"Mr. Plitski?"

The man put up his hand and added a few more figures on his calculator. "Sorry about that." He looked up. "I was in the middle of something. Can I help you?"

"Well I'm not sure." Harv looked around the sparse office. "Is this Special Projects Payroll?"

"That's us."

Harv took the envelope out of his briefcase. "Peter Burke in Marketing asked me to give this to you. He felt you could get some initial paperwork out of the way for a project I'm working on. I'm Harvey Gallagher, President of Gallagher & Associates. I'm a consultant."

"Ah, so this is going to cut down on paperwork, huh?"

"Well I don't think it will actually cut down any paperwork. Peter and I wouldn't dream of cheating you guys out of any crucial bureaucratic paperwork. This will simply give you a chance to start on it sooner so I can get paid sooner."

Plitski smiled. "Ah, a joke about paperwork. I like it. You wouldn't dream of cheating us guys out of any important paperwork." He laughed.

Plitski took the envelope and examined it. "It's just procedure with these things. I have to make sure the orange tape is unbroken."

"I understand." Harv was glad to be rid of the thing.

CHAPTER 20

The Boston traffic was sluggish as Harv drove home. On arriving at his apartment, he could immediately tell Sheila had been there. The place looked neat, and there was a note on the refrigerator saying "I'll be back." He opened a beer, sat back in his recliner, and called Chuck.

"Mr. Weitz's office," came Shirley's now familiar voice.

Harv took a swig of beer. "Shirley, this is Harvey Gallagher."

"Yes, Mr. Gallagher. I'm sorry Mr. Weitz is in a meeting."

"Shirley, this is extremely important. I don't think there's been a security crisis more important than this in the history of ADI." He had to talk with Chuck about his meeting with Peter. "It's something I'm working on very closely with Chuck. I know, no matter what meeting he may be in, I know he would want to be interrupted. Would you please tell him I'm on the line for him?"

Shirley was silent. "One moment please," she said crisply.

Harv knew he was stepping on Shirley's toes. She was gatekeeper to a key decision-maker and apparently unaccustomed to being strong-armed by outside consultants. But he didn't have the patience or inclination right now for excessive tact. This crisis gave Harv automatic access, and if Shirley resented it, she'd just have to get over it.

After a short wait, Shirley returned to the phone. "Mr. Gallagher?" Her tone was still cool, "Mr. Weitz will call you in five minutes. Can you wait that long?"

"Yes, Shirley, I can wait five minutes. But it's vital I talk to him then."

"Yes, I understand that. Is there a number where he can reach you right now?"

Harv gave her his number, even though he knew Weitz already had it, and within six minutes Chuck rang back. It was good to hear his voice. He told Chuck about the meeting with Peter, the probing, the bobbing and weaving on both sides. He wondered if he'd done the right thing, taking the envelope directly to Plitski.

"You can't second-guess yourself, Harv." Chuck's voice was calm. "In my opinion you did the right thing. If you hadn't gone directly to this Plitski guy, whoever he is, Peter would be suspicious. He'd know you suspected him."

"So, you've never heard of Plitski?"

"Not really. It's impossible to know everybody in this company, but I'm definitely going to check it out." He asked Harv to describe the man and reassured him that he'd done the right thing.

"Do you think Burke suspects I think he's involved?"

"There's a big difference between suspecting and knowing. He may suspect. He's no fool. He'd be wise to, at least, entertain the idea. But he doesn't know for sure in my opinion. And that's your main source of security right now. And that's the way we're going to keep it. I want you out of this thing."

"You sound more concerned than usual." Harv asked him if he'd returned Peter's telephone call, and Chuck told him Peter had just mentioned that he'd seen Harv in Maine. He said Peter didn't use the telephone conversation to discredit Harv directly but from the general thrust of the conversation he was expecting him to do it. He was laying the groundwork.

"Sounds like there's something you're not telling me." Harv took a long swig of beer.

"Just consider yourself to have done a tremendous job for ADI, Harv. And now it's over, and I want you to lay low for a while just like we discussed in my office."

Harv's thumbnail scratched off a corner of the label on his cold beer bottle.

"Listen, this guy you took the envelope to, exactly how do you spell his name?"

Harv spelled out Plitski's name as best he could remember, described the man's appearance, and told Chuck what took place. "I assume that's fairly standard procedure. I mean putting a purchase order through some bureaucratic machinations over in Payroll." Harv took another swig of beer.

"To a point it is," said Weitz. "To get a consultant paid on a secured project, the project leader has to develop an SPO, a Security Purchase Order, and get it over to Special Projects Payroll."

"Seems logical to me."

"But it's highly irregular to use the consultant

himself as a courier for that envelope. Something very unlike Peter Burke."

Harv changed positions on the couch and took a big swallow of beer.

"I'm looking here in our directory and it shows the name of Michael Plitski. He is, indeed, an employee here and the right guy to start a project like this."

Harv scraped off more of the beer label with his thumbnail. "Let me just talk about this a second, Chuck. First of all, I'm convinced in my gut this new assignment is bogus. I think he's trying to buy my loyalty, or silence or cooperation, or something like that."

"That's exactly what I think," said Chuck. "I think he's buying himself some breathing room until he can figure out what to do with you."

"That makes me nervous, but moving right along with this train of thought—once he figures that out, he'll tell me top management decided to focus on other things and has scrapped the project."

"Something like that. But there's more here, Harv. The guy is really laying down his cards for us. I mean look at the care and energy that went into creating that top security envelope. Dangling it in front of you. Having you take it over to Payroll so you could get paid." He paused. "Did the envelope have an orange tape sealing the flap?"

"Yes, the whole enchilada."

"He created a great prop."

"And you said that was highly irregular to have me deliver the envelope."

"Right. He went out of his way to provide proof to you that this is a real assignment. That's huge."

"The guy is so careful and manipulative."

"That's his weakness. We can read him like a book. He feels vulnerable. You penetrated his shield. He needs to buy some time with you, so he over-does this little bit of theater."

Harv took another swig of beer.

"Listen, Harv. It's vital you don't let on you suspect a thing. You understand?

"Yes, totally."

"OK, so the more you act like you think Peter's innocent, the less of a threat you are to him and the safer you are."

Harv said nothing for a moment. "It's still hard to digest the fact that Peter's in on this." He took another swallow of beer. "You're sure he's involved aren't you?"

"Do I have incontrovertible proof? No. Do I suspect him? Absolutely . . . Harv, like I said, I want you out of this as of now. You understand?"

"Don't worry, I'm out." Harv picked off more of his beer label.

"You make your travel reservations yet?"

"No, I just got in and called you. I'll do it as soon as I hang up. I'll make sales calls in Connecticut this week—Hartford mostly. Then I'll fly down to Philly for the weekend, then out to LA the following week."

"Just check in with me once a day and keep your phone on."

Harv looked up when he heard the clanking sound of his lock turning and waved at Sheila, pushing the door open with a bag full of groceries. He took a deep breath and waved, pointing to the phone in his hand. She blew him a kiss and walked over to the kitchen.

Chuck gave Harv his cell phone number. "Enter that number in your phone, Harv, so you can speed-dial me. I don't want you to have to go through a kabuki dance with Shirley when you want to talk with me. Just call my cell phone from now on."

As the conversation drew to a close, Chuck repeated his cell phone number and reminded Harv he needed to talk with him every day.

"Talking to ADI again; I can tell." Sheila unpacked groceries in the Kitchen. "All this top secret stuff you can't tell me about." She brought two chilled glasses of white wine over to the couch as Harv said goodbye to Chuck.

"Ah, wine." Harv grabbed the extended glass. "I just had a beer. I'll probably be smashed by the time the evening's over."

"A glass of wine is not going to kill you." Sheila gave him a kiss and headed back to the kitchen.

"Yeah, I can see it coming," said Harv. "Ply me with liquor and then you'll try to take advantage of me."

"Ha!" Sheila yelled in from the kitchen.

"I just hope you'll still respect me in the morning."

They finished off two glasses of wine each. Harv opened his laptop and made his plane reservations to Philadelphia and L.A. while Sheila puttered in the kitchen. He wrote down the flight information and sat back as the pleasant aroma of Sheila's chicken and onion concoction began filling the room.

"I'm flying down to Philadelphia Wednesday to get ready for your visit." Sheila walked over to the couch. "When are you getting in?

"Friday night. I just made the reservation." He

handed her a piece of paper with the Philadelphia portion of his flight written down. "Can you meet me at the airport?"

"Of course. I'll meet you, and we can go out for a nice late dinner. It'll be a great weekend."

"I'm going to be out of town after that though."

"Out of town?" She frowned. "You just got back from being out of town at that inn you raved about. Where are you going to be?"

"I can't tell you."

"Oh, God. More of this secret stuff with ADI. Honestly, those people are so secretive."

"It's no big deal. They're paying me to lie low for a few weeks. So after tomorrow, I'm just going to be out of town."

"Lie low? Is anything wrong?"

"No, no, just part of a security program I'm working on."

Sheila snuggled up next to Harv. "A few weeks is a long time. And you can't tell me where you're going to be? I mean besides Philadelphia?"

"It's part of a special security thing I'm working on. I'm not supposed to tell people exactly where I am." He took a sip of wine. "You know, top secret Defense Department government stuff."

"So you're lying low for a few weeks." Sheila looked at him with a cynical smile. "You don't have to be coy with me, sweetie."

"I don't?"

"Of course not." She raised her eyebrows with an all-knowing look. "You know one of my best qualities is my highly developed sense of intuition. You don't have to lie to me."

"I'm not. I'm . . ."

"You're going to that inn aren't you? The Seaview." She looked into his eyes and took a sip of wine. "I know how much you loved that place. I could feel it pouring out of you when you told me about it."

Harv opened his mouth but said nothing.

"I'm right aren't I? Somehow you got your client to pay your way to lie low at that inn."

"You are amazing." Harv shook his head. "That intuition stuff is incredible."

"But you're still flying down to Philadelphia this weekend." It was not a question.

"Absolutely. Actually I'll be seeing clients around here this week and then lying low next week. But don't tell anyone you figured it out about the Seaview."

She sat back with a smug look on her face. "It's pretty basic really. You love the place. You're an expert at getting clients to pay your way. It's isolated, a great place to lie low in comfort." She took a sip of wine.

"Don't tell anyone though, OK? You promise?"

"Oh, don't worry. Your secret's safe with me. But aren't you impressed how I just knew?"

"Awestruck. But don't ever call me there directly. If you ever need to talk to me, always dial my cell phone. That's important."

"OK, OK, but listen," Sheila turned to face Harv directly, "you don't have to go to Maine. You can stay with us. There's tons to do in Philadelphia. I've got vacation time coming. It'll be great."

"As tempting as that sounds, Sheila, I think not."

Sheila got up from the couch and put on a CD. "Well at least you're coming. That's the important thing."

* * *

Tuesday morning Harv stopped by his office, packed up his briefcase, and paid some bills. His part-time secretary was off that day, so he left a list of things to do and a short note saying he'd be visiting clients for the next week or so.

He drove to his apartment, parked on the street, and walked up the front steps. Then he heard it—a crack, a pop like a firecracker, the whoosh of wind over his right ear, and the sharp smack as something crashed into the brick around his front door.

Sandy fragments spat out over Harv as he dove down on the top landing—a stream of expletives erupting from his mouth. He turned and saw a black car cruising away. It looked like New York plates. It looked like the car he'd seen at Smith's house in Maine.

It's Burke. It's got to be Burke.

He wondered if it could have been a random shoot-ing but figured Burke was behind it somehow; pulling the strings; orchestrating it. The black car, the license plate. It had to be Burke.

He got a knife from the kitchen and dug the bullet out of the old brick outside his door. He put it in an envelope, wrote a note on a piece of paper, and stuffed it in the envelope with the bullet. After sealing the envelope, he wrote on the outside: *Chuck Weitz, Highly Confidential.*

His bedroom was still neat from Sheila's domestic

organizing. He got out his suitcase and put the envelope in an inside flap. He threw in enough clothes for an extended trip then loaded up his car and headed out.

On the way to ADI, he called Chuck's office. When Shirley told him her boss was in a meeting, he simply told her he was on his way to drop something off. Harv was pleasantly surprised to find Shirley in a good mood when he got there. She gave the OK for him to come directly to her office and promised to give the envelope to Chuck as soon as he got in.

Harv maxed out the speed limit on the Mass Pike on his way to Connecticut. It felt good to be driving fast. He wanted to cancel the two client meetings he'd set up but thought better of it. He'd just have to tough it out. The afternoon meeting went well, but he couldn't get rid of the knot in his stomach. He wondered if his hands had shaken during the meeting. He didn't care. The first meeting was over; all he had to do was get through the second one tomorrow and then he could really disappear.

Harv's phone rang while checking into the Ideal Motel on the Berlin Turnpike south of Hartford. The caller ID said Chuck Weitz.

"Chuck, thank Jesus."

"Hey, Harv, I got your envelope."

"Hang on a second, Chuck. I'm in the lobby right now checking in. I want to talk to you in my room."

"I can call you back."

"No." Harv looked up and lowered his voice. "I mean, no, I don't want to lose you. Just hang on two seconds."

He signed the register, got his key, and drove directly to the open space in front of his room. After closing and locking the door, he turned on the light and closed the drapes.

"Chuck, I was shot at, man. That bullet you've got whizzed right by my ear."

"I'm just glad as hell you're OK, kid. Where are you now?"

"In Connecticut."

"I want you farther out of town than that, and I want you to stay the hell out of town until I tell you different. Understand?"

Harv told him about the black car and the New York license plates. "It's got to be Burke. If not Burke directly pulling the trigger, then his henchmen. I know that's the same car."

Weitz told him the bullet was sent to the ballistics lab and they'd have a report in two days.

"What the hell kind of lunatic is this guy? I see him in a spy meeting and now he wants to kill me?"

"This thing has cranked up to a higher level, Harv. The stakes are pretty high. I didn't want to scare you when we talked yesterday. I just want you out of town. And we need to talk every day. If I don't call you, then you call me." He assured Harv they were making progress, and the ballistics report would help tie up some loose ends.

After the call, Harv went out to get a sausage pizza and stopped by a liquor store for a fifth of Jameson Irish Whiskey. Then he drove back to the motel, made sure his door was dead-bolted, and packed himself in for the night.

*   *   *

After the Wednesday meeting in Hartford, he drove back to his motel and called his secretary. "Ann, it's me." He closed the curtains, which housekeeping had opened, and sat down on the bed.

"Harv, you're calling on my cell phone, not the office landline. You know I'm in the office today."

"I know, Ann. Listen this is important. I wanted to make sure I got you and I want you to work from home for the next two weeks."

"Why? What's going on?"

"I can't tell you now. It's a security and safety issue, and I don't want you to set foot in the office until I give you the green light." He didn't want to tell her he'd been shot at.

"You're scaring me. Are you OK?"

"Don't be scared, Ann. Do not be scared. I'm just taking some precautions."

"Yes, but are you OK?"

"I'm OK, Ann. I'm OK. Just work from home until I tell you otherwise. You'll still get paid the same rate you have now. Have the office phone forwarded to your personal cell." He gave her the numbers of two clients he was working with at that moment. "Tape those two numbers to the back of your phone. Only answer if it's me or either of those numbers. Got it?"

"I've got it, but where are you going to be?"

"I'm not going to tell you, Ann, because this way you can honestly say you have no idea where I am, and you won't be lying." He looked at his watch. Hey, I've got to go."

"And you can't tell me what's going on?"

"Honestly, Ann, you're better off not knowing any-thing. Trust me. As far as you know, everything is normal." Harv looked at his watch, told Ann he'd check in periodically, and signed off.

It was mid-afternoon and both Hartford meetings were behind him. He felt good about his call to Ann. She was very capable and could easily handle any cli-ent details over the next few weeks. The only thing he had to do was make a plane reservation and stay safe for the rest of the day. He'd planned on going to Los Angeles after Philadelphia. Now, after the shooting, he'd hit the coast a little sooner. Harv got up, peeked through the closed curtain, and called Buzz.

"Good timing." Buzz walked over to Nickerson's desk. "We're in the tower room listening to some telephone messages that aren't very relevant. Let me put you on speaker." Buzz put his phone down on the desk as Carrie and Nickerson gathered around.

Harv told him where he was, about the shooting, and about his plans to fly to California. He began pacing around his motel room.

"Shot at?" said Carrie. "You were shot at? Like with a gun?"

"This is serious stuff, sport," said Buzz. "You get your ass somewhere far away. Like yesterday."

"I know. I know. I'm going to make my reservation for the coast as soon as I hang up. I'll call you when I get there."

They talked about the wire tap and how it seemed to be drying up as a source of key information. They talked about Peter Burke and some of the things they'd like to do to him.

"I could hack into his office email system and lace his outgoing emails with profanities," said Buzz. "Or even porno attachments."

Harv laughed out loud. "I can see top level communications to Bill Cobb filled with four letter words and porno. I love it." He poured some Jameson into a glass and took a swig. "Or how about ordering a stripper to go sing Happy Birthday to him at his office?" He took another swig. It felt good going down.

Harv started to feel more relaxed as they each contributed something to the list of things they'd like to do to ADI's senior vice president. The conversation morphed into a discussion about a sting operation they'd like to pull on Burke to put him behind bars. It made Harv feel good to talk about it. The Jameson helped. After twenty minutes, the strain of the last few days began to manifest itself. Harv was tired. The conversation wound down. He signed off and made a plane reservation for the coast.

CHAPTER 21

Los Angeles was cool and cloudy when Harv's plane touched down Thursday morning. He'd left his car at the Hartford airport and managed to get a red-eye flight direct to the coast. By the time he'd rented a car and driven to his hotel in Santa Monica, it was near noon. He was tired and needed to wake up. He checked into his hotel, had a late breakfast, and walked three blocks to the beach. After a quick jog he pulled out his phone and speed-dialed Sheila. When she didn't answer, he just hung up. He didn't want to leave a message. It was definitely the kind of thing he had to say directly. He felt bad about canceling again, but there was no other way. Peter knew he dated Sheila and could get to Harv in Philadelphia. Right now he needed total inoculation from the guy. He needed breathing room, time to think.

He was surprised how cool it was on the beach, but then he remembered how Southern Californians talked about June gloom. Right when the rest of the country is starting to warm up, Southern California suddenly gets cool and cloudy for a month. Harv walked past a volleyball game and called Chuck on his cell phone.

After two rings, Weitz answered and told Harv he

was putting him on hold until he could go to a secure area to talk. He excused himself from his meeting, walked into an empty office, and closed the door. "Sorry about that, Harv. I was in a meeting. Had to get to someplace private. What's up?"

"You mean since being shot at?"

Chuck laughed. "Yeah, since then."

"Well, since then my life's been pretty boring. I just wanted to talk to a friendly voice and let you know I'm in California."

"So you bagged Philadelphia."

"Burke could get me in Philadelphia. I was going to be at my girlfriend's parents, and he knows my girl-friend. He's met her. After the shooting I just wanted to get as far away as possible."

"I don't blame you, kid. You did good, Harv. You did good." Chuck asked for the name of his hotel just in case Harv's phone wasn't turned on and he needed to reach him. "Anyone else know where you are?"

"I told the Seaview crowd."

"You tell them everything?"

"Yes, I told them everything. They're my people, my posse. I told them about the shooting and everything."

"That's good, Harv. It's good to have someone to talk to when you're going through something like this."

"It was great. We talked about all the things we'd like to do to Peter Burke."

Chucked laughed. "Just as long as you don't actually do any of them . . . I know it's tough right now. Believe me, we're making progress. Just sit tight and give me a call tomorrow."

After a few more words if encouragement from

Weitz, Harv hung up and breathed in the sea air. He walked up to the water, crouched down and put his hand in. It was extremely cold. He walked up to an area where people were surfing in black wet suits and sat down on a raised area of dry sand. He dialed a few prospects and got an appointment with one of them for the next day in Long Beach. After a few more calls and several rejections, he looked at his watch. It was 2:05 PM. It would be late afternoon in Maine. He dialed Buzz. After getting no answer, he dialed the Seaview's main number and got Marge, who quickly tracked down Nickerson.

"Harv, is that you?" said the innkeeper.

"Yeah, it's me. I called Buzz first, but he didn't answer."

"Your genius inventor is out on the floating dock."

"He actually went in the water?"

"Yeah, he complained how cold the water was, but he managed to swim out there."

Harv laughed. "Tell him the water temperature there is only three degrees colder than the Pacific here in L.A.—practically the same."

Nickerson laughed. "I'll do that. Hey, let me see if I can round up some of the gang here. I know they want to talk to you. I'll call you back when I get 'em together."

Harv sat on the sand and looked out over the Pacific. He wondered what kind of material a wetsuit could be made of that would keep people warm in such cold water. He emptied sand out of his shoes.

When his phone rang, it was Carrie's name and

number on the screen. "We've got you on speaker in the tower room. Are you OK?"

"Yeah, I'm OK. I just wanted to let you know I'm now safely in California."

"That's the key word right now, *safe*," said Carrie. "If there's anything we can do to help, please tell us."

"I will. I will. Just talking to you guys is helpful."

Harv stood up, kicked a crab shell and walked parallel to the water. "It's a weird feeling, like everything's coming unhinged, combined with a kind of rage I've never felt before. I need to fight back somehow."

"I know, but listen to me," said Carrie. "You've got to stay safe. At least until we figure out how to fix this situation."

"You know," Harv stopped and looked out over the water, "I really liked talking about those things we wanted to do to Burke last night."

"Yeah, that felt good," said Carrie.

"If we can't actually do somethin' to the guy, the next best thing is talkin' about it," said Nickerson.

"I think the overall concept we came up with last night is viable," said Harv.

"You know," said Buzz, "if you could convince him you wanted to play on his team, he might open up to you and spill his guts. I mean if we were actually going to do this thing."

Harv stepped quickly away as an incoming wave crashed at his feet.

"To make it work, you'd need something to offer him," said Carrie. "Some token of good faith that showed him you were serious."

"That's a great point," said Harv. "He's not going

to buy my story unless I have something to show I'm the real deal."

They continued talking. They kicked around some of the ideas they had discussed the night before. Some got discarded. Parts of others were kept and re-configured. Finally, after twenty minutes, they had a consensus.

"Hey, people," Harv looked out over the ocean and smiled, "I think we've got the skeleton of a real plan."

"Well, it's fun to think about," said Nickerson.

"Yes, it is fun to think about." Carrie paused a second. "Let's give it a name."

"A name?" said Buzz.

"Yeah, we can't just call it *the plan*. We have to be specific; give it some individuality when we refer to it. A name only *we* know," said Carrie.

Harv threw a stone into the ocean.

"It's not like we're really going to do this," said Buzz.

"How about Project Burke?" said Carrie.

"You can't have the guy's name in the title of the plan," said Harv. "We need a code name so if anyone overhears us, no one else will know what we're talking about."

"Look, guys," said Buzz, "whatever we call this little caper doesn't matter because we're not really—."

"How about Project Bravo?" yelled Carrie. "That starts with *B*, the same as Burke."

"Not bad," Nickerson chimed in.

"I like it." Harv looked at his watch.

"Fine," said Buzz. "Project Bravo it is."

Harv's watch read 3:15. He realized he'd been talking for over an hour.

"Hey, I've got to go guys. I've got to call Sheila and tell her I'm not coming down this weekend."

"That'll go over big," said Buzz.

"Who's Sheila?" asked Carrie.

Harv told her about Sheila and how he'd had to cancel several previous meetings with Mrs. Whitmore. "I called once but she didn't answer her phone, and I didn't want to leave a message."

"Well you've got to tell her, sport," said Buzz.

"I know. If she doesn't answer next time, I'll just leave a message." He looked at his watch. "Hey, I've gotta go."

CHAPTER 22

The reading room at Philadelphia's William Penn Club was almost full, as it was on most Thursday nights. Members generally partied in their homes or at suburban country clubs on weekends, and most weeknights typically saw businessmen entertaining clients before catching a late ride home. But on Thursday night, one would often see members and their families in town for dinner at the club.

During peak hours, people sat in the reading room for drinks and pleasant conversation prior to being seated in the main dining room. It was relatively informal and conducive to private discourse without the intrusion of waiters, busboys, or wine stewards. A bar was set up with an assortment of hors d'oeuvres. People just got up, helped themselves, and signed a chit for the bartender.

Old books on floor-to-ceiling shelves covered one of the walls, while hunter green wallpaper and large, gold-framed paintings adorned the other walls. The furniture was arranged in private clusters, each consisting of big, leather chairs, one or two coffee tables, and several end tables.

At one cluster the Whitmore clan sat, conversing in well-modulated tones over pâté and gin. It was mostly gin, anyway. Mrs. Whitmore had a gin and tonic, Mr. Whitmore a very dry martini, and Sheila nursed a banana daiquiri, decked out with a small, lime-green umbrella.

"I don't see why we can't just bring him here to the club Saturday night," said Mrs. Whitmore. "I think he'd like to get out and see a little of the city."

"I don't think so, Mother." Sheila rearranged the parasol and straw in her daiquiri. "I'm certain that what he'd really like is a nice home-cooked meal."

"Well I gave Ronada the weekend off and I'll be damned if I'm doing any cooking."

"Relax, Mother, I'll cook."

"You've turned into a pretty good little cook, princess," said Mr. Whitmore.

"Thanks, Daddy."

"You say this young man was a hockey player or something?" Mrs. Whitmore took a sip of her gin and tonic.

"He was one of the stars of the hockey team at Boston University before I met him at Penn."

"That's right." Mr. Whitmore nodded. "When we had lunch with him he said he got his undergraduate degree at B.U."

Mrs. Whitmore held up her hand and looked over her shoulder at a Japanese woman in a bright red, white, and orange kimono. An American couple and a Japanese couple walked up to the adjacent cluster and sat down.

"Did you see that fabric? It's gorgeous." Mrs. Whitmore shifted her large torso, changing position in her chair to see the other people more comfortably.

Mr. Whitmore looked over and took a long pull on his martini.

Sheila put her hand up to her mouth and spoke softly. "Did you notice how the Japanese woman kept standing until her husband was seated?"

Mrs. Whitmore smiled with a combination of disgust and arrogance. "I know. It's grotesque isn't it?"

"They're what you call the more traditional Japanese." Mr. Whitmore took a bite of foie gras on a cracker. "You see them from time to time."

"I guess they all haven't become civilized yet," Sheila observed.

"So you're going to do the cooking, princess. What are you going to make us?"

"There's a couple of dishes I make pretty well," said Sheila. "There's this chicken thing I do with wine, and I make a pretty good veal scaloppine."

The Japanese woman got up and walked across the room to the hors d'oeuvres table. The Whitmores ceased their conversation and watched as the woman got a plate, filled it with selected goodies, returned to her chair, and placed the plate on the coffee table in front of her husband.

"I've heard they treat their women like second class citizens;" Sheila peered over the top of her tiny parasol, "I mean the traditional Japanese."

"It's barbaric." Mrs. Whitmore stared over her right shoulder. "That poor dear creature. I wonder if she realizes how exploited she is."

"To them it's natural," said Mr. Whitmore. "I'm sure she doesn't think twice about it." He paused and took another sip of his martini. "So anyway it looks like you're going to try to win this guy over with your cooking huh, pumpkin?"

"I've already got him won over, Daddy. It's just a matter of taking that final step."

"And that doesn't happen," interjected Mrs. Whitmore, "until I meet him and get to know him."

"Yes Mother." Sheila rolled her eyes and looked at her father.

Mrs. Whitmore picked up her drink. "What time is this Harvey fellow arriving anyway?"

"Tomorrow afternoon, Mother. I told you. And don't worry; I'm picking him up."

Mrs. Whitmore drained her gin and tonic then held up the empty glass, clinking the ice back and forth, smiling across the table expectantly at Mr. Whitmore.

He got up, walked across to his wife. "Same?" he asked, taking her glass.

"This time with two lime slices." Mrs. Whitmore reached for a canapé with her empty hand.

"I think I'll have another too, Daddy." Sheila drained her daiquiri.

"Sure, pumpkin." Mr. Whitmore smiled and took the two glasses for refills.

At the bar, he was joined by a business associate, and the two men talked while waiting in line to get their drinks. The Japanese wife then got up and walked over to the bar, carrying an empty beer mug. Mr. Whitmore and his associate nodded politely as she joined them in line. While talking about golf scores and interest rates, the two men towered over the brightly-colored, kimono-clad Japanese woman.

Mrs. Whitmore finished off the last appetizer.

"Our table should be ready soon." Mr. Whitmore returned and handed each woman her cocktail.

"It better be; I'm starved." Mrs. Whitmore took a sip of her new drink.

"They're really crowded tonight, huh Daddy?"

"Yes, I'm afraid it's a typical Thursday."

They talked for a while, sipping their drinks, discussing Harv's upcoming visit as Mrs. Whitmore and Sheila continually shot glances over at the Japanese couple.

"I think I'm going to visit the little girl's room," announced Mrs. Whitmore.

"That sounds like a good idea, Mother." Sheila took a quick sip of her drink and stood up.

Mr. Whitmore got up and walked over to help his wife out of her chair. As the two women departed, he walked outside to the porch, pulled out a small cigar, and lit it. Smoking of any kind was not allowed inside the club, but outside it was fine. At home, Mrs. Whitmore would not allow him to smoke cigars in her presence because the odor offended her, so he learned to love the outdoors and steal a few moments of private puffing here and there during her absences.

His wife's extended visits to the powder room used to annoy him. He didn't understand why it always took so long and why she, and women in general, always went in groups. Over the years he'd given up trying to figure it out and learned to appreciate little diversions like smoking cigars and quietly meditating during her excursions. He'd come to really enjoy these peaceful moments of lavatory leave. The longer the better.

After an all too short period of time, Mr. Whitmore

noticed his wife coming back to the room. He instinctively put out the cigar in an adjacent ashtray and returned to his family. As his wife and daughter approached, he walked over to help Mrs. Whitmore back into her chair.

"They've still got that awful wallpaper in there." Sheila sat down while Mr. Whitmore made a gallant attempt to help her back into her chair as well.

"You smell like cigar smoke, Alan." Mrs. Whitmore sniffed the air.

"Just a few puffs, dear."

"You get plenty of time during the day." She waved her hand in front of her face. "God it smells dreadful."

They chatted until Mrs. Whitmore put her hand up and focused her attention on the adjacent cluster. The Japanese couple was standing, obviously taking leave of their American companions. The American man stood and shook hands with his guests, while his wife remained seated and smiled politely. The Japanese couple bowed, said a few parting words, and then walked toward the door.

"Must not be staying for dinner." Sheila kept her eyes riveted on the Japanese.

"A lot of people just come in for a drink," said Mr. Whitmore, "especially if they have to catch a flight or keep on a tight schedule."

"Shh!" Mrs. Whitmore held up her hand again, her eyes following the Orientals out of the room. "My God! She actually has to walk behind him."

The Japanese couple walked to the large doors leading out of the room. The man exited first, his wife following closely behind.

Back at the house, Mr. Whitmore retired to his study. Sheila walked into the parlor, pulled her phone out of her other purse, and checked it for messages. There were two. The first from her roommate. The second from Harvey, canceling his weekend visit.

"Something unexpected has come up. I feel terrible about this." Harv's voice sounded tense. "You already know where I'll be. I'll call you."

"Damn!" Sheila slammed her phone down on her purse as her mother entered the room.

"What happened to my little lady that I raised so carefully? What kind of talk is that?"

"Harvey can't make it."

"He what?" Mrs. Whitmore dropped the magazine she was holding.

"He isn't coming this weekend. Something came up."

Mrs. Whitmore's eyes glared. She paced across the room. "Something has come up? Something is always coming up with this young man." She continued pacing. "This is the last straw. This is ridiculous." Mrs. Whitmore retrieved a handful of M&M's from a bowl on the counter and began eating them.

"Mother, now calm down. I know this is important. Harv told me all about it, and I know it has to be a serious crisis."

"Well, tell me this. I'd really like to know. What's so excessively important that he has to cancel again for the umpteenth time?"

"It has to do with business, Mother. It's top secret. Harvey's a very important consultant, and he works on some top secret things. His clients can be very demanding."

Mrs. Whitmore shook her head. "I don't know, Sheila. I mean this is the third time he's done something like this. Or is it the fourth? I can't remember; there've been so many."

"I know he's going through a crazy time right now, some important secret things with one of his clients. I know he'll be calling me."

"What's all this cloak and dagger business anyway?" Mrs. Whitmore turned toward her daughter. "Did he say where he's going to be?"

"Yes, he told me. No one else knows, but I know."

"You know exactly where he'll be? I mean the exact place?"

"Yes, I've got it written down. Why?"

"How long is he going to be there?"

"A few weeks. Why?"

"Well I tell you what we're going to do," said Mrs. Whitmore. "I've had it with this on-again off-again, now-we'll-see-him, now-we-won't business. This is exactly why the family trust is written as it is. If this young man can't come to see me, then I'm jolly well going to go see him and get this thing over with."

"What?" Sheila's eyes widened.

"That's right; where is he?"

"In Maine, but—"

"Well I'm booking us on the next convenient flight to Maine—maybe next weekend. We'll take a cab to wherever he is."

"Mother that's wonderful."

"I didn't get to where I am by being shy and retiring,

young lady. I've always managed to meet who I want, when I want."

"I hope it'll be OK. I mean I hope Harvey won't mind."

"Don't tell him ahead of time, because he'll just say 'no.' It will be a nice little surprise for him. If he loves you, he'll be delighted."

"Yes, it'll be a surprise all right."

"I'll meet him. We'll come to some conclusions, and you can get on with your life. One way or another."

Sheila began looking up flight schedules.

"Besides, I think this will be a good experience for you. You'll be able to see this young man in a different environment." Mrs. Whitmore smiled. "In the middle of all this secret business. I think you'll get a much clearer picture of him after this."

Mr. Whitmore read quietly in his study, comfortable in his easy chair, oblivious to the tempest swirling outside his walls.

After considerable discussion, Sheila and her mother agreed to fly up to Maine a week from Saturday. Sheila felt certain Harvey would still be there then, and it would give Mrs. Whitmore enough time to rearrange her busy schedule.

With flight reservations made for Portland, Maine, the two women walked down the hall to make coffee. The door to Mr. Whitmore's study was closed when they passed, and tiny puffs of cigar smoke under the door went unnoticed as they hustled into the kitchen.

CHAPTER 23

Friday morning Harv got up early to beat the freeway traffic and met with Haitachu Electronics, the Long Beach prospect he'd made the appointment with. The meeting went well; he even got to talk with the vice president of Marketing, who promised he'd give Harv a chance to submit a proposal on the next consulting project. He called Chuck just to check in and spent the early afternoon calling more prospects, to no avail.

Harv got back to his hotel around four o'clock and realized the next two days were going to be dull. Usually he looked forward to weekends, but he was away from home and had nothing to divert his brain from the Peter Burke situation. He called the Seaview crew and talked more about Project Bravo, flushing out specific details. That made him feel better.

After the phone call, Harv laid back on his bed, dreading the boredom the next few days would bring. He took a deep breath, sat up, and phoned his old roommate from Penn, Matt Gallo. He'd kept in touch with Matt over the years and had even stayed at his place on two of his west coast trips. It would not be out of character for him to call and drop by over the weekend. He had to do *something*.

Matt sold bonds for one of the big brokerage houses

and, from what Harv could observe over the years, was doing very well. Matt answered the phone and told Harv he was free Saturday afternoon. They agreed Harv would come over for lunch.

"I'm living with this new chick, Harv. You'll love her."

"What happened to what's-her-name, Rachel?"

Gallo laughed. "Hell, Rachel was a fucking moron. Irene is deep, somebody I can really connect with. You'll see."

At noon Saturday, Harv headed his rented car down Pacific Avenue and hung a right on Driftwood in Marina del Rey. Matt's place was just off the beach.

Harv parked on the street, walked up to the front door, and rang the bell.

When Matt opened the door, he looked like he hadn't changed a bit. "Good to see you, man," he said.

Harv shook hands and walked in.

"Why didn't you tell me you were coming out? You could have crashed here."

"It was a last minute thing." Harv looked around. "My client's picking up the tab. I didn't want to impose at the last minute."

"Hell, I'd just clear some shit out of the guest room. No big deal." Gallo walked into the living room and its attached dining area.

Harv followed and saw a woman rummaging around the adjoining kitchen in bare feet and a floral housedress. She had long brown hair, sunken cheeks, and very tan skin. It was hard to tell how old she was.

"Harvey Gallagher." The woman put down her spoon and walked toward Harv with open arms. "I've heard so much about you, I feel I already know you." She gave him a big hug.

"This is Irene," said Matt.

"Irene, it's great to meet you." Harv looked around the living room and noticed how the decor had changed from his last visit. He looked at Irene. She didn't look like an *Irene*. Then he realized he didn't even know anyone with that name except one of his mother's friends.

"I hope you're hungry."

"Actually, I am." The fast food he'd been eating the last few days hadn't been sitting well. "I'm really looking forward to some home cooking."

"Great!" Irene turned triumphantly back to the kitchen. "Lunch is almost ready. I've got a tofu, Vegemite quiche that's about to come out of the oven."

"Sounds yummy."

"We're kind of like vegetarians these days, Harv. Irene has opened up so many new worlds for me."

Harv nodded and walked around the living room, admiring the artwork on the walls.

"Isn't that one incredible?" Matt walked up as Harv stared at a framed picture of a big brown free-form shape. "Irene made that." He nodded his head. "That's an abstract interpretation of Rosemary Clooney made out of rosemary leaves. You know the herb, rosemary?"

"Wow," said Harv.

"It's the whimsical intrinsicality that spoke to me while I created it," Irene chimed in from the kitchen. She had clear visual and audio access to the living room. "We like it because of its artistic dynamism. It's so non-linear, don't you think?"

"Absolutely," said Harv. "It's non-*something*. I was just groping for the right word."

Matt smiled. "Irene's developing quite a name for herself in food art."

"Food art?"

"Yeah, the primary medium has to be edible . . . very biological. Primal. It's too bad you weren't here last month. Her very best piece sold—a pasta interpretation of Sylvester Stallone on a background of aged pecorino cheese."

Harv shook his head. "God, I wish I could have seen it."

"The pithy innateness of it was rather overpowering," said Irene, bringing a serving platter out to the table.

"It must have been incredible."

They sat down and Matt opened a bottle of white wine. He poured a small portion of it in his glass, sniffed it, tasted it, nodded, and passed the bottle to Harv.

"I know you're in Boston, Harvey. Tell me all about the northeast capitalist empire." Irene passed Harv her quiche concoction. "Matt tells me your clients are part of the famed military-industrial complex. It sounds positively evil. I'm enthralled. Talk to me."

The meal passed somewhat uncomfortably. Harv did his best to tell Irene what he did for a living. Matt played cultural ambassador for most of the meal, building conversational bridges between Harv and Irene.

"So, what are you driving these days, Harv?" asked Matt.

"I just rented a mid-sized Honda at the airport."

"No, I mean at home, your car. What kind of wheels do you have?"

"Oh, my wheels." Harv took a long sip of wine. "You know, I've switched to the round ones, and they're working much better."

Irene laughed.

"Tell me, Irene," Harv said quickly, "I've been admiring that sculpture in the center of the table. Have I seen that somewhere before? In a magazine or somewhere?"

Irene's eyes lit up. "That's my interpretation of Rodin's famous work, *The Thinker.*"

"Ah, yes. That's why it looks familiar. Great interpretation."

"Irene got totally screwed out of an award with that piece."

"The judges were just too unsophisticated to appreciate it," said Irene. "I mean my work is not for everyone."

"You see, Harv, it's made out of pasta," said Matt.

"Yes, I can see that."

"But what you don't see," Matt continued, "and it was on the little sign she had in front of the piece at the show, what you don't see is that it's made out of gluten-free pasta . . . gluten-free."

Harv took another sip of wine. "Ah, gluten-free pasta."

"It takes extra thinking to eat gluten-free food."

Harv raised his hand. "And this piece is *The Thinker.* I get it. Wow!"

"All her stuff is deep like that, Harv. Not everyone is smart enough to appreciate it."

Irene shook her head. "When an artist's world view is on a more evolved plane than those judging their work, it can be very difficult."

"Yes, I hate it when that happens." Harv looked at his watch.

Matt topped off all the wine glasses and continued to initiate conversation.

Harv smiled when his phone rang. On seeing *Charles Weitz* on the caller ID, he excused himself from the table.

"Harv, this is Chuck."

"Hey, what's up?" Harv walked to the door and pointed outside while nodding to his host. He opened the door and walked outside.

"Harv, there's one new development I wanted to share with you."

"A new development. Did you find out something about that bullet?" Harv walked and stood next to his car.

"No, something else . . . We've been watching your place for the last few days."

"Watching my place?"

"Yeah, surveillance, daytime only. For security reasons mostly, to make sure you were safe, see if any bad guys were hanging around. You know, your office and your residence on Marlborough Street."

Harv lowered his voice. "Well spy away; I don't have anything to hide."

"Harv, listen to me. We've been keeping an eye on your office and residence and one of the things we've found out is that someone else is watching too."

"Someone's spying on me?" Harv looked around and noticed it was turning into a sunny day.

"Spends most of the day watching your office, then at around five o'clock goes and stakes out your apartment for a few hours."

"Who?"

"Guy named Vick Chenko, local P.I., sleazy reputation. Cops have had a few run-ins with him. We just got a make on him ten minutes ago and I wanted to give you a call to make sure you stay put."

"Jesus." Harv took a deep breath.

"Listen, Harv, from what we're piecing together here, my guess is Peter Burke hired this guy."

"Surprise, surprise."

"I think he wants to know your schedule to help plan his attack."

"That's real comforting."

"Look, that's why it's important you don't tell anyone where you are. Just stay put for a few days. Let us work on this."

"So, it's back to the bullet, Chuck. You get anything back yet?"

"Came back yesterday. The round is from a Smith and Wesson 357 Magnum."

"Sounds serious."

"It's a serious weapon, Harv. I'm not going to lie to you."

"Did the test give you any clues to who did it? Who shot at me?"

"There's a good chance we can link that bullet back to a specific gun, Harv. That must have been pretty soft brick because the round is in decent shape. There are some pretty good striation markings on it. They're usually unique to a specific gun. When that gun turns up in our investigation, we'll link it to this bullet and have the shooter."

Harv leaned on his car and watched a bikini-clad woman walk into a neighboring residence. "Can't you trace it through some gun registration or something?"

"Depends on the state, Harv. And goons don't follow gun laws anyhow . . . Look, we're slowly building a case. We're getting more information every day. Just keep a low profile for a while and stay safe."

Harv returned to Matt's, apologized for the interruption, and made his best effort to finish Irene's lunch. He used the phone call as an excuse to cut the visit short. The news that someone was spying on him was like a punch in the gut. He felt violated.

*   *   *

Back at his hotel, Harv dialed Buzz, who did not answer. He dialed Carrie and ultimately got the crew assembled in Nickerson's office.

"Hey, dude, sorry I missed your call," said Buzz.

Harv flopped down on his bead. "I don't think I've acquired full dude status yet. A few lessons on a surf board, then maybe I'll qualify."

"We had some guy here looking for you today," said Carrie.

"What? . . . Who?" Harv sat up.

"Just some guy, a big guy, blond hair. Seemed friendly enough," said Nickerson. "Marge and I were the ones who talked to him. Told him we never give out any information about our guests, except to the police."

"That's it?"

"That's it. He said 'thank you' and drove off."

"Did you see the car?"

"Didn't really get a good look. He was parked around back."

Harv got up, began pacing around his room and told them about the guy watching his office and apartment. "Peter's really playing his hand like Chuck said he would isn't he?" He looked at his watch. "You know, I hate this . . . the hiding, the running. I can't accept it."

Carrie said, "I know, Harv but—"

"It's not me. I mean it's not my personality type to hide in a situation like this. And right now I am really, really pissed off."

They talked about Project Bravo. Harv was glad to see the others had been thinking about it and had fleshed out some of the details.

"You know," said Nickerson, "we've got the makings of a nice little sting operation here."

"It's a beautiful sting," said Harv.

"It's a head-fake-reverse to be precise," said Buzz.

"A what?" asked Carrie.

"A head-fake-reverse. It's a maneuver used in military strategy. I use it in chess sometimes."

"So how is Project Bravo a head-fake-reverse?" Harv parted the drapes and looked outside.

"It's simple. Like a running back in football, you head fake left and go right. You take a fundamental element of any battle, like how strong you are or where you're located, for example. You sell your opponent on believing certain things about that element. Then you completely reverse yourself and change the reality of that element, and while your opponent is grappling with his erroneous assumptions, you use that time to implement a plan to bring about his total destruction. Assuming you've got an effective plan of destruction."

"We've got one," said Carrie.

Harv grabbed his room key, opened the door, and walked toward the beach. "Again, how is Project Bravo a head-fake-reverse?"

"Look," said Buzz. "Your big head-fake is location. Obviously Burke doesn't know where you are right now. You actually *are* in California; so you lay down some very traceable footprints out there, even get Burke to call you there if necessary, then completely reverse yourself, fly back to the Seaview, and implement Project Bravo. It's classic."

"Hey guys," Harv stopped walking, "this thing is do-able."

"What are you saying . . . exactly?" said Nickerson.

"I'm saying I want to do this thing, not just talk about it. We can do this."

"Now hold on, sparky," said Buzz. "You asked me what a head-fake-reverse is and I told you how this situation is—"

"I'm not going to go on hiding from that bastard. I'm not going to let him turn me into a cringing dog, just reacting to whatever he might decide to do."

"Hey guys," said Carrie, "let me just throw something out. I love what you're saying, Harv. And I want to do this too, but let me just play devil's advocate for a second. Don't you think it would be better or safer to let this guy, Chuck Weitz, take care of Burke?"

"Chuck is terrific at what he does, Carrie, but he can only do so much here." Harv paused while crossing the street onto the beach. "It's me Peter wants, and because of that there are things I can do to nail him that Chuck just can't do. Chuck can't lure him to the Seaview like I can. He can't get him to incriminate himself like I can." He looked out over the Pacific. "Hey, I don't want to force this on anyone. This is my problem. I can understand if you don't—"

"This problem's for all of us," said Nickerson.

"Absolutely," said Carrie.

"I mean I didn't know I was even going to say this stuff until I just said it. But I know we can do this."

"You've got plenty of moxie, son," said Nickerson. "I like that, but let's not get swept up in somethin' before thinkin' it through. I want to do this. Don't get me wrong. But I don't know for sure if I can even get the chopper."

"The helicopter isn't a total necessity," said Harv.

"No, but it'd be better to have it," said Nickerson. "I'm just sayin' let's give ourselves twenty-four hours to step back, think this through, and iron out a few details before makin' a complete commitment."

* * *

Sunday morning Harv woke up early and took a jog on the beach. Then he showered, dressed, and drove to Dave's Sunshine Diner in Santa Monica. He ordered hash browns, scrambled eggs, and coffee.

He jotted down notes on his legal pad while finishing off breakfast. After eating, he looked up the number and address of South Star Manufacturing, an ADI subsidiary located nearby.

It was a little past eleven when he called Buzz. When no one answered, he called Carrie.

"You're early," said Carrie.

"I know it isn't twenty-four hours yet, but I thought I'd give it a shot."

They talked for a while. Carrie wanted assurances he was doing OK. "Let me get everyone together," she said. "I'll call you back in a few minutes."

Harv ordered a second cup of coffee and jotted down more notes while waiting. When his phone rang, he heard Carrie's familiar voice. "OK, Harv, we've got you on speaker."

"You doin' all right, son?" said Nickerson.

"Yeah, I'm still in one piece."

"Hey, I've got some good news," said Nickerson. "I can get the chopper."

Harv banged his fist on the table and smiled. "You can actually get a helicopter? That's awesome."

"Crowley's got a friend in Belfast who'll let me use his and I've got a former client in Portland who just gave me his OK. I just have to show 'em my papers, go for a test spin and we'll have our choice of either one."

"Well it's a *go*, people." Harv looked around again and lowered his voice.

"It's a definite *go* on this end," said Carrie.

"It's going to be real fun screwing this guy to the wall," said Buzz.

"Listen, I'm going to get Burke to call me out here

to really let him know I'm actually here. I know how his mind works. And to really place the ultimate footprint, I'm going to call on South Star Manufacturing."

"What's that?" said Carrie.

Harv took a swig of coffee. "Burke is always telling me that on my west coast trips, I should check out South Star. It's a subsidiary of ADI here in LA."

"When you start laying down these footprints, you'd better move fast," said Buzz. "You don't want Burke caching up to you."

"Don't worry, I'm calling on South Star, phoning Burke, then heading straight to the Seaview."

*   *   *

Harv made a plane reservation for Hartford, leaving Monday afternoon. He figured he could pick up his car and make it to the Seaview late that night.

Monday morning he packed, checked out of his hotel, and dropped in on South Star Manufacturing. The Plant Manager was in a meeting, but when told that Harv was a consultant for ADI and that Peter Burke had suggested he drop by, Jose Martinez postponed his meeting, walked into the lobby with a big smile, and gave Harv a tour of the plant.

After his visit, Harv dropped into a diner down the street from the plant and confirmed that he could make and receive a call on the landline public phone. He didn't want to use his cell phone. He wanted a landline with an LA area code. A crisp twenty dollar bill convinced the manager to allow a short call to Boston and to receive an equally short call back. Harv wrote down the diner's phone number then grabbed a table, ordered toast and coffee, and thought through his upcoming call. He looked around the room, took a deep breath, then walked up to the public phone and called Peter Burke.

He couldn't remember a time when he'd ever gotten directly through to Peter. He was always busy and had to call back. Harv hoped Burke would be busy again and have to call the diner. That would be a great footprint. He figured if the callback ploy didn't work, and he miraculously did get through to Peter, it wouldn't be the end of the world. He already had the South Star footprint. But a direct callback would be great.

"Peter Burke's office." Lois's voice sounded the same as ever.

"Lois, this is Harvey Gallagher. Is Peter there?"

"Hi, Harv. Hang on a second; let me check and see what he's up to."

Harv turned and watched a customer pay her bill. He noticed her calm, peaceful face and wished he could be half as relaxed.

"His meeting is just breaking up in his office now, Harv. Can you hold on a second?"

"I'll tell you what, Lois; why don't I just give you this number where I am right now and he can call me?" He lowered his voice. "My cell phone isn't working right now. Something about the signal."

"Uh, OK, sure."

Harv gave her the diner's number and hung up. Since the cashier would be answering the return call, he gave her his name and got the manager to give her the green light for handling Harv's call. When he got back to his booth, coffee and toast had arrived. He put cream and sugar in his coffee and stirred loudly. He looked around the diner. Everyone looked wrapped up in their own thoughts, some on laptops, others scrolling on their phones, others chatting quietly. He wondered if any of the other customers were in the middle of a sting operation. His thoughts were interrupted by the cashier walking up to his booth.

"Mr. Gallagher? That was fast. Your phone call is here."

"Oh, thank you." Harv got up and walked over to the phone at the front desk. He took the receiver and walked as far away as the cord would go.

"So where the hell is area code three ten?" Peter's voice sounded friendly.

"Hey, Peter, Thanks for getting back to me."

"What is that code? California or someplace?"

"Yeah, it's one of those L.A. area codes. I'm on my way to a sales call. Listen, the reason I called—I stopped by South Star Manufacturing this morning."

"Well, you finally made it."

"I just wanted to tell you quickly how impressed I was."

"Oh, yes," said Burke," it's state-of-the-art stuff. Who'd you see there?"

Harv could picture Burke calling South Star and checking things out immediately after the call. "Jose Martinez, a hell of a nice guy. Gave me a tour and everything."

"So where are you staying?"

"I'm on my way across town. I have no clue where

I'll be staying tonight. I may drive up the coast to Silicon Valley after that."

Peter pressed him on the details of his itinerary and Harv dropped the names of the places he'd visited.

"Uh oh, I'm going to be late for my appointment, Peter. I have to try to make a sale. Gotta run."

"Give me a call when you—"

"If I can. Gotta go."

Harv hung up and smiled. He could see Peter's mind working, trying to figure out who he might be calling on, where he might be going, and how he could get to Harv.

He walked back to the table and sat down. The nervous twinge down his back surprised him. He realized the only time Peter would know his exact location would be right now, at this exact moment. He took a big gulp of coffee, put some cash on the table, and headed for the airport.

CHAPTER 24

Steve Smith looked out the window of his living room for any sign of his expected visitors, then he called Peter Burke. Peter had been furious at Smith for allowing his meeting to be crashed but had calmed down over the past week, assuring his colleagues he would take care of the situation.

They were best friends back in prep school and had kept in touch during college but drifted apart after that. It wasn't until Peter had taken a job in New York City that the friendship was reestablished. By that time Smith had gotten divorced, made a bundle selling commercial real estate in Manhattan, and was thinking of moving to Maine for a more leisurely life style.

The phone rang several times before Burke picked up.

"They turned down our latest offer, Peter."

"What the hell?"

"Nickerson said 'no' flat out. But I think he may be softening a bit. I'm not sure. He seemed a little less hostile this time."

"He'd better soften up a lot and soon. Things are getting dicey down here at the office. That Gallagher is a loose end I can't accept. I don't know what the hell he knows and what he doesn't know. He's acting different; like maybe he suspects something."

"He doesn't suspect anything. I told you that was a total coincidence. It was a simple bee sting. They had to get into my office. End of story."

"I sent some of my New York boys to take care of Gallagher, but apparently the guy's still at large."

"Peter, I don't know what you mean by *take care of*, but you're starting to scare me. Believe me, we can handle Gallagher. You've got to calm down and relax."

"I'll relax when this is over. They want to turn us down? I'm going to crank this thing up a few notches. I want one more demonstration out of your hayseeds. I want the biggest, scariest demonstration yet."

"I was planning on one anyway. In fact I'm expecting my two contacts any minute now." Smith looked over his shoulder out the window. "As soon as Nickerson turned me down, I called them. I owe them a little money, and I was going to bring up the idea of another demonstration."

"That's fine but this one's got to be big, Steve. I mean more than big. I mean scary big. I mean freaky and totally intimidating. I can't wait any longer."

Smith cringed as he looked out the window to see two motorcycles roaring up his steep driveway. "Hey, they just arrived."

"Remember, this has got to be big."

"I hear you. Listen, I've got to go."

Smith hated having holler rats come to his house, but there had been some talk in town about seeing them at his office, and he wanted to minimize any way of linking Cove Realty with Blade and his cohorts. So he put up with them. He realized they could get things accomplished that he could not. They could do all the dirty work that needed doing and keep him distanced from the whole thing. It had worked well so far but that didn't make dealing with them any more appealing.

Smith came out of the house with an irritated expression on his face, motioning his visitors around behind his garage. "You guys trying to wake the dead?"

Blade and Carl Chavone slowed down and cruised past Smith to the back of the garage.

Inside the house, Blade helped himself to a beer from the refrigerator as they sat down around the kitchen table. Chavone lit up a cigarette.

"Use an ash tray," Smith yelled. "You guys can live like pigs in your own place but when you come here, show some manners." He slid a plastic ashtray toward him.

"Hey, I was gonna use my pocket," Chavone yelled back.

"Just use the damn ash tray."

Smith reached in his briefcase and threw two envelopes down on the table. Both men picked them up, opened them, and examined the packet of bills inside.

"It's all there. You don't have to count it."

"It's a pleasure doin' business with you," said Ouellette as he jammed the envelope in his pocket.

"There's one more project I want to talk to you guys about." Smith stood up and got himself a beer from the refrigerator. "It's the Nickerson place. I gave them a higher offer the other day and they turned it down."

"Gee what a surprise," said Chavone.

Smith took a big swallow of beer and sat down.

"I want you guys to create another demonstration over there.

"Another one?" Blade lit up a cigarette.

"This one has to be bigger and scarier than any you've ever done. The biggest yet. I want to completely demoralize those clowns. And I'll give you two grand each to make it happen."

Chavone jammed his cigarette down into the plastic ashtray and slowly blew out a stream of smoke. They talked about the inn, about Nickerson and about their past attempts to get the Seaview.

"We don't have any more time to play around with these people." Smith took another tug at his beer. "With business down the way it is, I think a huge demonstration is just what we need. I want this to be huge."

Blade got up, walked to the other side of the kitchen, and then turned slowly toward the table. "Ya know, there's somethin' I've been thinkin' about in the back of my mind that just might work for that old inn."

"What is it?" said Smith.

"I don't want to tell you now. I haven't worked out the details in my head yet, but it could be huge."

Smith shook his head. "You guys work out the details. Make sure it's doable. Make sure it's huge and then blow it by me. And make sure it's done in the next week. This next Saturday would be ideal."

"This next Saturday?" Blade frowned.

"You said you already had a starting idea. You guys can do it then." He got up and looked at a calendar on the wall. "Today's Monday. You've got all week. We're under some time pressure here. My people want to make something happen soon." He took a step toward the kitchen door. "And most important, guys, nothing, absolutely nothing is to happen to that Inn."

The two motorcycles headed home toward Crotchet Mountain. They turned down the old logging road to Glen Hollow through the deep woods. Past the dirt road to Blade's house, the main road forked left down to a deep valley where a driveway snaked back to a gray, unpainted house. It was Chavone's place, and they knew they could talk in privacy until five o'clock when his mother and sister returned home from the mill.

"What a total jackass." Chavone stretched out on a chair.

"If he wasn't payin' us good money I'd smash his face in." Blade pounded his fist into the sofa he was sitting on. "He thinks he's so much better then us."

"He says 'Just use the damn ashtray,'" Chavone sneered. "How 'bout I use your goddamn face?"

"There's a lot of money to be made from that bastard though." Blade got up to rummage through the refrigerator. "Remember that idea I was talkin' about?"

"What idea?"

Blade grabbed a beer from the refrigerator and opened it. "It'd be a perfect cover for a huge demonstration—a cleansing."

"A cleansing? You mean like with the church?"

"Yeah, it's perfect." Blade returned to the big chair. "All those torches, all that fire, the chanting, the dancing. Scary as hell. The guests would freak."

A cleansing was a frequently used ceremony the Glen Hollow church used for exorcizing and expunging evil. If the church thought there was an undue amount of sin or evil in a particular location, they would all light torches and encircle the place in question. They'd dance around, chanting ancient incantations, waving their torches to scare away evil spirits.

The church performed cleansings about twice every year or so, usually in and around Glen Hollow. Not just limited to buildings or places, the ritual could also include people. If some poor soul was suspected of cheating on his wife or having impure thoughts, he just might find himself dragged out of his house one afternoon, tied to a tree, and encircled by a bevy of singing, chanting, torch-wielding parishioners. It was an offshoot of the old Puritanical witch burnings, except that no one got burned. Fire was used as a cleansing agent, waved around on torches.

Every once in a while over the years they had attempted a ceremony near the town of Black Hill Cove. Ned Crowley had caught them at it twice but it took forever to break things up. He had to call for back-up and by the time help came the ceremony was over.

"A cleansing at the Seaview, huh?" Chavone picked at his beard.

"Yeah! Why the hell not? With all that dancin' and torch-wavin' the guests'd pack up and leave in no time. We could, like, let it be known there was a lot of evil goin' on there."

Chavone laughed. "Like it's really a cat house or somethin'."

"Hey, I like that." Blade smiled, pointing at his friend. "My old lady would eat that up. We could spread a rumor like that around here in no time."

CHAPTER 25

Bracing ocean air greeted Harv when he opened his eyes Tuesday morning. He had arrived after midnight and didn't get a chance to talk with anyone about Project Bravo. He rolled over and looked at his watch. It was 10:15 eastern time, early by California standards.

He showered, shaved, and looked out his big window at the water. It felt good being back at the Seaview. Despite an occasional pang of doubt, Harv knew he was doing the right thing. Maybe Chuck could help; maybe he couldn't. But one thing Harv knew for sure—there was no way Chuck or anyone else could come up with a solution as crippling to Peter as the plan he and his friends had devised. It had the element of devastating surprise. It would be on his terms and on his turf.

He walked out on the porch and saw Nickerson, Carrie, and Buzz sitting at the far table.

"Well, Sleeping Beauty finally wakes up," said Carrie, draining her coffee cup.

The breakfast buffet had already been closed down, but Carrie had a stack of pastries waiting for Harv under a metal cover.

"God, I slept well." Harv sat down and poured himself a cup of coffee.

"Well, good, you needed it." Carrie took the lid off the pastries.

They talked about his flight and drive up from Hartford.

"Anything interesting show up on our little wire tap while I was gone?"

"Actually we got one new nugget of information," said Buzz. "Apparently they bought a deep-water fishing boat for transporting prototypes, plans, and so forth out of the country."

"Could you tell who the other party was talking to Smith?" asked Harv.

"No, it was a voice I didn't recognize." Buzz looked at a transcript of the call. "It was a guy named Frank, and the boat's moored down near the mouth of the bay on the west shore."

"Said it was just shy of Owls Head Lighthouse," said Nickerson. "The place I showed you when I took you out about a week ago."

"After that it was just Smith getting chewed out by our friend Nick again for allowing you to crash his party," said Buzz.

"We haven't gotten much in a while," said Carrie. "They're either laying low because of our intrusion or are communicating in other ways like maybe cell phones, or e-mail, or another phone somewhere." She pushed the pastries toward Harv. "If this thing dries up as an information source, I'm not going to miss it all that much at this point."

"It'd be nice to have," said Buzz, "but it's already coughed up the key information we need."

Nickerson held up his hand while trying to finish

chewing a mouthful of doughnut. "The chopper in Portland doesn't have the kind of transmitter we need, but the one I got through Crowley does. I'm drivin' up to Belfast today to check it out—take it for a test run. Gotta make sure I can still operate the thing."

They talked about the helicopter and how it would be used as a back up.

Buzz looked at Nickerson. "So you've definitely talked with Crowley about the equipment on this bird?"

"Yeah, the transmitter is totally compatible with the ground station at his office. The owner will show me which slot in that transmitter to put the memory card into. He tells me all I have to us just put the card into that slot and hit *send*. The system will compress the file to the proper format and zap it to Crowley."

"Sounds good. Should be a piece of cake."

Nickerson nodded. "Of course if things go as planned, you can just drive the memory card up to Crowley at the police station. You won't need me." He reached for his coffee cup. "Ned's got the local magistrate and a sheriff standin' by at the station either way. You give them probable cause and they'll raid that damn real estate office."

"Hopefully we won't need you," said Carrie.

"But if you do, I'll be at the helipad in Belfast up the bay. You have any problems, you call me. I'll get to you and have that memory card up in the air, out of harm's way, and broadcastin' in seconds."

Carrie looked over at Harv. "So, are you ready to start, sleepyhead?"

"All systems are go," said Harv.

Carrie read off a list of things they needed to buy. Drywall and lumber had to be purchased at the lumberyard. Buzz had to get some couplings and cord extensions from the electrical supply store in Corvellisville. Harv had to buy the special mirror at Coastal Glass.

"Do you think it's safe, your walkin' around out there?" Nickerson looked at Harv.

"I think so. I really need to see the mirror in person to make sure it's exactly what I want. Besides, Coastal Glass is way over in Milton. When I put on my sunglasses and hat, no one will recognize me."

"Believe me," said Carrie, "that get-up covers half his face."

Harv smiled and drained his coffee. "OK, boys and girls, let's hit the stores."

CHAPTER 26

Light spilled out of the little church's windows twenty minutes before the service. Beneath the darkening sky and overhanging trees, the place took on a glow of importance. Elsa Ouellette scurried around the sanctuary, polishing candlesticks, lighting candles, and dusting off pews. She looked forward to announcing the upcoming cleansing. It had been six months since the last one and, from what her son had told her, it was definitely time for another.

Elsa removed the dark green minister's robe from the closet and put it on. She had brought her antler headpiece from home and carefully placed it on the table by her pulpit. It would not be worn tonight. Indeed it was worn only on special occasions like cleansings, fertility rituals, Easter and the like. She would, however, pick it up and hold it high overhead on several occasions to help drive home a point. Elsa fully understood the role of theatrics in a good sermon.

The antlered headgear, worn by all church members, was a tribute to the deer, a sacred beast in Glen Hollow culture. It was the deer which Indians slaughtered and brought as a gift to keep the early settlers alive when they first arrived in the Hollow. And so the animal, having given up its life so they might live, was deified; its antlers thenceforth attached to religious headgear for the most sacred of ceremonies.

Sally Thompson, the piano player, arrived and started arranging her music. "I see you brought your horns tonight, Elsa," she said.

"Yeah," Elsa smoothed out her robe, "big doin's comin' up, Sally, big doin's this Saturday."

"I heard all about it." Sally got her choir robe out of the closet. "This Saturday; I've got it marked down."

Members of the choir began straggling in, all ten of them, seven women and three men. They slipped on their white robes, took their places behind the pulpit, and started warming up as Mrs. Ouellette ignited the last two candles on the altar.

Soon the faithful flock began trekking through the door. By eight o'clock the place was packed, with several people forced to sit on temporary folding chairs in the back. After the obligatory opening hymn and an anthem by the choir, Mrs. Ouellette rose, walked to her elevated pulpit, and launched into her sermon.

She started slowly with several passages on sin from the Bible. Then she announced her discovery that the Seaview Inn was a place of terrible sin and that, indeed, the level of evil behavior going on had gotten so bad that a cleansing was required.

Loud rumblings of approval wafted through the congregation with occasional hallelujahs, as people nodded their heads in agreement.

Blade walked in with Carl Chavone and stood at the back of the church next to the people in folding chairs. As the congregation mumbled and nodded, he looked at his friend and smiled.

Mrs. Ouellette raised her voice a decibel and went on to tell about past cleansings—stories they had all heard before but never failed to arouse emotions. She repeated how important cleansings were and said that without cleansings, they would all be engulfed in evil.

The lighting had been arranged so her shadow was cast on the sloping ceiling above and behind her. It was a long, angular, disjointed figure that hovered above the congregation, vibrating with energy in the flickering candlelight. The antlers were lifted high overhead, leaving their own ominous shadow like twisted vines reaching down from on high to envelope the church.

"Fornication, adultery," she screamed, "evil, lewd, and sinful behavior of the worst kind."

The congregation became agitated. People yelled, "Scourge. Cleanse in the name of the Holy Mother."

"If we don't take action soon," Elsa continued, "the Antimadonna will descend upon us to pave the way and make a permanent home for her son the Antichrist, the devil himself."

"Scourge! Cleanse!" The yells and screams of self-righteous condemnation bellowed up from the people.

Three men volunteered to build a rough wooden replica of the inn, which would be put on a ten-foot pole and burned in effigy the night before the cleansing. Elsa went over the details. Everyone would bring torches, as they always did at such events. The Cleansing was to be held at three o'clock in the afternoon that coming Saturday. Parishioners were to meet at the church at two o'clock and drive in a caravan to the inn. At exactly 3:00 P.M. all would be ready for the sacred ceremony to begin.

"As the fire rises high unto the heavens," wailed Mrs. Ouellette, "so too will it cleanse and annihilate the evil which surrounds it."

"Amen," said the congregation in unison.

Elsa made a few last remarks, and the choir led worshipers in the closing hymn, *Fire of Thy Salvation*.

While everyone was still singing, Blade gave the thumbs up sign to Chavone, and they left the building.

"I think I may try to juice this little ceremony up a bit," said Blade as the two men walked outside.

"Whadya mean?"

"I mean fire on torches is one thing, but a real fire, say a fire in the woods around that inn would really freak those people out."

"A real fire." Chavone picked at his beard. "Ya know, we can't hurt that inn."

"I know. I'm talkin' about a fire in the woods. Far enough away to keep the inn safe but close enough to scare the hell out of people."

"I guess that could work," said Chavone as the two men walked slowly down the dirt road to the Ouellette home.

"I may just wander over to the Seaview in the next few days and scout out their woods. See if I can find the perfect spot for my own little ceremony."

CHAPTER 27

Harv held the drywall while Nickerson hammered it onto the new studs. They'd removed the old closet wall and were replacing it with a new one, two feet farther out into the parlor, creating more storage room for Nickerson and more maneuvering room for Buzz. The two-way mirror, which would adorn the new wall, leaned against the corner chair.

Buzz had all the electrical supplies laid out on the table. With a pile of artificial flowers in front of him, he concentrated on cutting a petunia in half and hollowing out the center with an X-Acto knife. He took the newly dissected flower and taped it carefully around a microphone with its petals encircling the mouthpiece.

"There," Buzz held up his creation, "it looks like a flower to me." He brought it over to show the others. The dark black webbing of the mouthpiece was nicely recessed in the center of the flower petals.

"Looks like a combination between a black eyed Susan and a petunia," said Harv.

"You don't even know what a petunia looks like," said Buzz.

"Does look like a flower though," Nickerson looked closely at it, "except for the fat stem. You put that in a group of other flowers and hide the stem, and no one'll ever know."

Buzz drilled a hole in the bottom of the wooden flower bowl for the microphone cord, then drilled a hole in the center of the table and threaded the cord through it.

"How you going to hide the cord?" Harv looked over from the new closet.

"I'm going to tack it underneath the table and down the inside of the leg to the floor." He grabbed a roll of brown packing tape. "When I cover it with this, you'll never see it."

Nickerson looked over and nodded. "The man knows what he's doin'."

"It appears that way at times," said Harv, "but he still needs close supervision."

Buzz ignored the comment and continued working. When the last strip of tape was applied, he drilled a hole in the floor under the table leg. He pushed the microphone cord through to the basement, ran it under the floor joists, and up through another hole he'd drilled in the closet floor.

As Harv and Nickerson placed the two-way mirror in the opening they'd prepared, Buzz put the video camera on a tripod and brought it, along with a stool, into the new closet. After sitting down, he looked through the lens at the table on the other side of the mirror and adjusted the focus.

"Looks good from here." Buzz picked up the microphone wire coming up through the floor and plugged it into the camera.

"I'm gonna have fun with this closet when we're

done." Nickerson, packed glazing compound around the new mirror.

They hammered in the front molding and then stood back to admire their work.

"Looks good," said Nickerson.

"Like a mirror is supposed to look," said Harv.

"Can you guys see me?" Buzz yelled from inside the closet.

"Just a mirror hanging on the wall," said Harv. "We'll just stain and varnish the framing. Paint the wall. It'll be perfect."

Buzz emerged from behind the mirror. "Wherever he moves, I'll follow him. Just keep him near that flower."

"Not bad." Nickerson nodded his head just as Harv's cell phone rang.

Seeing Chuck's name on the caller ID, Harv walked over to the corner of the room.

"Hey, stranger." The sound of Weitz's voice brought Harv to attention. "I hadn't heard from you so I just thought I'd call to make sure you were safe out there."

The words *out there* sounded strange. Harv had to concentrate. He was supposed to be in California. "Yeah, I'm OK. How are things going?" Harv looked over at Buzz and Nickerson, raised his eyebrows, and walked outside where he could get a better signal.

"Things are moving right along. But more importantly, how are things out there? I tried calling you yesterday but couldn't get through."

Harv realized he'd left his phone in his room the day before. "Yesterday was a crazy day, Chuck. I left my phone in my room . . . at the motel room out here in California. By the time I realized it, I was already late for a sales call. I might as well try to make a living while hiding from Burke."

"It won't be too much longer, Harv. You keeping out of trouble?"

"So far I guess." Harv felt a little guilty talking to Chuck. He didn't like misleading him, but he was certainly not going to tell him about the Burke trap he was setting. Chuck would put a stop to it immediately or at the very least complicate things.

"You've been so quiet out there lately, I just want to make sure you're not planning any of your wild, hot dog schemes you don't tell me about."

"Who me?"

"Yeah you."

Harv smiled. "Hey, if I was planning one of those schemes I don't tell you about, I certainly wouldn't tell you about it. That would change the very nature of the scheme itself. Then it would become one of those schemes I do tell you about. In which case you'd be the first to know."

Chuck laughed. "Listen, Harv, I'm serious. We're dealing with some pretty unsavory people here and I want you to be careful."

"I hear you."

"That's it, kid, I got concerned when I couldn't reach you. Just wanted to make sure you were OK." Chuck repeated his warning for Harv to be careful and told him he'd let him know when it was safe to come out of hiding.

CHAPTER 28

Thursday morning Claude Ouellette sat out on his front porch and held a wooded object in front of his well-trained eye. To an outside observer the thing may have looked like a fat wooden bowl, but any resident of Glen Hollow would know he was making another of his antler headpieces. About two-thirds of all ceremonial headgear in the Hollow were made by Claude. He'd started making them for close friends about twenty years ago. Folks were impressed with his craftsmanship, and word spread. He charged fifty dollars, which people willingly paid. A good antler headpiece was a family heirloom passed down from one generation to the next.

He had promised Fred Rutledge he'd have his new headgear completed for the cleansing on Saturday. Since it was already Thursday morning, Claude realized he'd have to rush to get it completed in time.

Fred had inherited his father's headpiece at age thirteen when the old man was killed falling out of a tree. At age eighteen, when he reached his maturity in the church and was first allowed to wear the piece, it didn't fit properly. He put up with it, but at age thirty-five he wanted his own horns.

One of the reasons people liked Claude's headpieces

so much is that each was custom made to the wearer's head size and shape. He got blocks of wood from the mill and turned them on his old, foot-powered lathe into the rough shape of a bowl. Upon getting a new order, he would then take careful head measurements, gouge out the inside of the crown, and drill two holes for the antlers.

"Saw Fred Rutledge down at the grocery." Mrs. Ouellette poked her head out onto the porch where Claude was working.

"Ayea." Claude inserted a horn into one of the crown holes.

"Just wanted to make sure you'd have his headpiece done for the ceremony Saturday."

"Ayea." Claude grimaced with concentration, rotating the horn to the proper angle. "He can pick it up tomorrow afternoon. Saturday mornin' for sure."

Antlers, which were supplied by the people themselves, were always a tricky issue. The tendency over the years was to use horns that were too big. People regarded it as a status symbol to get bigger and bigger antlers. The problem was that the bigger the horns, the harder it was to keep your balance. There had been some serious problems. Five years ago Mary Drummond nearly got her eye poked out during the fertily dance at her daughter's wedding. Ben Fletcher, wearing a massive eight-point rack, was right next to Mary in the dance ceremony. In a moment of spiritual fervor, he threw his head back, lost balance, and went careening backwards, catching Mary an inch from her right eye with one of his points. Gladys Archambeau wore antlers that were way too big for her petite frame and nearly punctured her husband's kidney two Easters ago. She was walking behind him on the way to church, slipped on some mud, and couldn't keep her balance. She fell forward, poking one of her horns right through her husband's coat an inch above his left kidney.

"I'm gonna have to put double chin straps on this thing 'cause Fred's horns are so big," Claude said as Elsa slipped back into the house.

He inserted the second antler in its glue-filled hole and held up his project to evaluate. He figured he'd have it done just about on time. He'd finish the horns and do the padded cloth lining today. If he really pressed it, he could give the wood its standard coat of brown paint and let it dry over night. Some people wanted the outside covered with leather, but most folks thought that was an affectation. Rutledge, like most people, wanted it painted brown. The chinstrap was the final step and could be added tomorrow. Headpieces tended to topple off people's heads unless secured by leather straps under the chin. Claude always took extra time with the chinstraps.

Carefully placing the headpiece down, he rolled up his pant leg and looked at his newly carved peg. The moose was coming along nicely, but the leg was a long way from finished. He decided he'd wear his special peg this Saturday, the one hanging on the bedroom wall. It was reserved for ceremonial occasions. After all, a cleansing didn't happen every day.

*   *   *

Mrs. Whitmore drove her cream-colored Mercedes past the gates, up her driveway, and emerged with a new hairdo. She walked around to the side door of the big stone house with a happy bounce to her step. It was the look of someone in control, someone on a mission.

"Sheila, I'm home," she sang out, turning the word *home* into a long two-syllable note.

"Ooh, I love your hair, Mother." Sheila walked into the kitchen. "Who did it, Raymond?"

"Of course, Raymond." Mrs. Whitmore put her purse and packages down on the counter. "You don't think I'd have that incompetent Bulgarian woman touch me again do you?" She looked at her daughter's hair. "I see you got yours cut too."

"How do you like it?" Sheila said, spinning around quickly.

Mrs. Whitmore grabbed her daughter's shoulder and turned her around, focusing her analytical gaze on Sheila's head. "It's all right, dear, but I don't know why you won't use Raymond." She tweaked the back of Sheila's hair lightly with her hand, fluffing out some of the hair.

"He's too expensive, Mother. And besides, I like my hair."

"It's fine, dear, fine. Just the feathering is a little clumsy, that's all. But it's fine."

Sheila went into the den and retrieved a big map, which she spread out on the kitchen table. "I've got the map and our route all marked out." She smoothed out the folds. "Here it is north of Portland on the coast of this huge bay."

Mrs. Whitmore glanced at the map. "We're going all the way up there?" She pointed to a red circle on the map.

"Yes, it's supposed to be an adorable little town."

"Black Hill Cove," Mrs. Whitmore said, looking at the map. She removed an envelope from her purse and opened it. "The tickets say our plane gets into Portland at eleven in the morning, Saturday." She looked carefully at the tickets and put them back in her purse. "Allowing time to get our luggage and grab a cab, we should get to your young man somewhere between two and three o'clock Saturday afternoon."

"He's going to be so surprised," said Sheila.

"Never be afraid to surprise your man, dear. It's when you stop surprising him that you should be concerned. Never let him take you for granted."

"I guess you're right."

"Absolutely, princess. Believe me. Keep him off balance and always keep your eyes focused on exactly what you want." She glanced at her fingernails. "God, my nails look absolutely dreadful." She paused and looked closely. "My nail girl was sick today, so I had this other girl do them, and they're all wrong. I think she was Chinese or something. I can never tell about those people."

"Didn't you say anything when she did them?"

"No," Mrs. Whitmore extended her chubby fingers, examining her outstretched fingernails, "she worked on them while Raymond was doing my hair and I didn't pay any attention. I only talked to Raymond. Then when she finished, I didn't look closely at them."

She took a deep breath and shook her head. "But I just noticed them in this light, and they're dreadful."

Sheila walked over and looked at her mother's nails. "They're fine, Mother. You're overreacting."

"The gloss is wrong, the color is wrong." She looked at her nails carefully. "Other than that they're wonderful."

Sheila smiled. "Mother, I'm going to the mall to get a pair of shoes for the trip." She grabbed her purse from the table.

"Well you've only got today and tomorrow to get anything you need, and pack. We leave bright and early Saturday morning."

"I know." Sheila picked up her mother's car keys. "I'm so excited. Harv will just die when he sees us."

"Aren't you going to have lunch first?"

"No, I'll grab a bite at the mall." Sheila opened the door and dashed out.

CHAPTER 29

Carrie held the kitchen door open while Buzz brought his prototype weapon out to the parking area behind the inn.

"Where's your uncle?" asked Buzz.

"He and Harv are putting the furniture back in the parlor. Harv said he was coming right out. He really wants to see this."

Buzz had made considerable progress field testing his weapon while Harv was in California and wanted to put it through its paces again. He put the device down on the lawn next to his car at the far edge of the parking lot and connected it to the battery pack and instrument panel. The weapon's guts were housed inside the plastic casing of a Craftsman large-sized hand drill. A two-inch copper rod extended out the open front, and a small tube was mounted on the top with a cable connected to the main housing.

"All right, a little dog and pony show." Harv came out the back door with a stack of paper plates. "We can use these as targets."

"The problem now is I don't know what the tolerances are for a human subject." Buzz adjusted the control panel. "I don't know what numbers on these knobs yield too much voltage and what's too little." He tightened a wire inside the panel while Harv walked into the woods to hang the plates on trees. "Same with the laser mode." Buzz turned to Carrie, "I could create a light tickling on the skin or drill a hole through someone's skull."

Harv returned to the parking area and watched as Buzz turned on his weapon and took aim. A thin blue light flashed out and zeroed in on one of the paper plates, hanging back in the woods. Buzz pulled the trigger, and the plate bounced backwards with a crackling sound.

"That's incredible," said Harv. "You really can't miss, can you? I mean with that light thing and all."

Buzz nodded. "The electric mode has a light component and the laser emits a beam. That's the beauty of it."

They all took turns with both the electric and laser modes until all five plates were knocked down.

Harv went back into the woods to re-attach the plates. He had attached four of the targets and was walking over behind a large tree to pick up a fifth when he felt an arm wrap around his neck and sharp steel dig at his throat.

"Hey, mister smart-ass, we meet again." Blade's unmistakable voice grated quietly into Harv's ear.

His first instinct was to struggle but the more he moved, the harder the knife dug into his skin.

"How does it feel to have someone surprise you from behind?"

Harv didn't say anything. He thought if he could maneuver out from behind the tree, Buzz could get a clear shot with his weapon. He figured they must be wondering what was keeping him. He dug his heel into the dirt and slowly rotated toward the clearing. Blade didn't resist as much as he might have, placing all his concentration on keeping his grip around Harv's neck.

The steel dug in harder. "Maybe I should cut you up a bit, pretty boy. Teach you a little respect."

Harv grabbed Blade's knife arm to relieve the pressure and pushed off with his right leg, rotating out to the edge of the clearing. He could see the side of Buzz's car through the opening.

"What's-a matter?" Blade laughed. "You ain't goin' nowhere."

A blue light flickered and danced through the leaves. Harv saw it creep slowly up his arm. He stood perfectly still in an effort to give Buzz a stable target. The last thing he wanted was to move just before Buzz fired and get hit himself. He watched the light slowly travel up his arm and stop on Blade's right forearm. Then he heard a crackling, popping sound. Blade yelled out in pain and released his grip. Harv turned, landed a solid upper cut to Ouellette's midsection, and backed away, rubbing his neck. The knife hadn't punctured the skin, but his neck was sore.

He thought of having it out with Blade right there, a knock down fight to get it over with, but he thought better of it. He had a lot going on right now. Nailing Burke was his sole priority, and he didn't want to jeopardize it with a fight. Instead, he walked out of the woods, back to his friends, knowing Blade would follow.

"Nice shot," he said, walking up to the car.

"I could barely see," said Buzz. "Who was that?"

Blade's motorcycle exploded out of the woods, and Buzz's face lit up with a smile. "All right! A little human field research." He whipped a small notepad and pencil out of his breast pocket and gave them to Carrie as Blade's cycle roared up toward the car. "Mind taking a few notes?" Buzz smiled at Carrie.

About twenty feet in front of the car, Blade brought his motorcycle to a stop and turned off the engine. "Well, what do we have here? Runnin' to your little friends for protection?"

Harv turned around, leaned casually on the car, and smiled. "Actually, Maurice, it's you who needs protection."

Blade laughed. "I need protection huh?" He got off his bike and put down the kickstand. "Somehow I'm not feelin' too scared right now." He looked at all three adversaries and smiled.

"So, Harv, this must be your little friend Maurice I've heard so much about." Buzz casually aimed his weapon straight ahead. "You didn't tell me he was so funny looking."

Ouellette gave Buzz a long slow glare. "Another wise-ass."

"Yeah, he's funny looking all right," said Harv. "You know, Maurice, even though your personal grooming regimen could use some re-thinking, you could still get a job with the Highway Department painting lines down the center of the road with that haircut of yours."

"OK, that does it." Ouellette transferred his knife to his right hand and headed toward Harv. "I should have finished you off back in the woods."

The blue light flashed on Blade's pant leg. He jumped back and grabbed his calf. "What the hell?"

"Sixteen hundred," said Buzz to Carrie, "penetrates clothing, minor topical sensation."

"Jeez," said Harv, "here I'm trying to give the guy some solid career counseling and he comes at me with a knife."

"Ungrateful as hell." Carrie finished her entry on the notepad.

"Yeah," Buzz readjusted the controls, "you think you know a guy."

"What the hell is that?" Ouellette rubbed his leg.

Another blue light flashed, producing no reaction whatever.

"Fourteen hundred seems totally ineffective. That's our low end." Buzz readjusted the controls.

Blade came at Harv again. This time the blue light landed on his right forearm as he screamed with pain, dropping his knife and grabbing his arm.

"Eighteen hundred seems effective with moderate neuromuscular degeneration at twenty feet," said Buzz.

Carrie continued to write.

"I'm serious about this painting gig," said Harv. "They could strap you upside down on a clothes rack with wheels, dip that Mohawk in white paint, and you'd be all set for painting lines on the highway."

"You're dead." Blade looked at Harv and rubbed his arm.

"Hell," Buzz readjusted the controls, "put a beveled edge on that plume and he could do window trim."

Blade picked up his knife and rushed toward Harv.

This time the light beam caught him in the chest and sent him backwards off his feet onto the grass.

"Twenty-one hundred. Approaching the high end," said Buzz. "Total neuromuscular breakdown at fifteen feet. This is tremendous data."

Blade got up on all fours, grabbed his knife and shook his head. "What the hell is that thing?"

Carrie finished her entry.

Ouellette got back up on his feet.

"Switching to laser mode." Buzz threw a switch on the instrument panel. "L-42 to start with."

A blue light flashed on Blade's leg with no effect as he regained his composure and circled for another assault.

"No one does this to me," he said, "no one." He sprang at Harv, low like a cat, when another arc of blue light hit him in the left arm. Ouellette's scream echoed across the back lawn as he rolled over on his side, grabbing the wound. Smoke floated up from where the laser had burned his shirt, and blood stained the cloth.

"L-75 seems to be the high end," said Buzz. "Couldn't go much higher without causing serious injury."

"You're dead, fella." Ouellette looked at the blood on his right hand. "This ain't over." He got up slowly as another blue light hit his arm. He swatted the spot like a mosquito had just bitten him.

"OK," said Buzz, "L-50 seems to be the low end range. We have a much narrower window of viability with the laser. I'll readjust the knob on a two-to-one ratio. This is incredible data."

Blade bent over, retrieved his knife and walked back to his motorcycle. "You're all dead." Holding his wound, he mounted his bike and cranked the starter. The engine growled twice before he switched it into gear and rode slowly past the Cherokee, looking straight at Harv. "You're history, pal." He gunned the accelerator as the cycle sped off to the driveway and out of sight.

CHAPTER 30

Conversation was limited in the Seaview launch Friday morning when Buzz steered Harv out into the bay. Harv was primed. He'd rehearsed the phone call and planned for every contingency. He knew Peter would be taken off guard. Harv was the aggressor, Peter the victim. Harv's role was to execute his plan. Peter's role was to react, to figure out what was happening, and try not to get snared. Harv liked his own role better.

He knew he could get a good signal from the tower on top of Crotchet Mountain; he didn't want any broken transmission caused by trees, or other peoples' electronic devices. The bay had worked well for his calls to Chuck. It would work well for this call.

When they got far enough out, Harv took out his phone and punched up the number.

"Mr. Burke's office." Lois's voice sounded so familiar. But it also seemed strange somehow, like deja vu experienced through a warped prism.

"Hi, Lois. This is Harvey Gallagher."

"Hi, Harv. Haven't seen you in a while." She sounded friendly as ever.

"Yeah, I've been traveling." Harv took a short breath.

"You calling for Peter, I assume?"

"Yeah, is he there?"

"I'm afraid he's at a meeting right now."

Harv nodded his head; at least Burke was in town. "I see. Do you know when he'll be back?"

"Well, I expect him back from this meeting just before lunch." She paused a moment as if checking a schedule. "Then he's having lunch with the agency. Then he's going to be out all afternoon."

Harv thought what a nice woman Lois was and wondered if she even suspected what a bastard she worked for. "So you're going to see him just before lunch? What, around noon?"

"I'd say twelve fifteen. I've got some reports he's got to sign. Then his lunch reservation is at twelve forty-five."

"Lois, this is extremely important. When you see Peter, will you tell him I called and that I'll call him at twelve fifteen?"

"Sure. You want me to have him call you?"

"No, that's OK. I'll call him exactly at twelve fifteen. Tell him it's very important." He knew Peter had his cell phone number and could call him at any time, but he didn't want to leave the ball in Burke's court; he didn't like the loss of control. He wiped sweat off the palms of his hands. "I've got great news for him." He knew Peter couldn't pass up a message like that, especially coming from him under the current circumstances.

"I'll tell him."

"Thank you, Lois. I appreciate it."

Harv jammed the phone into his pocket and looked

at Buzz. They decided to go back in, kill off the morning with a little fishing, and return later.

Buzz started up the launch and headed to shore. "So, these Nickersons. They're damn nice people."

"Of course they are. They're great." Harv looked out over the water.

"All three of them, Bart, Marge . . . and Carrie."

"Yeah, all three. They're great people."

Buzz looked at his watch and slowed down. "Listen, Harv. It's me, your best friend. We tell each other everything, right?"

"Most everything. What are you getting at?"

"This gal, Carrie. I know she's gorgeous, so that may be influencing my observations, but am I seeing something more than friendship between you two?"

"What?" Harv looked incredulous.

"I mean, I just want to know if I'm imagining things. I know you're going with Sheila, and she's been talking about marriage, and I thought it was serious stuff, so maybe I'm crazy, but am I seeing some sparks between you and Carrie?"

Harv shook his head. "Are you crazy? . . . I don't know where the hell you're getting this."

Water slapped against the side of the boat as Buzz carefully steered around a floating log.

"I've got a girlfriend. I'm going to meet Mrs. Whitmore. That's all there is to it. End of story."

Buzz nodded his head and maintained his course.

"And besides, I don't have time for anything like that. My life is complicated enough. I just don't have the emotional energy right now to deal with anything like that."

"I hear you, pal." Buzz goosed up the motor.

"So let's just take this subject off the table right now, OK?" Harv looked at his friend. "The only thing relevant in my world right now is this plan, getting Peter Burke."

"I hear you, man. No problem. I promise, I won't bring it up again."

"Thank you."

They killed off the morning with a little fishing. Buzz caught a mackerel on a blue popper lure and let it go. After an early lunch, it was exactly 12:15 when they headed back onto the water. Buzz cut the motor and Harv took out his phone. Burke's phone rang once; it rang twice. Harv wondered what was going on; Lois always picked up by the second ring. It rang three times. Four times.

"Hello, Peter Burke's office," came the familiar voice at last.

"Hi Lois. It's Harv Gallagher."

"Oh, Harv. Hang on a second. Let me put you on hold."

Harv became immediately concerned. This wasn't how he envisioned it happening. Lois was supposed to say 'Yes Peter's here. He's expecting your call. Here he is.' Harv waited and rubbed his phone on his pant leg to dry off some water that had splashed up.

"Sorry about that, Harv," came Lois's voice again. She sounded stressed. "Peter's running late. Let me put you on hold one more time."

"Did you tell him I called?"

"Oh, yes. I told him. Hold on a second."

Then it hit him. Of course, this would be just like

Burke. The message that Harv called had obviously taken him off guard. This was Peter's way of reestablishing control, of reclaiming the agenda. He would make Harv wait, put him off balance. Harv felt like a fool for allowing himself to be sucker punched right off the bat. But he saw it and was on top of it. He relaxed a little and wondered what mindless, make-work task Peter had Lois doing to create this sense of preoccupation. Probably dictating some bogus memo.

He waited.

"Harv," Lois's voice seemed even more stressed when she got back on the line, "we're in a little bit of a rush right now. Can I get Peter to call you right back? You still have your same cell phone number?"

Harv shook his head. *Unbelievable.* Peter was playing his little control game. The guy was already bobbing and weaving to maximize his position. Harv knew he had to be careful and keep the initiative.

"Listen, Lois, the message I have for Peter is of such importance that he would be furious if he didn't get it now. I promise you that whatever Peter is doing right now is nowhere near the importance of what I have to tell him."

Lois took a deep breath. "OK, hold on."

Harv could envision Peter's surprise at what Lois was now telling him. The pressure to bend his agenda would be unexpected.

After a long pause, Peter got on the phone. "Hey, Harv, what's up?" He sounded friendly enough.

"Peter, how you doing?"

"Fine, fine, so what's this incredibly important message you have for me?"

Harv gave Buzz a thumbs-up. "Well, Peter, it's one of those things that would be far better face-to-face but I just stumbled onto this information I want to share with you."

"Where the hell are you anyway?"

He could feel Burke maneuvering and probing. "I'm back home."

Burke said nothing at first. "So what's this information you have?"

Harv took a deep breath. "Listen, Peter, I don't know about you but for me things have been a little weird after seeing you at Smith's place last week."

"Weird?"

"Yeah, I mean you said you're involved with Smith in some real estate deal, and I know Smith is a real wheeler-dealer and involved in some things up in Black Hill Cove."

"Oh, really."

"And I just want you to know that whatever you're involved in, I'm behind you one hundred percent."

Burke was silent. "I'm still listening."

"Peter, here's the deal. I know that if you're involved in a project, it's going to be successful and it's going to make money. I've seen you make so much money for your employers over the years it boggles the mind." He could hear Burke's ego lapping up the flattery. "The real bottom line is, Peter, that if you're involved in a project, I don't care what it is; whether it's legal, illegal or paralegal, it's going to make money and I'd like to be a part of it."

Peter said nothing for what seemed an hour. "Is that all you have to tell me?"

Harv shifted the phone to his other ear. "No, the real bottom line is this." He felt relieved at finally getting to the meat of the conversation. "Obviously I'm not naive enough to think you'd deal me in just because I'm such a swell guy. I've got an entry ticket I think you'll find pretty interesting. I know you want the Seaview Inn, you and Smith, and I know it's been impossible to get up until now." He paused for a moment, but Burke was silent. "Peter, I stayed at that inn when I was in Maine. I overheard something. A conversation between Nickerson and his sister-in-law, Marge. A conversation the two of them thought was totally private. The substance of that conversation, Peter, is something that would be very helpful for any potential buyer of the Seaview to know." Harv looked at Buzz. "Something I think could help you."

The silence coming from Harv's phone lasted an eternity. He took the phone away from his ear and looked at it. He listened some more.

"Look, Harv, I'm not saying whether I want the Seaview Inn or not. But as you say, this is the kind of thing we should talk about in more detail face-to-face."

"Listen, why don't I meet you at the inn?" Harv looked over at Buzz. "Kind of neutral ground, away from ADI. We can meet at the inn. We can meet in total privacy and talk."

Burke was silent.

Harv pressed on. "I'll meet you at the inn whenever you can get there. We can talk. You can tell me about your project and I can tell you this information that I know would help you."

Harv waited for Burke to say something. He

wondered if he seemed too anxious, if he'd pressed too hard.

"Well, there are a few things I could probably get done up there," Burke said after a long silence. "Tell you what, I'll be there Saturday and we can talk."

Harv felt a little relief. "A week from tomorrow?"

"No, tomorrow."

Bang! The adrenalin shot through Harv like fire-water. He had no idea Peter would move so soon. He wasn't mentally ready for one day's notice but didn't want to blow it. "Great, the sooner the better." He threw a tense look at Buzz. "When do you think you'll get there?"

The line was silent for a second. "Considering normal driving time, I ought to get up there around mid-afternoon, around two or three o'clock."

"It's a date."

Harv signed off, jammed the phone into his pocket, and screamed, "It's tomorrow, man."

"Tomorrow? Like in twenty four hours?"

"That's right. Take me home Jeeves. We've got work to do."

*   *   *

Smith had taken Friday off and was sitting on his back deck doing paperwork when his phone rang.

"Steve, this is Peter."

Smith sat up quickly from his chaise lounge, removing the stack of papers from his lap. "Hey, how's it going?"

"Listen, I'm coming up there tomorrow."

"Tomorrow? A little notice would be nice."

Burke told him about his conversation with Harv.

"I thought you said you weren't sure about this Gallagher guy. You trust him now?"

"I'd say it's fifty-fifty. But we, at least, need to see if this thing is legit. I'll be there around two or three."

"You know I've got the big demonstration taking place tomorrow. The one you wanted. The freak show."

"Wonderful. So much the better. If Gallagher's plan is bogus or falls through, your little party may just put things over the top for us."

*   *   *

Buzz and Nickerson drove to the helicopter in Belfast and tested the equipment. Take-off and landing on the helipad went without a hitch. Everything went smoothly when they sent a practice video to Crowley.

Marge Nickerson talked to the kitchen help about putting together some sandwiches for a picnic on Blueberry Island the next day. They wanted to get as many guests off the property as possible when Burke arrived, and Marge thought a Seaview-sponsored picnic with free food would lure some of the guests off-site.

Harv spent the afternoon rehearsing his talk with Peter. Carrie played the part of Burke. They placed his chair in the proper position to get a good shot of his face through the camera lens.

After Carrie had convinced Harv he had rehearsed enough, they went for a swim in the bay. Sitting out on the floating wooden dock, Harv looked back at the front of the inn. He thought the place looked best from the water, like the picture on the brochure with its chimneys poking upward, surrounded by trees and mountains. He noticed how good Carrie looked in her pink, floral bathing suit. Nothing outrageous, a one-piece. A hint of cleavage. It appeared to be made out of very thin material. It was wet. Her body looked firm, tan, well-proportioned. The water made her skin glisten.

Harv immediately started talking about Sheila. He told Carrie about Mrs. Whitmore and about Sheila's various attempts to get him to meet her.

Lying on her back, Carrie rolled over onto her side and told Harv how she had been in a relationship for the past three years. A lawyer in Portland. She said there had been some talk of marriage, but lately the two seemed to be growing in different directions.

The wake of a passing boat made the wooden dock undulate up and down. It felt good. Harv looked out toward open water and watched a big two-masted windjammer sail by.

*   *   *

That night they all had a light dinner and met in the tower room at nine o'clock for a little pre-sting celebration.

Buzz opened all the windows to let in the cool night air off the bay, and Nickerson lit a fire in the fireplace.

"You know there's not much to celebrate yet." Harv squeezed a lemon on an open oyster.

"We can celebrate the successful phone call." Marge

put a tray of Havarti cheese and stone-ground crackers on the desk. "Your guy has taken the bait. He's coming. That's definitely something to celebrate."

"You got a decent number of guests signed up for that picnic of yours?" Nickerson poked at a log.

"The Grinnells are coming, Mr. and Mrs. Finch, and the new couple from New York, so we've got a total of six," said Marge.

"Every little bit helps," said Nickerson.

Harv looked at his watch. "Just think, guys, within twenty-four hours we'll be going head-to-head with our friend, Mr. Burke."

"Just think how great it'll be to have this over with," said Carrie.

"You are so ready for this." Buzz reached for an oyster. "You're going to clean his clock."

Harv dug his thumbnail into the wet label on his beer bottle. "I know."

CHAPTER 31

Saturday morning Harv woke up at five thirty and noticed an eerie silence outside his window. The food, beer and laughter had all combined to take the edge off and bring on a light sleep, but at five thirty he was wide awake and wired. He lay there thinking about the upcoming day, what Peter might do, what he himself would do in response.

At six o'clock he was in his sweat suit and sneakers, tiptoeing down stairs. Despite the dense morning fog, enough early light filtered through to guide him down to the bay where he began jogging along the path. No thought of time or direction. He just ran. Morning for the rest of the world was just around the corner, but this was his time. The day was a coiled spring ready to erupt, and he held the trip hammer. He had control, and he didn't want the day to start quite yet.

*   *   *

Mrs. Whitmore tipped the cab driver an extra ten dollars and asked if he would "mind taking the bags over to that black gentleman by the door."

"The Skycap?" asked the cabby.

"Yes, the Skycap," said Sheila, grabbing her car-ry-on bag.

The drive to Philadelphia International Airport had gone quickly since there was little traffic on Saturday morning. They checked Mrs. Whitmore's two suitcases and headed for the gate.

"Honestly, Mother, I don't know why you're taking all those bags. I've got all I need in this little carry-on."

"A lady is always prepared for any eventuality."

"But we're only going to be there two days."

"Nevertheless, you never know what you might need." They passed through the metal detectors and into the gate area. "You don't know what the weather's going to be like. You don't know if it's going to rain or what kind of restaurant we may go to. You'd be well advised to take heed of what I'm saying, young lady."

"Yes, Mother." Sheila rolled her eyes.

*   *   *

Fred Rutledge drove his rusted, blue pick-up onto the Ouellette's front yard and walked to the house. His headpiece had been ready Friday night but he didn't leave the mill until late, and figured he'd pick it up before the ceremony.

"Fits like a glove," said Rutledge, securing the chin-strap. He walked around the Ouellette's living room, performing a few gyrations of the ancient cleansing ceremony dance, careful not to hit anything. He turned sideways and looked at himself in the mirror. After more admiration he gave Claude fifty dollars and removed his new headgear.

The two men talked about the cleansing as they walked outside to Fred's car. Rutledge held out his new headpiece and smiled, then he looked up when the sound of two motorcycles roared up from the road.

Blade and Chavone rode slowly up to the house. They turned off their motors, grunted hello, and walked inside.

"Maurice is gonna be at the cleansing ya know," said Claude. "He's not gonna wear a headpiece, but at least he's promised to be there."

Rutledge nodded and carefully placed his new headgear in the back seat of his car.

"I think maybe his attitude is startin' to improve a little."

*   *   *

At noon Harv and Carrie walked down the front lawn to the docks, each with a basket of food for the upcoming picnic.

Mr. Grinnell was out on the front lawn taking pictures and walked up to them. "So, they're conscripting the guests to help now I see."

"Carrie tells me this is supposed to be part of the fun," said Harv.

Carrie nudged Harv with her arm. "You're still coming to the picnic aren't you, Mr. Grinnell?"

"Absolutely; Joyce and I both are coming."

"I did a head count this morning. We should have almost a full boat."

"I should be able to get some good pictures from there." Grinnell tapped his camera.

"You'll definitely get some good shots," said Carrie. "The view is beautiful from there."

"Incidentally, Harvey, I've been meaning to ask you. Do you have a brochure or a web site or anything about your consulting firm? From our talk yesterday it sounds pretty interesting."

"My web site is on my business card. I think I still have a few in my car."

"Great. Give me one before we leave, will you?"

"Sure."

"We may be in need of your services."

Harv and Carrie continued down to the docks. "A prospective new client." Harv said. "Not bad."

"I was talking with Mr. Grinnell yesterday. He likes you." Carrie put her basket down on the dock and climbed into the boat. "He said you seemed to be 'a solid young man.'"

"*Solid*, huh?"

"Yeah, *solid*."

*   *   *

By 2:45 a collection of old cars and pick-up trucks began accumulating in the Seaview parking lot and driveway. Most had come together in a caravan, but others straggled along on their own and parked wherever they could find a spot. Some parishioners sat in their cars, while others got out and talked among themselves, putting on their headpieces in anticipation of the ceremony. Everyone brought their own unlit torches with rags wrapped around one end,

secured by wire, and soaked in worshipers' acceler-
ant of choice.

Blade and Chavone sat on their motorcycles in the
driveway, telling late arrivals to park along the road.
They wanted to make sure there was plenty of room
for Peter Burke when he arrived.

Buzz hovered in the parlor, waiting for the word
to jump into his closet, where the video camera sat
in readiness. Two blank memory cards were in his
pocket as back up.

Harv paced the foyer and front porch, looking for
Peter's car while Marge Nickerson punched numbers
on her calculator behind the front desk.

Carrie handed out life jackets to her guests as they
boarded the launch. After helping Mrs. Finch with
her jacket, she turned on the motor and took off for
Blueberry Island.

*   *   *

The airport taxi pulled up in front of the Captain
Hawkins House in the center of Black Hill Cove. Sheila
and Mrs. Whitmore had decided on that particular
hotel because the travel agent had recommended it
and because they didn't want to spoil the surprise
by making reservations at the Seaview.

Mrs. Whitmore reached in her purse, pulled out her
wallet and peeled off a collection of hundred dollar
bills. "This should take care of things."

"Yes ma'am." The driver made a halfhearted
attempt to get change from his pocket.

"Forget the change, but would you mind taking

the suitcases into the lobby?" Mrs. Whitmore spoke in a miffed tone as she struggled to open the car door herself.

The cab driver opened his trunk and carted the three bags up to the old hotel, followed by both women. Arriving at the front door, Sheila and her mother paused, giving the driver room to put down the bags and open the door for them. Instead, he opened the screen and held it ajar with his foot while stepping through into the lobby with the suitcases. The screen door slammed behind him.

Mrs. Whitmore shook her head. Sheila opened the door, and the two women followed the driver into the lobby.

"Oh, Mother, it's darling."

"A little rough around the edges for my taste." Mrs. Whitmore looked around.

After checking in, they spent the next twenty minutes unpacking clothes, putting on make-up, combing their hair, and generally freshening up. At 3:05, Sheila and her mother went downstairs to secure transportation.

Mrs. Whitmore walked up to the front desk. "Would you mind calling us a cab?"

The old lady at the counter reached for an information brochure and handed it to her guest. "Number's at the top of page two. Public phone's on the other side of the lobby."

Mrs. Whitmore shook her head and walked across the lobby. Sheila took the brochure and promptly called the only cab company listed.

"Not for two hours? Are you sure?" said Sheila.

After asking if there was another taxi company, she rolled her eyes and hung up.

"Did I hear you correctly?" said Mrs. Whitmore. "They won't be able to pick us up for two hours?" Her voice was loud.

"That's what they said." Sheila shook her head. "Their one, and apparently only, functioning taxi has three other calls before ours. Their other cab is in the shop." She looked through the phone book attached to the phone. "They said Saturday was a real busy day."

"There must be another cab company."

Overhearing their conversation, the bellhop chimed in from the stairway. "If you're talkin' about Farnsworth," he said, "it's the only one in town."

"That's who it was," Sheila pointed to the brochure and read out loud, "Farnsworth Taxi Service."

"Well there's got to be another way." Mrs. Whitmore paced back and forth.

"Exactly where ya goin'?" asked the bellhop.

"To the Seaview Inn," said Sheila.

A sour look came over Mrs. Whitmore's face. "It's no one's business where we're going," she whispered to her daughter.

"Just a minute." The bellhop held up his hand. "Maybe I can help." He walked over to the front desk and had a brief conversation with the manager. Then he returned and explained to Sheila and Mrs. Whitmore that he had a boat at the public docks across the street and that he'd be willing to take them directly to the Seaview by water for a price. "It's just down the cove and out into the bay a piece," he said.

Sheila smiled. "That sounds like fun, Mother."

The sour look on Mrs. Whitmore's face disappeared. "I must admit it does sound like kind of an adventure." She looked at her watch. "We can make a grand entrance by water. Your Harvey friend can bring us back here for dinner."

"Business is kinda slow here right now." The bellhop looked over at the front desk. "Don't mind takin' some time off to help out."

"Oh, Harv will be so surprised." Sheila clapped her hands, smiling.

After agreeing on a price, the bellhop introduced himself, took off his red jacket, and hung it in the front closet. "I'll be back," he said to the manager as he and the Whitmore women left for the Seaview.

CHAPTER 32

The collection of old cars in the parking area and Seaview driveway had grown dramatically. Some vehicles were parked in the woods, others by the roadside. Elsa Ouellette gave instructions to a large group of people clustered under the trees, several already wearing their antlered headgear. Blade and Chavone maintained position on their cycles at the driveway entrance.

Then it came.

Heads turned to look at the dark green Lexus as it made its way down Vista Road and cruised into the driveway. Tinted glass obscured the inside. Blade motored up to the vehicle as the power window descended, revealing the expressionless face of Peter Burke.

"The parking lot at the inn is packed, Mr. Burke."

Peter nodded. "I'll park as close as I can, but I'm going to turn my car around to face the road. Do me a favor. Any more cars come, have them park in the street so I can get out easily."

"Will do," said Ouellette with an uncharacteristic tone of respect. He'd only met Burke on two other occasions but knew Smith deferred to him.

"I understand you people are putting on a big demonstration today."

"A cleansing ceremony with the church. It's gonna be huge."

"The bigger the better. Just don't do anything to hurt that inn."

"No worries," said Blade as the power window went up. The Lexus moved slowly up the driveway and turned around.

Harv saw Burke first. He ran into the parlor and yelled, "Showtime!"

Buzz walked immediately into the closet and shut the door.

Harv mustered as much composure as he could and walked out onto the porch to greet his guest. Burke arrived wearing a blue blazer with open collar. Somehow the man seemed less imposing on neutral ground. In his office or his home he had an aura of power and invincibility, but here in front of the Seaview, he took on more human dimensions. Maybe that's because Harv knew he was a man walking into a trap. Shaking Burke's hand, however, Harv took in the full measure of the man's intensity. The grip was firm. The dark eyes blazed, observing everything. The smile, friendly but businesslike.

They talked a while on the porch. Harv asked about the drive up. Peter was cordial, but it was obvious he wanted to get down to business. After a bare minimum of small talk, Harv suggested they go into the parlor for some privacy. Peter walked into the big foyer, looking around with a subtle smile on his face, taking in every detail.

As they turned to enter the parlor, George Ferguson, the dining room manager, walked through the foyer with an armful of table cloths.

"George?" Peter looked at the man and smiled. "George Ferguson. How the hell are you?"

The man looked up and walked over to Burke. "Yes, I'm George Ferguson. How do you know my name?"

"It's me, Peter Burke. I used to work here."

Ferguson looked closely. "Oh my God, Chip Burke." He smiled. "Yes, I do remember you." He extended his right hand around the pile of table cloths to shake Peter's hand. "You haven't changed at all, now that I look at you."

"Neither have you. You look great. I can't believe you're still here."

"The Nickersons treat me well. I'd be a fool to leave this place."

Burke looked at his watch. "I've got to meet with Harvey here," he nodded in Harv's direction, "but afterwards I'll find you and we can catch up."

"Sounds good." George smiled.

After proceeding into the parlor, Burke was offered the target chair, located at the proper position.

Harv closed the door and pulled up a second chair to its assigned location. "You want anything to drink? Coffee? Ice tea?"

"No, I'm all set."

Harv sat down and looked at Burke. "So . . . *Chip*, huh?"

Peter smiled. "Yeah, I jettisoned the *Chip* and used my given name in grad school . . . a little more professional sounding."

"Good decision." Harv smiled. "And you know George Ferguson apparently."

"Yeah, worked here as a waiter during college."

"So that's when you fell in love with this area, I'm guessing."

"Something like that."

Staring directly at Burke, Harv leaned his elbows on the table. "Before we start, Peter, I want to thank you for driving up here." He tried to generate as much saliva as possible in his dry mouth.

"Well, as I said, I had some things I could take care of up here anyway." He looked around the room; eyes probing, expressionless. "And from your phone call, there's probably some things we need to talk about."

"I could be way off base here, Peter but my instincts tell me there may be some common ground."

"Well you never know." Burke remained relaxed during a long silence. "Tell me, Harv, what makes you think I'm so interested in buying this inn?"

Harv leaned back in his chair. "Well, Peter, I wasn't sure at first. But I know Smith was making offers to Nickerson, and I know you're involved with Smith. The notion that Smith's offers were related to you was just guesswork. But the fact that you're here right now tells me maybe I was right."

Peter smiled for the first time. "OK, Mister Gallagher, let's just suppose, for the sake of argument, that I *am* interested in buying this inn. Before we go any further, tell me about your sudden interest in real estate. Your interest in joining my team."

"It's not sudden, Peter. I've always been interested in real estate investing. I'm starting to do pretty well now, largely thanks to you. And I've got some money saved." He saw someone with antlers on their head walk past the window and paused a second. "Most important, I have total faith in your business judgment." The expression on Burke's face warmed up. "On top of all that, this inn is incredible. I'd love to be part of a real estate trust or whatever that owned this thing."

Burke sat back and smiled. "You know, kid, I think my first instincts about you were right. You do remind me of myself when I was your age."

"I regard that as a compliment."

Burke nodded his head. "Be that as it may, Harv, let me ask you, what's this little entry ticket you talked about on the phone?"

Harv told Burke how the inn's chef would often take in a fish Harv had caught and cook it up for dinner for him. Although that part was true, Harv invented a story about one particular time he took a freshly caught striped bass into the kitchen and the chef wasn't there. The story continued with Harv taking it upon himself to go into the pantry and put the fish into the big refrigerator, and just as he was closing the door, he heard Nickerson and Marge enter the kitchen. He didn't want them to know he was in the pantry, so he kept quiet while the two Nickersons talked.

Harv was happy to see that Burke's body language indicated he was buying into this yarn. "While the Nickersons thought they were totally alone, the conversation between them soon launched into a discussion of how bad-off the Seaview was financially."

Burke's inscrutable facial expression warmed a bit.

"They were saying that business is way down and they would like to have accepted the last offer from Smith except that they hate Smith and hate Cove Realty."

"Why do they hate Smith?"

"I have no idea. I only know what I heard. Anyway, they said if they had to sell the place, they'd rather sell it to anyone but Smith."

Burke released his laser-like gaze upon Harv, and nodded. "Pretty interesting stuff. And they never found out you were in there?"

Harv laughed. "I waited about ten minutes after they left the kitchen then high-tailed it out the back door at the far end of the kitchen. No one saw me."

"Pretty interesting." Burke repeated himself.

"I figure it's always good to know all you can about a situation. The substance of that conversation should be pretty helpful."

"It is, Harv. It certainly is."

"And here's the last thing I want to kick in, just to show my good faith."

Burke smiled.

"I've done some reading about real estate. If you were to find yourself a good real estate lawyer, you could set up a nifty sub rosa purchase situation and the Nickersons would never know Smith was behind it."

Burke nodded his head. "I like the way you think, Mr. Gallagher. I like the way you think."

"So, I'm guessing you're creating a real estate trust, and you want the Seaview to be part of it?"

Peter laughed. The guarded reticence was gone.

"No, not quite. Let's just say for now that this inn is a very interesting place." He looked around the room. "It has some attributes that make it ideal for my purposes."

They talked about the inn, how old it was, its unique architecture. Peter mentioned that the inn's dock was in deep enough water to accommodate sea-going vessels.

"So how's all this going to make us a pile of money?"

Peter smiled. "Impatience," he said, shaking his head.

"No. I didn't mean to be pushy."

"I know, I know." Burke put up his hand. "Impatience is an ingrained part of American business these days. Impatience with getting new technology to return a profit quickly. And I have to say my little side venture is a principle cause of it."

"Impatience, like the short pay-back time frame our manufacturers demand from their new products?"

"Exactly," said Burke.

"Like the ridiculously short pay-back imposed on the Mustang Project?"

Burke's eyebrows went up. "You're hitting a little close to home there, Harv, but yes, like the Mustang Project . . . exactly like the Mustang Project."

"Chuck Weitz told me there's a lot of pressure to make new products succeed quickly because foreign agents often steal our pre-production technology and beat us to the market."

Burke smiled. "Let's just say I'm very familiar with that situation. Very familiar."

"And you said your little side venture plays a role in this dance . . ."

"Harv, you initiated this meeting. You shot straight with me about your entry ticket. You did that in good faith and I appreciate that, so I'll give you an answer. Yes, we do play a role. And there's big money involved, but I'm not going to say any more."

Harv heard noises coming from outside the inn and saw people passing the window in antlered headpieces. He shook his head and put it out of his mind as best he could. Burke required all his concentration. "Is that what this is about, Peter, technology, not real estate?"

Burke smoothed down the lapels of his blue blazer and looked around the room. "It's technology destined to end up in Russia or China anyway. We just shortcut the process and get it in their hands a little sooner; that's all."

"And get paid for it."

"I'm not going to say any more, Harv. You're a smart young man and maybe there might be some room for you on my team." He looked at his watch and glanced out the window. "But we're going to have to talk details at another time. I have to talk to some people."

The noise outside was impossible to ignore, and Harv suspected Burke knew what was going on. If the guy knew nothing about it, he would have commented on it by now. Noises seemed to be everywhere. Strident voices started coming from the living room. As Harv tried to block out the clamor and refocus on Burke, the parlor door burst open and a large, well-dressed woman walked in, followed by Sheila Whitmore.

Harv looked up with his mouth open. He never thought of locking the door because most all the guests were off the premises. "Sheila, what the hell?"

"I didn't come all this way just to wait around." The woman walked briskly up to the table and looked at both men. "Hello, I'm Katherine Whitmore."

Harv's face turned white as he stood up and shook hands. "Uh, hello, Mrs. Whitmore, I'm Harvey Galla-gher." He looked blankly at Sheila and then at Peter. "Uh, this is Peter Burke."

Peter stood up and shook her outstretched hand as Harv looked around helplessly for Marge Nickerson, who was nowhere to be seen.

Sheila came up, grabbed Harv's arm and gave him a peck on the cheek. "Surprised to see us?"

"Uh, surprised is not quite the word." He put his hand over hers and began escorting her toward the door, looking briefly at Peter. "Sorry about this," he said as Peter smiled politely.

"Hi, Mr. Burke," Sheila looked over at Peter.

"Yes, hello there." Peter managed to sound cordial.

"Listen," said Harv softly, "I'm right in the middle of something very important."

"I know. I just couldn't wait to see you. Do you know there are people with horns on their head running around outside? When are you going to be finished anyway?"

"Soon, very soon. But you're going to have to wait outside for a bit."

"Sure, we just wanted to say hello. That's all." She looked over at Mrs. Whitmore. "Come on, Mother." She released Harv's arm and walked over to grab her mother's. "Let's go Mother. Harv will be done in a minute."

Mrs. Whitmore looked miffed. "Well I suppose we can wait if we must."

"I'm delighted to have a chance to meet you, Mrs. Whitmore." Harv ushered the two women to the door. "I shouldn't be too long."

"We can watch the weirdos outside while we wait," said Sheila.

"Are you associated with those people outside, young man?"

"No, Mrs. Whitmore. I have absolutely no idea what's going on out there." Harv looked out the front window. "We'll talk in a little while. I'm looking forward to it." Through the window, Harv could see Marge Nickerson talking with the revelers. He reassured Sheila and her mother he wouldn't be too much longer and returned to the parlor where Peter was looking out the window.

"Do you have any idea what's going on out there?" Harv closed the door.

"Not a clue," said Burke.

Harv felt sure he was lying but didn't care. He needed to resume the conversation and get Peter talking again. They sat down and began talking about corporate espionage in general terms. No matter how hard Harv pressed, however, Peter refused to talk in any more detail about his special side venture. The conversation wandered in generalities. As Harv tried to steer the dialogue back to Burks's operation, an unexpected noise shot through the parlor to his right. Mrs. Whitmore exploded into the room again.

"I am through waiting," she said in a loud voice.

Harv was numb. He never thought anyone would burst into a private meeting twice. "Mrs. Whitmore!"

"I am returning to the Captain Hawkins House and we can perhaps meet for dinner." She was clearly angry.

Harv got up and walked over to her. "We're almost done, Mrs. Whitmore, but you do whatever you feel you have to." He looked over at Peter and shook his head. "Right now I'm very busy."

"There are no cabs to be had in this town, the driveway is blocked with old cars," she looked out the window. "I came by boat. I'll be waiting in one of those boats I saw down by the dock. I trust you can find someone around this establishment to take me back to the village."

Sheila entered the parlor with a surprised look on her face and walked up to Harv. "I'm sorry, sweetie, but Mother is tired. It's been a long day."

"Sheila, I'm very busy. I'll be done soon. But right now I have to finish up." He escorted both women out of the parlor.

"I'll take care of it, sweetie. Don't worry. I'll get someone to take her back."

Mrs. Whitmore walked through the foyer and out of the inn. Then she marched briskly down the front lawn, past the dancing parishioners toward the dock.

After a few quick words with Sheila, Harv returned to the parlor to see Peter standing, sliding his chair back under the table.

"Harv, I've got to go." He quickly looked at his watch.

"Call me next week and we'll talk about things. I need to make a few phone calls and talk to some people."

There was a momentary lull in the chanting as Burke walked over to the front and side windows to view the exhibition outside. On his way back toward the parlor door he walked past the new mirror, only a foot away.

Then it happened.

The subtle noise that invaded the parlor was unmistakable. Harv heard it, and he knew Peter heard it. No one figured the automatic focus on the video camera would ever be a matter of concern. When it made a radical readjustment to refocus, it extended and contracted the lens with a quiet humming sound. It was an electronic, automatic feature that functioned unobtrusively during rehearsals. With two people sitting at the table or walking around the room, there was minimal need for refocusing—certainly not quick refocusing from one extreme to another. The little hum was never noticed.

Burke's demeanor changed. No longer the affable comrade rushing out of a friendly meeting, he was now the wily prey with his guard up. It was hard to say exactly what about the man was different; something to do with the set of his jaw. His mouth was more tightly drawn, and his dark eyes blazed. He looked around the room, probing, processing data like a high-speed computer.

He looked closely at the mirror, running his fingers along the exterior molding where it met the wall. "Interesting mirror, Harv." He tapped the glass. "At first it looked like a regular mirror. Now I see it's actually built into the wall." Burke glared through Harv. The look of sadness on his face was profound.

He knows.

"What's behind the mirror, Harv?"

Harv's stomach churned. "I don't know." He tried to sound casual.

"You know, some of these mirrors are made so you can shoot a bullet right into them and they don't shatter. It just makes a little bullet hole." Peter slowly rubbed his hand along the base of the mirror. "I wonder what would happen to this one." He reached under his jacket, pulled a Walther PPK from a shoulder holster, and pointed it at the mirror.

"Hold it," said Harv.

"Yeah, hold it," came Buzz's voice from inside the closet.

"Well, what do you know, a talking mirror." Burke pointed the gun directly into the mirror. "Open the door, son." He jiggled the locked closet doorknob with his free hand and raised his voice. "Do it now and no one will get hurt. I just want the video." He pointed the gun quickly at Harv then resumed his aim at the mirror.

The ease with which Peter handled the weapon surprised Harv. He'd never had a loaded gun pointed at him. He was scared, and he was angry—angry that someone could hold the power of life or death over him simply by pointing a gun.

"Yes sir." Buzz unlocked the door and emerged with his two arms raised, each clutching a memory card. "Here it is" Buzz said as he tossed one of the cards high into the air toward Burke.

As Peter reached to catch it, Buzz underhanded the other card to Harv and lunged with both hands for Burke's gun arm.

"Run!" Buzz held Peter's right forearm with both hands, forcing the gun to point skyward.

Harv caught the card and raced out the door. He worried about Buzz but knew Peter wouldn't be crazy enough to hurt him. After all, he didn't have the card anymore, Harv had it. Harv was the one in danger now. He ran through the living room past Sheila in the foyer.

"Hi, I'm so glad you're done, sweetie." Sheila looked surprised to see Harv running. "What's . . .?" She turned as he ran past her. "What's going on? . . . Harv?"

He dashed out the front door and saw his car was blocked by a mass of vehicles.

The cleansing ceremony was well underway with antlered parishioners chanting and dancing in circles on the front lawn. Harv didn't have time to react to the spectacle. Jamming the card in his pocket, he bounded across the lawn through the dancing parishioners, most of whom had already ignited their torches. He wound his way down to the waterfront like a halfback, going for a touchdown.

Inside, Peter gave Buzz a karate chop to the neck, knocking him down. Dashing out of the inn, Burke was met by Blade and Chavone at the bottom of the front steps.

"What gives, Mr. Burke?" said Blade. "I saw Gallagher runnin' outa here like a scared jack rabbit."

"The video," Peter took a bead on Harvey with his gun. "He's got a memory card. I've got to get it." He pointed his gun forward then lowered it, unable to get a clear shot through the dancing parishioners.

As Burke headed for the water, Blade took off after him and grabbed his shoulder. "Hold on, Mr. Burke. I know every rock, every island in that water out there. Let me get the thing. I need to hurt that guy, Mr. Burke. I'll get that video-thing for you." He pulled out a gun from under his vest and smiled.

"You get that card and bring it directly to me at Smith's house and there's an extra five grand in it for you. It's a small memory card." He held up his hand with his thumb and forefinger a few inches apart. "Probably in his pocket."

Blade's face lit up. "Yes sir."

CHAPTER 33

Harv saw two boats tied up at the dock. One had a gas tank sitting up on the pier, waiting to be reconnected to the motor. The second boat looked completely intact, hooked up, and ready to go. It had only one drawback—Mrs. Whitmore sat expectantly in the middle seat. On seeing Ouellette heading toward him, Harv jumped in and asked Mrs. Whitmore to get out.

"Young man, I've been sitting here for the past ten minutes waiting for someone to take me to my hotel, and I am not moving from this spot."

Harv grabbed her arm in an effort to physically remove her, but was interrupted by a bullet glancing off the dock piling.

Harv jumped at the sound and looked up. Seeing Blade halfway down the lawn, he released Mrs. Whitmore's arm, unhooked the mooring lines, and sped away from the dock.

"That's more like it." Mrs. Whitmore smoothed out her dress, oblivious to the bullets splashing around her.

Looking down the barrel of Peter's gun was one thing, but being shot at was quite another. Harv's sole compulsion at that moment was getting to Nickerson as soon as possible. He thought of calling him, but couldn't use his phone while operating the boat at full speed, and right now he wanted to create as much distance as possible between himself and Ouellette. He knew it would take Blade a little time to hook up the gas tank, and he wanted to take full advantage of that delay. Cranking the motor up into high gear, he held onto the seat with his left hand and steered with his right as the boat bounced around in the choppy water. He quickly felt the outline of the memory card in his pocket and shoved it down as far as it would go.

In front of the inn, Marge Nickerson pleaded with the revelers to stop. She couldn't call Crowley because she knew he and his deputy were both standing by at the police station as part of the sting operation.

The chanting grew louder as parishioners broke out into smaller groups of five and six people, each cluster dancing around in circles, singing and wailing loudly.

Blade hauled the full gas tank onto the remaining boat and attached it to the fuel intake. After starting the motor, he unhooked the lines and took off in pursuit.

On Blueberry Island, the picnickers unloaded their gear on a flat knoll overlooking the bay. Carrie set up a game of horseshoes then spread out two big blankets. Mr. Grinnell crouched down with his camera and took some pictures of a passing sailboat.

Peter got a busy signal on his phone and jammed it back into his pocket. He walked around the parked cars to his Lexus, spun his wheels, and sent a stream of pebbles into the air as he took off.

Sheila stood on the porch near the steps. Her eyes wide, her mouth open, breathing heavily. She moved quickly back and forth along the railing, looking at the ceremony.

Buzz wandered out on the front porch, rubbing his neck and stopped at the railing to take in the spectacle.

"My God, Buzz what are you doing here?" Sheila ran up and gave Buzz a hug. "What's going on?"

Buzz shook his head. "I swear to God, Sheila, your timing is incredible."

"What do you mean?" She looked out over the lawn. "What the hell's going on?"

Buzz told her he was helping Harv with a consulting project. "As far as what's going on out there, I have no clue."

Mrs. Whitmore looked behind her and scanned the shoreline. "Young man, my hotel is in the village, and the village is that way." She pointed at the land rapidly receding behind her. "Why are you heading in the opposite direction?"

"Mrs. Whitmore, I told you to get off the boat." He quickly looked over his shoulder. "There's something I have to do first, then I'll figure out what to do with you."

Harv brought the boat down to a more manageable speed and called Nickerson.

"You sure you're being shot at?" Came the familiar voice.

"Positive." Harv wiped some splashed water off his phone and told Nickerson about Ouellette chasing him in the other boat.

"You get the memory card OK?" asked Nickerson.

"I got it, but I need your help." Harv looked back at his pursuer.

"I take it all hell broke loose at your sting operation or you wouldn't be calling me."

"Unbelievable. More than you could imagine. A holler rat demonstration with torches and everything." He told him about Burke discovering the video camera, about Buzz's deft toss of the memory card, then he looked as another bullet pinged off the outboard casing. "Right now I'm being shot at."

Nickerson assured him he was taking off immediately and that he had a gun in the cockpit with him. "I'll put a few holes in his flooring. I should say *my* flooring. That's my boat I'm gonna be shootin' holes in. Five or six holes will bring in enough water to get him off your tail." He paused as the rotor picked up speed for lift-off. "I'll call you when I get close. Remember the safety flair we talked about?"

"Oh yeah, the orange bag with the little orange gun."

"In the compartment under your seat. When I call, shoot it up in the air. I'll find you.

"I'd appreciate it."

"I'll decommission Ouellette's boat—it's well insured. Then I'll lower the winch line and you can send up the card."

"Listen here, young man." Mrs. Whitmore's voice interrupted the call. "I don't know who you're talking to on that phone or what you're involved in, but I asked to be taken back to my hotel, and I expect to be taken now. Turn this boat around this instant."

Harv finished his conversation with Nickerson and put the phone back in his pocket. "I'm sorry Mrs. Whitmore but—"

A loud ping rang off the top of the motor casing.

Looking back over his shoulder, Harv noticed Ouellette had gained considerably on him. He immediately cranked the motor back into high gear, causing Mrs. Whitmore to lunge backward, nearly falling off her seat.

As another bullet glanced off the hull, Harv began swerving the boat left and right to become a more difficult target. He'd seen enough police shows on television to know about moving in a serpentine pattern when being shot at. Mrs. Whitmore's large torso lurched back and forth, nearly falling into the water at one point when Harv made an extra quick turn to avoid a half submerged log.

"Stop this instant," she screamed. "Help! Help me someone." The matron held onto her seat and looked out across the water. "Young man, what in the world are you doing?" Water splashed up over the side, spraying her face, hair, and dress as the boat changed direction again and again through the choppy water.

The craft's tortuous path took it between Blueberry Island and the mainland, a path directly in front of the picnicker's grassy knoll. Blade, on the other hand, headed for the far side of the island, giving him a more direct route to the lower bay. Harv was too preoccupied with steering the boat to keep looking over his shoulder and didn't notice Blade veer off around the other side of the island. It was all he could do to concentrate on maintaining his serpentine pattern while driving as fast as he could to get away. He hoped Nickerson would arrive in time or that Blade would run out of bullets.

Up on the grassy knoll of the picnic grounds, Mrs. Finch pointed to a boat in the distance. "There's a boat zigzagging toward us. Maybe some more guests are coming."

Carrie picked up her binoculars and looked out at the water. "I can see it." She shielded her eyes with her left hand. "It looks like one of our boats."

As the boat got closer, the picnickers stared at it.

"Whoever it is, why are they driving like that?" asked Mrs. Finch.

They gathered around Carrie and her binoculars.

"I've got news for you." Carrie maintained her steady gaze through the field glasses. "That's our boat, and that's Harvey Gallagher, one of our guests, at the wheel." She paused. "But I have no idea who that is with him."

Mr. Grinnell picked up his camera and looked through the telephoto lens.

Carrie kept her steady gaze as the boat got closer. "It's some woman."

"Must be another guest." Mr. Grinnell adjusted the focus and gazed at the boat.

"I can see her," said Carrie. "She's looking out over the water like she's looking for someone . . . looking for help."

"She looks upset," said Mr. Grinnell.

"Maybe it's your mother," said Mrs. Finch.

"No, it's definitely not Mom. I can see her clearly. She's a large woman, but I have no idea who it is." Carrie adjusted the focus on her binoculars. "It's a complete stranger."

Mrs. Whitmore wiped salt water from her eyes, smearing the thick mascara.

"Hey, Harv," yelled Carrie. "Over here."

Harv was too preoccupied with his nautical problems to notice the waving picnickers, much less hear them over the loud outboard.

Mrs. Whitmore stood up in a crouching position, grabbing the gunwale with both hands and began inching her way toward Harv.

Hearing footsteps behind him, Harv turned and saw the large woman coming toward him. "Mrs. Whitmore, sit down."

"I'll turn this boat around myself if I have to." The matron held on tight as the boat bounced in the choppy water.

"Mrs. Whitmore, for God's sake you're going to fall overboard." Harv let go of the steering wheel and rose to grab the woman's elbow in an effort to make her sit down.

The picnickers stared in silence. The boat's motor kept driving it forward.

Not to be deterred, Mrs. Whitmore let go of her grasp of the gunwale and grabbed Harv's arm. The two struggled for a moment before Harv sent the woman sprawling on her back-side between two seats into a puddle of cold water. The impact of this sudden weight shift caused the boat to lurch and tip dramatically to the left, bringing a wave of fresh seawater over the two passengers.

Without looking up, Harv grabbed the wheel and instinctively resumed his serpentine pattern toward the southern edge of the island.

The picnickers stood gaping as the launch sped away. Mr. Grinnell looked helplessly at Carrie with his mouth open.

"He's been under a lot of stress lately," Carrie said, raising her binoculars to watch the boat continue its course.

As Harv rounded the southern end of the island, he was surprised to see Ouellette bearing down on his left flank. Blade had gained considerably on him. A dull *thunk* sound drew Harv's attention to the side of his boat where a fresh bullet hole appeared below the gunwale. Spying the helicopter off in the distance, he grabbed the safety flair gun and shot it into the air. He maintained his zigzag pattern, swerving back and forth, making himself as difficult a target as possible until Nickerson arrived.

The water got rougher, and fog began rolling in from the sea as it became apparent a major change in the weather was underway. Mrs. Whitmore held onto her seat with both hands. The wind had blown her hair into a wild bird's nest, sticking out in all directions.

"Help me," she screamed, looking across the water. "Dear God, somebody help me."

The helicopter swooped down on Blade, distracting him, making it harder to draw a bead on Harvey. Ouellette squeezed off two shots at the chopper, one bouncing off the wheel strut, the second missing completely. He unloaded one last errant round at Harv before his pistol clicked harmlessly out of ammunition. Throwing the empty weapon on the floor, he steered directly at Harv's boat.

Harv's radical driving pattern had slowed him

down considerably. Combined with the additional weight of Mrs. Whitmore, his craft was losing ground. Blade was just fifteen feet off his left side and closing fast.

The chopper swooped down again and hovered over Ouellette as Nickerson leaned out the open door and fired four bullets through the boat's flooring. While Blade was looking up to avoid his new adversary, Harv noticed a change in the water's surface ahead of him—a small spot where the water stopped shimmering, revealing the dull black of a submerged rock, barely hidden by the rising tide. He swerved quickly to avoid the obstacle. Distracted by the chopper, Blade didn't notice the quick turn and drove his speeding boat directly into the rock.

Harv heard the sickening sound of metal crashing into solid granite and turned to see a fireball hurtling into the air. Blade's body went flying ahead, landing ten feet in front of the craft's final resting place. Mrs. Whitmore screeched while Harv looked on with a mixed sense of horror and relief. No matter how gruesome the accident, it was hard not to feel good about the fact that his life was no longer in danger.

He circled back around to look for Ouellette as Mrs. Whitmore shielded her face from the searing heat. Harv figured his pursuer must be dead, and the thought of recovering a broken corpse repelled him. Nevertheless, something inside forced him to make the effort. Through the black smoke, he saw a body floating on the surface and headed toward it. He couldn't believe he was actually making an effort to recover or possibly even save someone who was just shooting at him, but there was no time to think about it.

As he got closer, Harv saw Blade's arms moving and his head rotating out of the water to breathe. Motoring up next to him, he reached over the side and grabbed the back of Ouellette's collar as the phone rang in his pocket.

"You all right?" asked Nickerson.

"Yeah, I'm OK." Harv held Blade's head up out of the water. "Our friend here is a little banged up though."

"Don't try to move him. I'll send down the safety harness."

Overhead, the belly of the chopper opened up and a body harness descended on the end of a thin cable.

"Just put the two lower straps under his legs and the upper ones under his arms. You can see where the fasteners are."

"The hell with that." Harv grabbed the memory card from his pocket. "I'm sending up the card." Blade raised his head out of the water, gasping for air while Harv secured the card in the sack Nickerson provided. "This son of a bitch was just trying to kill me. He can damn well wait."

"Sounds good to me." Nickerson paused. "Who's that woman in the boat?"

"My girlfriend's mother. I'll explain later."

Mrs. Whitmore leaned forward and screamed in the direction of Harv's phone. "Help me. Whoever you are, please help me." She lowered her voice. "My dress is ruined."

"Yes, well maybe next time someone tells you to get out of a boat, you'll listen." Harv grabbed hold of

Blade's collar again while the harness and memory card slowly ascended. Mrs. Whitmore screamed up at the helicopter for help, but the whirling propeller drowned out her pleas. Nickerson retrieved the card, slapped it in the transmitter then lowered the harness.

After securing Blade in the straps, Harv watched the cable rise up to the chopper.

"I hope you don't have any illusions about hauling me up there like some piece of meat, young man. You will take me to my hotel immediately." Mrs. Whitmore attempted to smooth out her dress.

"This is not a subject for debate, Mrs. Whitmore," said Harv as Nickerson pulled Ouellette into the chopper. "You're going up next. Mr. Nickerson up there is very capable. He'll take you directly to the helipad on shore and call for someone to take you back to your hotel."

Harv called Nickerson on the phone. "I've got to check out that boat they mentioned down near Owls Head before Peter can spook it." He explained who Mrs. Whitmore was and what needed to be done with her.

Nickerson agreed, saying he'd arrange to have her picked up.

It took a while to get the harness on Mrs. Whitmore. She squirmed and fussed as Harv struggled with the straps in the rocking boat. She slapped him soundly on one occasion, but Harv was too quick for her and too strong. Eventually the thing was secured, and Harv motioned for Nickerson to haul away.

The winch started to pull, but Mrs. Whitmore got no further than a foot off the boat's flooring.

"What's the problem?" Harv spoke into the phone while Mrs. Whitmore kicked her feet wildly.

"Damn cable's jammed. I'm gonna have to let out more line and go up higher."

"Is my video broadcasting?"

"It's sent."

The chopper rose higher into the fog as more cable poured out of its belly. It was barely visible now. Mrs. Whitmore continued to squirm and complain as the boat rocked in the choppy water. When the line snapped taught, the woman's feet rose off the floor again and stopped.

"Harv?"

"What's up?"

"Damn winch is broken. It's not a cable jam; it's the winch itself."

"What does that mean?"

"It means I can't bring her up."

"Hell, you brought up the memory card and Ouellette."

"I guess that's all she had in her," said Nickerson. "Is this passenger on the hefty side?"

Harv looked at Mrs. Whitmore. "Yeah, I'd say you were probably correct in that area."

"Well it's an old winch, maybe it's temperamental, who knows."

Harv thought for a moment while Mrs. Whitmore fidgeted with the straps. "Can you fly her over to the helipad like this, keeping her just above the water?"

"With her danglin' in the harness?"

"No," screamed Mrs. Whitmore. "Don't even *think* about it... you... you maniac." She tried to unfasten the straps but her weight kept everything too taut. "Unhook me this minute."

"Yeah, can you do it in this fog?" Harv swung her kicking feet up over the side of the boat where they just touched the rolling water.

"I suppose I can do that," said Nickerson. "I've got instruments."

"No, let me down. I demand you let me down this instant." Mrs. Whitmore's screams became louder as she looked down at the gray water below her.

"Mrs. Whitmore, I'm going out farther in the bay toward the ocean. The water is going to be rougher. There may even be more gunfire. I don't think you want to come with me, and I don't have time to take you anywhere." Harv brought the phone close to his mouth and yelled. "Can you keep it just about at this altitude? Maybe up a hair."

"Can do," said Nickerson.

"No!" Mrs. Whitmore screamed as she hovered over the water. "I want to be taken to my hotel immediately. What kind of lunatic are you?"

Harv smiled. "This is the fastest and safest way to your hotel." He put the phone to his mouth. "Bon voyage," he said as the chopper gunned its engines, taking the screaming matron out over the rolling water of Penobscot Bay.

CHAPTER 34

Harv shifted out of neutral. The gas tank was nearly half empty, and he hoped he had enough fuel to get to Burke's boat and back. He was physically and emotionally exhausted, but he knew the boat could be a big deal and felt compelled to check it out. If he could get a vessel name or registration number, it would be another nail in Burke's coffin; another way authorities could nab him. Harv was pumped with adrenalin; he was angry, and he was nearly there. The water grew choppier as he headed out toward the inlet. The fog was thickening. He checked his gas tank and pressed on.

Nickerson watched his instruments carefully, mindful of the strange woman dangling at the end of his cable. "You get that, Ned?"

"This is serious stuff," came the voice of Ned Crowley from the police station. "This guy's vice president of ADI?"

"Executive vice president. You get enough yet?"

"Hold on. We've got the local magistrate right here."

Nickerson turned around and looked at Ouellette, moaning behind his seat. He had a nasty gash on his head.

"OK, Nick," said Crowley, "we've got enough for reasonable suspicion.

"How soon can you get there?"

"Got some paperwork to do. I'd say fifteen, twenty minutes maybe."

"Hope you're in time. You ought to check out Smith's house too."

"We're goin' there next."

Nickerson kept his eye on the instruments, carefully monitoring his altitude.

*   *   *

Marge Nickerson and Sheila stood on The Seaview's front porch, watching the parishioners work themselves into a spiritual lather. Buzz retrieved the video camera from the closet, inserted a fresh memory card, and began recording the spectacle.

Horned worshipers chanted and danced in circular formations on the front lawn, each holding a flaming torch. They splintered off into groups of five or six in small circles, spinning and dancing. Then they all joined up into one large circle with Elsa Ouellette in the center, raising her torch in the air with her bony right arm, exhorting the faithful, leading them in wild, maniacal song. Again, they broke off into groups, singing and chanting. It was a low repetitious chant, combined with a high shrieking, almost wailing sound. The words were in an arcane French/Latin dialect.

*   *   *

Harv kept his eye on the rocky coastline as he made his way down the bay. He was glad he knew where Owls Head Lighthouse was. He remembered Nickerson taking him out fishing and pointing it out. "Any farther past that lighthouse and you're in the Atlantic Ocean," Nickerson had said.

As the water got choppier and the sky darker, Harv thought of turning back several times. Then he saw it. Sitting proudly high on top of its rocky cliff, Owls Head lighthouse looked down over the water. Harv saw two fishing boats anchored well off the shoreline. He slowed his launch down considerably as he drew closer to the two boats. He knew the closer he got to shore, the more submerged rocks he'd find, and he didn't want to end up like Ouellette. A nervous glance at the gas gauge showed it well below half. He'd never make it all the way back, but couldn't worry about that now. He'd give Nickerson a call. As Harv maneuvered toward the first boat, two men came out on deck and looked at him through the fog.

"You lookin' fer somethin'?" one of them yelled.

"What?" Harv stalled for time to get closer.

"You want somethin', bud?" said the second man.

Gliding closer, Harv saw the name *Sea Witch*, painted in black letters on the stern. He figured that would be easy to remember. He yelled out, asking if they had any extra gas. They said "no" and kept staring as Harv motored toward the second craft. While passing *The Sea Witch*, he tried looking at its registration number on the bow, but it was too complicated. In his exhausted state, he'd never remember. The name would have to suffice.

Approaching the stern of the second boat, he saw the name *Lady Claire*, another easy one. No one came out on deck, and the vessel itself looked unoccupied. He turned his craft around in the rolling water and headed back up the bay.

After a few minutes, when *The Sea Witch* became hidden in fog, Harv reached in his pocket for the phone and called Nickerson. "How are your two passengers doing?"

"Little ways to go yet. Don't forget, I've got to go real slow with this woman at the end of my line." Nickerson threw rag back to Ouellette who was awake enough to grab it and hold it on his bleeding head.

"I don't suppose your guys have reached Cove Realty yet."

"Haven't heard anything."

Harv told him about the two boats and asked if he could write their names down just in case. "I'm going to run out of gas at some point." Harv looked at his gauge. "I'll need your help after you drop off your two passengers."

"I'll come get you if you need me." Nickerson looked down at the water through the fog. "I hope I can find you in this pea soup."

*   *   *

The wheels squealed as Burke turned his car onto West Shore Road heading into town. He grabbed his phone and dialed Smith again.

"Where the hell were you when I called five minutes

ago?" Burke turned the steering wheel sharply with his left hand.

"I was on the office phone talking to a new listing, why?"

I'm on my way there now. All hell has broken out." He told Smith what happened. "We've got to clear out those files. Who's at the office now? Anybody?"

"Just Ruth. But what—"

"Give her the day off. I want her outa there." Burke jammed the phone back in his pocket, and gunned his car up to sixty miles an hour on the narrow road. He looked at his watch. A muscle twitched on his jaw.

Turning onto Main Street, he slowed down and pulled up across from Smith's car, parked directly in front of Cove Realty. Smith emerged through the open door with an armload of files and put them in his front seat.

"Is all the stuff here or do you have some files at your house?" Burke hustled past Smith through the front door.

"Most of it's here," said Smith, walking to the back office, "lists of international contacts, the target technologies you worked up, surveillance photos. I've got some canceled checks back at the house."

Quickly, the two men attacked the main filing cabinet, carrying files out to Smith's car.

As Smith emerged from the office with a laptop computer and more files, a sheriff's car pulled up behind his Range Rover out front.

"Well isn't this special," said Crowley, getting out of the big black cruiser. He ambled over to Smith's car and looked in. "Ooh and look, someone's selected a whole bunch of readin' material for us."

"What are you talking about?" Smith ran up to his car. "This is private property, my personal files."

"Now quiet down, son." A uniformed sheriff got out of the driver's side. He was older, with gray hair and pulled a piece of paper out of his breast pocket. "No need to get riled up. Here's the warrant. We're impounding all these files." He walked up to Smith. "And the laptop."

"You're crazy," Smith yelled, looking up at the building's open door. "I have rights." He grabbed the warrant and looked at it.

Burke poked his head out of Smith's back office and saw the commotion through the front window. Immediately he put down the last armload of files, picked up two flash drives from the desk drawer, put them in his coat pocket, and dashed out the back door.

*   *   *

"This ought to be good." Buzz adjusted the video camera's focus as parishioners gathered in another big circle.

"For God's sake, Buzz, how can you be so calm." Sheila stared out at the spectacle before her. "Do you know what's going on?"

"I have no idea, Sheila." He zoomed out to get a wider view.

Through eerie fog, the flickering torches gave an ominous quality to the ritual as Elsa walked up to one of the smaller groups and spoke to them. These were the Young Pilgrims, a group of young parishioners who had achieved their full maturity in the church within the last several years. Not only did they receive special religious indoctrination from Mrs. Ouellette, but they were also called on for the more energetic aspects of church worship. As Elsa raised her torch over the twelve antlered acolytes, they turned and ran to the tower side of the inn, screaming and chanting.

"Buzz, what are they doing now?" Sheila turned to watch the horned youths disappear around the corner.

"Fascinating." Buzz paused his recording in anticipation of the group's re-emergence around the other side.

Sheila gripped the porch railing. "They're circling us. I can hear them out back." She glanced left and right.

When Marge Nickerson walked out on the porch, Sheila ran up to her. "What is this?" What in God's name is happening?" Her face was red.

"Just a little local color." Marge shook her head and walked up to the railing. "Should be over soon." She turned to an employee next to her. "Sally, do me a favor. Would you and Scott go and fill a couple of buckets with water?"

The Young Pilgrims appeared from the other end of the building and rejoined the main body of worshipers on the front lawn.

As revelers re-established their big circle and began chanting again, a blood-curdling scream rose from the group. It was a woman's scream. At first Buzz wondered if the noise was part of the ritual, but it was too wild, too emotional. A second scream caused Elsa Ouellette to stop and investigate.

The chanting stopped.

Ethel Burkhart stood, looking out over the water, pointing and screaming at the top of her lungs. It was a wild, uncontrollable shriek, filled with horror and surprise. Then Tom Nolan began screaming, his eyes fixed out over the big bay. As Elsa peered out at the water, her eyes widened, the angular jaw dropped, and a look of terror swept over her face. She raised her bony arm, shaking her torch in the air, her body quaking as she tried to speak.

"The Antimadonna!" she screamed. "We are too late . . . the Antimadonna!"

In the distance, hovering just over the water's surface, emerging through wisps of fog, Mrs. Katherine Vandenberg Whitmore screamed from the end of her winch wire. Nickerson had changed his mind about dropping her off at the helipad. Increasingly concerned about taking her on such a long trip, he decided to take her to the Seaview's front lawn. Flickering torch light made its way through the fog, giving him a good idea of his target area. He had done an excellent job of keeping her feet just above the water. Fog concealed the chopper and obscured the cable holding the angry matron aloft.

"She walks on water," yelled Elsa. "Run for your lives."

Parishioners shrieked as the strange apparition came at them over the water. The wind had blown Mrs. Whitmore's thickly-sprayed hair in all directions. Her dress billowed out around the harness. Her mascara dribbled down her cheeks, and her arms flailed about in rage. She screamed wildly. The chopper's whirring blades, muted from their lofty altitude, sent down ominous sounds like the beating of other-worldly wings hidden above the fog.

"Run for your lives," shrieked Elsa through the pandemonium. "Run for your very souls."

Screams spread across the lawn. Occasionally a recognizable word made its way through the racket, but the primary sound was uncontrolled screaming. Antlered revelers ran in all directions, trying to get their bearings in the confusion. They dropped their lit torches on the grass. Spouses looked for mates. Others looked for their cars. Some removed their sacred headpieces and carried them while fleeing. Most, however, ran first and thought about their heavy antlers second.

Several parishioners lost their balance and fell down. Sylvia Blake was severely gored in her left buttocks while getting up. When Claude Ouellette ran, his peg leg sank into the soft soil, forcing him off balance. The antlers made his shift in equilibrium more severe, sending him falling on his face.

Chavone ran for his motorcycle, and took off toward the road.

The shrieking got louder as Mrs. Whitmore moved deftly off the water and over the front lawn, closer to the fleeing parishioners.

Two of the women got their horns inextricably locked together. Bent over at the middle, they screamed and jumped up and down in frustration, trying to untie their chinstraps. Big Jake Cranford grabbed the two by their belts, one in each hand, and carried the entwined women, kicking and screaming, to his pickup where he dropped them in the back and took off on the side lawn, bouncing off several cars as he sped down the crowded driveway.

Sheila, Marge, and most of the staff stood and watched, as parishioners scrambled across the front lawn to their vehicles.

"Outstanding." Buzz continued to tape.

Sheila looked at the figure hovering over the front lawn. Slowly, she descended the porch stairs, her eyes locked on the disheveled, screaming apparition. As she walked forward, her mouth fell open. "Mother?" Sheila ran up to Mrs. Whitmore. "Mother, what's happened to you?" After a brief struggle with the harness, she managed to free the exhausted woman, who collapsed into her arms.

On seeing the cable dangle weightlessly below him, Nickerson hauled it up by hand and flew to the hospital.

Marge picked up a pail of water, and began dousing the smoldering torches on her lawn.

CHAPTER 35

The meter on top of Harv's gas tank read zero. Occasionally the needle bounced up above the empty mark, but that had stopped a while back. He was now running on fumes and knew he wouldn't make the inn. On reaching the southern end of Blueberry Island, he headed for the channel, running closer to the mainland. It was the route he'd come out on and offered calmer water.

As the craft turned up the channel, its motor sputtered and died. Harv immediately called Nickerson.

"I've dropped off your lady friend and I'm about five minutes from the hospital, Harv," said Nickerson. "I can get a can of fuel at the helipad there and get it down to you . . . If I can find you."

Harv told him he'd shoot off another couple of flairs but privately didn't feel totally confident about Nickerson finding him. It was a big bay and the fog was getting thicker. He wasn't even sure the body of land off his bow was Blueberry Island. The fog made everything look different.

He began rowing, glad the tide was coming in rather than going out. After a few minutes, his hands got sore, and he could feel blisters forming. He was thankful to be near land. If worse came to worse, he could always row over to shore and phone the inn.

He got into the steady rhythm of rowing, and began to make more headway. The oars groaned in the oar-locks and slapped the water.

After ten minutes of rowing, a faint sound trickled through the air behind him; a new sound. Unrecognizable at first, it just lay dormant in the back of his consciousness as he strained at the oars. He heard it again and paused a moment. It sounded like voices rippling over the water. He turned and scanned the island's shoreline but saw nothing. He resumed rowing and headed for the new sounds.

*   *   *

"So who is it?" asked Mrs. Finch as Carrie looked through the binoculars at the lone boat moving toward them.

"I can't tell yet," said Carrie.

The guests looked out over the water.

"When he turned around, it looked like Harvey Gallagher, the same guy we saw zigzagging past us a while ago, fighting with that woman." Carrie continued her steady gaze. "There's only one person in the boat though . . . and he's rowing."

Mr. Grinnell looked over. "You mean that strange woman isn't with him anymore? Maybe she's lying down."

"I don't think so," said Carrie, still looking through the binoculars. She readjusted the focus, and paused. "Yeah, that's Harv."

Mr. Grinnell walked over and looked through his

camera. "I only see one person in the boat." He adjusted his big lens.

"Yes," Carrie continued her gaze, "that's definitely Harv. That's his shirt . . . his hair coloring . . . and that's our boat." She nodded her head. "That's him." Putting down the binoculars, she turned and walked toward the water. "I'm going to get him."

Harv wasn't sure whose voices he heard. If the body of land was Blueberry Island, like he thought it was, then maybe the picnic was still going on. He wasn't sure, and he didn't care. He was ecstatic to know there were other human beings nearby.

As the oars continued to groan, he soon heard the distinct hum of an outboard in the distance. A quick look over his shoulder revealed a launch heading through the fog straight at him. A bit more rowing and he turned again. This time the boat appeared larger. He looked closely. He wasn't sure about the color, but it looked like a green bow slicing through the fog. A solitary figure standing at the controls, the brown hair blowing . . . It was Carrie.

Harv stood and waved, yelling out her name, filled with instant relief—not just relief at seeing a friendly face or being rescued. It was more. He realized the entire plan, the sting, the tension were all mercifully over. There was nothing anyone could do to affect the outcome anymore. For better or worse, the plan had played itself out and was behind him. It had worked. All players had completed their roles, and now at this moment in time, Harv knew it was over.

Carrie cut the motor, glided up next to Harv, and threw her arms around him. It was a natural, spontaneous hug which had the added benefit of stopping her boat from gliding on past. He hugged her back.

She asked if he was OK and if Burke had spilled his guts. They stood there in the gray, choppy water holding onto each other to keep their boats from drifting apart.

"What was that zigzagg, back-and-forth driving all about?"

"I was being shot at."

"Shot at?" Her look of curiosity instantly changed to one of concern.

"Blade was chasing me, shooting at me." He showed her the scar on the motor casing and two bullet holes in the hull.

"Oh, my God," she squeezed his arms, "you sure you're OK?"

He assured her he was, and told her what happened to Ouellette.

"Who was that strange woman in your boat?"

Harv shook his head. "Sheila's mother, my girlfriend's mother." He told her how Sheila had surprised him in the middle of his meeting with Peter.

Carrie wasn't listening anymore. She couldn't stop laughing. "That was your girlfriend's mother? The mother you never met before?" She lowered her head and tried to stifle the laughter as best she could, but it wouldn't be kept down. After all the stress, and now the instant release of pressure, Carrie found things much funnier than she normally would. At that moment, the vision of Harv zigzagging through the water, struggling with his future mother-in-law in the boat was the funniest thing in the world to her. "Nice first impression," Carrie sputtered.

Harv looked at Carrie, her face flushed, her white teeth flashing, trying in vain to keep from laughing. The humor was contagious, and he began to see the situation as absurdly funny. He told Carrie how he'd found Mrs. Whitmore in the boat and how she'd demanded to be taken back to her hotel. When he got to the helicopter rescue and described the poor woman dangling at the end of the cable, it was more than either of them could handle. Loud, unrestrained peals of laughter rang out over the water. Carrie told him how the picnickers had seen him struggling with Mrs. Whitmore in the boat.

"You saw that?"

"Yes, you were right in front of us. Didn't you see us?"

"No. I was just trying to get away, and keep from being shot."

Carrie doubled over, holding onto the gunwale of Harv's boat to keep from drifting away. Harv's knees buckled as he laughed uncontrollably. The picture of Mrs. Whitmore being spirited across the water at the end of a long cable was now the funniest thing he'd ever seen. Regardless of its implications for him personally and his relationship with Sheila, the humor of the situation overshadowed all else. The more Carrie laughed, the funnier it seemed. He was tired; he was slaphappy, and he couldn't help it. They spent the next few moments doubled over in crippling convulsions, trying to keep the two boats from drifting apart.

From sheer exhaustion, the laughter gradually

subsided. They stood there holding on to each other to keep the boats together. Her face was inches away.

He looked at her.

She looked back, holding his arms tightly.

Then he kissed her . . . full on the mouth. It was a completely spontaneous act. Her lips were soft. She parted them slightly.

Harv pulled back, staring into her face. A warm feeling rushed through him.

Carrie smiled, looking back at him. "I'm going to have to rescue you more often, young man." She wiped a laugh tear from her eye, keeping hold of Harv's arm with her other hand.

After regaining some level of composure, Carrie circled around, tied a rope to Harv's bow and towed him to the picnic grounds. The water was getting choppier, the fog thicker, and rain clouds darkened the sky.

Harv called Nickerson and cancelled the gasoline order. He thought about the kiss. It was not like him. He never did anything spontaneously. He was shocked at how good it felt.

Mrs. Finch and the new couple started packing up the picnic gear in anticipation of the downpour.

Mr. Grinnell met the boats and caught Carrie's tie line. "Are you all right, son? I thought you might tip over for a second."

"I am now." Harv jumped out of his boat and tied it up. "I'll tell you about it when we get back to the inn."

Carrie walked up to the picnic area with Harv and smiled. "Hey, Commodore, don't mind Mr. Grinnell. He was very worried about you out there on the water."

"Yeah, I don't know how 'solid' I looked struggling with Mrs. Whitmore."

Carrie smiled. "She looked pretty 'solid.' "

Harv threw his head back and laughed.

Everyone helped load up the remaining gear. Harv bailed out his boat and lined it with several blankets and seat cushions. He secured ten freshly opened oysters, got two cold bottles of Lowenbrau, and placed it all within easy reach under the seat of his boat.

With Harv's boat tied behind and the picnickers all loaded into the lead vessel, Carrie started the motor and headed for home. Harv lay down on the padded floor of his boat with his back propped up by two seat cushions wedged against a picnic cooler. He stretched out his legs under the seats with his beer and oysters on the blanket next to him.

Carrie looked out the back of her launch at Harv as he popped an oyster in his mouth. "Comfy?" she yelled.

"Extremely," Harv yelled back as he splashed along in the rolling brine.

CHAPTER 36

Carrie put artichoke dip and crackers on the porch table and sat down between Buzz and Harv. Buzz rubbed his neck where Peter had whacked him. Harv sat there with a beer in his hand, looking out over the water. He couldn't see much through the fog but felt peaceful just sitting there, watching an occasional boat find its way through the wispy clouds. The bad weather kept the other guests off the porch. Most were getting ready for dinner.

Buzz described the strange, horned ritual like an anthropology professor who'd discovered a lost tribe in the jungles of Borneo. Harv shook his head, smiling with detached amusement. When Buzz got to the arrival of Mrs. Whitmore at the end of her winch wire and the hysteria on the front lawn, Carrie started laughing again.

Harv tried not to laugh. His gut ached from rowing, and he was tired. "Please, seriously. I can't handle this." He put up his hand in protest. "I'm in a weakened condition."

Buzz smiled. "Well you can see the video when you recover." He opened a cold beer bottle. "It's a definite collector's item."

"Oh yes," Harv sat back in his chair, "I want my own copy of that video. I'll pay you for a copy of that video."

Carrie looked up and smiled when Nickerson bounded up the porch steps.

"Home from the wars I see," said Harv.

"Took a while." Nickerson walked over to the table and sat down. "Had to unload Ouellette at the hospital then stopped by the police station and saw Crowley."

"They get the files OK?" said Harv.

"They've got the files and are takin' Smith up to Augusta," said Nickerson.

"All right!" Carrie stretched the word *right* into two syllables.

"So they got there in time," said Buzz.

"Just barely." Nickerson ordered a beer from the waiter.

"What's in Augusta?" asked Buzz.

"Crowley has some contacts there. I guess he thinks they can do a better job of doin' what has to be done up there."

"I like the sound of that," said Harv. "How about Peter?"

"You'll like the sound of this even better. Smith looks like he's gonna be real cooperative," said Nickerson. "The Sheriff phoned Ned and told him Smith was very talkative in the cruiser on the way to Augusta."

"And Burke?" Harv took a very quick swallow of beer.

Nickerson's face looked more somber. "That's a temporary loose end we've got to talk about."

"Burke got away?" Harv sat up straight.

"Ned says they nabbed Smith in front of his office, but when they went inside, no one else was there."

"Damn!" Harv slammed his fist on the table.

"They've impounded the car he left out front, so they know he was there. Smith admits he was there. He must have scampered out the back door."

"So, he's on foot," said Carrie.

"He's on foot and Ned's put a dragnet around the town."

Harv shook his head. "Burke could rent a car, take a cab . . ." He looked out at the water.

"Not in this town he couldn't," said Nickerson. "There are no car rental companies in Black Hill Cove. Ned's talked to the only cab company we have, and the state boys set up road blocks on the only roads out of town."

"Sometimes it pays to be a small town." Carrie looked up and smiled as the waiter brought Nickerson his beer.

Harv gazed out over the water while everyone gave their dinner orders. He watched a big white fishing boat pass by. Its oversized rear cabin area and high, sweeping bow gave it a distinctive look. He'd seen a few others like it out there.

When the waiter left, Nickerson filled his pipe, and leaned back in his chair. "There's no way Burke's gettin' out of Black Hill Cove."

"When did they put up the road blocks?" Harv kept staring out at the water.

"Ned says as soon as they saw that Lexus with the Mass plates in front of Smith's office, they ran the number and figured out what had happened."

"I don't know." Harv shook his head and continued to look out at the bay. "That man is the wiliest bastard on the face of the earth."

Nickerson sat up straight and packed down the tobacco in his pipe. "Harv, it's understandable you might be nervous right now but—"

"He just might want to kill me, that's all."

"Listen to me. Bill Norton has closed down his pharmacy for the day, and he and Ned have rounded up the citizens' action committee to call everyone in town and let 'em know Burke's on the loose. Anyone sees anybody lookin' remotely like Peter Burke, any stranger requestin' transportation, they call Ned. Plus Ned got his deputy to watch the Seaview."

"Anderson is actually watching the Seaview?" Carrie looked out toward the driveway.

"That's right. He followed me here from the station and is parked out at the entrance right now. Everybody comin' in here goes through him. And he'll be relieved at midnight by one of Crowley's state buddies, so we'll have twenty-four hour coverage 'til Burke is found."

"I guess that's kind of reassuring." Harv took a deep breath.

"Believe me, Harv, there's no way Burke is gettin' out of Black Hill Cove, and there's definitely no way he can get to you. We've even got two boats out patrollin' the bay lookin' for anything suspicious."

"I'm sure Peter's far more interested in saving his own skin right now than getting any revenge against you, Gallagher," said Buzz.

They continued talking about Peter Burke, speculating on where he could be and how far he could have gotten. When dinner arrived, Harv looked out at the bay and saw the white boat turn around and slowly head back the other way. With the fog, and with twilight coming on, the view wasn't clear, but there was something familiar about the craft, especially with the new view of its stern.

"Hey, your meal's getting cold." Carrie interrupted Harv's thoughts.

He redirected his attention to the stuffed lobster in front of him, as the conversation moved onto lighter subjects, including the horned ritual on the front lawn.

While they talked, Harv looked out at the water again. He watched the boat turn back to the left. He'd seen it from a variety of angles and first thought it might be a different boat at each sighting. But he was beginning to realize it was the same boat, going back and forth. He told them about the boat he saw on his trip to Owls Head.

"What are you staring at out there?" asked Carrie.

"That white boat. The size, the shape. It looks like the *Sea Witch*. You have any binoculars I could borrow?" Harv stood up at the table, keeping his gaze out over the water.

"I put them back in the office," said Carrie. "You want them now?"

"Even sooner if possible."

"You're determined to let your dinner get cold aren't you?" Carrie got up, patted Harv on the shoulder, and went to the office.

On his way down to the dock, Harv removed the binoculars from the leather case.

"What are you looking for?" Carrie took the empty case from Harv and followed him.

"I'm not sure." He walked over to the farthest piling on the dock, leaned against it, and looked through the lenses at the slow-moving vessel. "The angle isn't right yet. I need to see the nameplate on the stern. I think that boat may be the one I saw out there. And it just may be the one they talked about in that telephone conversation."

"The one they want to use to take stuff out of the country?"

"It could be." Harv continued to look out over the water. "If I'm right, it's going to turn around and head back the other way in a few minutes."

In less than five minutes the boat made its move.

"It's turning," said Carrie.

Harv leaned against the piling and looked through the binoculars. He couldn't see much at first. Fog obscured the view, and it took a while to bring the moving craft into focus. As wisps of fog rolled by, he zeroed in on the nameplate.

"Damn!" He steadied his gaze. "There's no way I can read the name. But it looks a hell of a lot like the *Sea Witch*." He continued to look as the boat maintained its course to the southeast.

When they sat back down at the table, Nickerson signaled the waiter to bring their plates back from the kitchen where he'd sent them to keep warm. "You say that boat's been cruisin' out there for a while?"

"I noticed it when we first sat down." Harv looked out at the water. "The thing is, I'm almost positive it's the *Sea Witch*".

"I take it you couldn't get the name just now." Buzz wiped his mouth with his napkin, and leaned back.

"No, the fog's too thick, and it's too far away. But it looks just like the *Sea Witch*. If it's not, it's sure as hell the same *kind* of boat."

They each picked at their dinners, looking up occasionally at the white craft, cruising out on the water. Buzz described more of the antlered ritual he'd taped. Harv took one last bite, pushed his plate away, and looked out at the water.

The waiter came and poured coffee.

"You know," said Nickerson, "Ned said to call him if we saw anything at all unusual." He looked out at the boat and then at Harv. "If you say it looks like the boat you saw out there, maybe Ned ought to know about it." He got up, wiped his hands on his napkin, and excused himself from the table.

Harv tried not to think about the boat as it glided silently over the water. He poked at his dessert, looked up, and watched the craft disappear behind the rocky outcropping. He knew what would happen next. In a few minutes it would reappear, heading back up the bay. He watched, but the craft was getting harder to see. Although the fog had dissipated, darkness was settling in fast.

When Nickerson returned to the table, he looked different. There was a quickness in his manner and a seriousness in his face. He sat down and looked at Carrie. "Ned says there's supposedly a tunnel under the Seaview."

"What?" Carrie's mouth dropped open.

"He just got finished talkin' with the state boys in

Augusta. They said Smith just told 'em there's a tunnel under this place."

"Absurd," said Carrie. "A tunnel to where?"

"To the bay." Nickerson stared at the water.

"How would Smith know if there's a tunnel?" Buzz looked out at the front lawn.

"Burke apparently happened across a tunnel when he worked here years ago. That's why he wanted to buy the place, according to Smith. They wanted to put buyers and sellers of stolen technology up at the Seaview and smuggle them and the goods in and out of here through the tunnel. That's what Smith's sayin' anyway."

"That's ridiculous," said Carrie. "I know every inch of this place. You know every inch. Our family has been in every nook and cranny of this place for generations. If there was a tunnel, we'd know about it."

No one spoke for a moment.

"It kind of makes sense though." Harv sat up straight. "Peter said this place had some special char-acteristics. Why else would they have had such a single-minded focus on this specific place. There are other inns they could have tried to buy.

"Maybe they didn't want the Seaview because of its pretty architecture," said Buzz, "and maybe they didn't want it because of the nice view." He looked across the front lawn. "Maybe they wanted it because it has a tunnel." He pointed to the rocky outcropping to the right. "And if there is a tunnel to the water, that's the only place it could come out."

Nickerson stood up, walked to the railing by his

chair, and looked out over the lawn, his eyes darting back and forth from the Seaview to the bay.

Carrie's eyes danced along the shoreline and back to the inn.

Buzz gazed across the table at Harv. "You know what I'm thinking?"

"Yeah, I think I do," said Harv.

"I'm thinking if that boat out there is the boat you think it is . . . Burke's boat."

"The *Sea Witch*."

"Whatever," said Buzz. "If that *is* Burke's boat, and if there is, in fact, a tunnel under this place, then there's a good chance Peter Burke is in that tunnel right now waiting for the right time to climb aboard that boat and make his getaway by sea."

"You got it." Harv tapped his fork on the table.

"Now wait a minute," said Carrie. "In the first place, I seriously doubt there's a tunnel, and in the second place, how could he have gotten here?"

"This is Peter Burke we're talking about. Believe me he'd find a way." Harv looked at his watch. "It's been nearly four hours. Something tells me there *is* a tunnel and somehow he's figured out a way to get there. He's climbed that hill to the tunnel opening out there on the water."

"He could have stolen a little boat and stashed it behind the rocks. The cove in town is filled with little boats. Or hot-wired a car, drove to the water and swam," said Buzz.

"The whole town's looking for him and no one's found him. He's got to be somewhere," said Harv.

Nickerson walked to the steps and down onto the

front lawn. The others followed, their eyes darting back and forth from the Seaview to the bay.

"Nickerson pointed to the high, rocky outcropping off to his right. "You're right, Buzz. If there is a tunnel, it would have to come out there."

"No question." Harv walked up beside him. "I've jogged all around the shoreline and that's the only possible place."

"I've seen that area many times from the water and it's covered with bushes and vines," said Nickerson.

"If my theory is right," said Harv, "he's hiding behind those bushes and vines, hiding in that tunnel opening right now, peering out at that boat."

"I thought the bay was being patrolled," said Carrie.

"It is." Nickerson continued walking out toward the rocky knoll. "Gus and Tommy Weeks are both out there lookin'. But they can't be everywhere."

"If I'm right," Harv lowered his voice, "he's waiting until dark to make his move."

Buzz looked at his watch. "I've got news for you, sparky. It's nearly dark now."

Walking back to the porch, they talked about Burke, what kind of transportation he could have gotten, and how he could have maneuvered his way to the Seaview.

"If that is the *Sea Witch* and it's here to pick up Burke," Carrie turned and looked out at the water, "why isn't it just moored out front? Why is it going back and forth?"

"That'd be even more suspicious." Nickerson climbed the steps back up to the porch. "A boat movin' is no big deal. All boats are movin' out there. But a moored boat, in that part of the bay, just sittin' there'd sure get my attention."

"If that is the *Sea Witch*," Harv followed Nickerson back up to the porch, "Peter probably called it on his phone and told them to hover in front of the inn until nightfall. And if there is a tunnel, and he thinks no one else knows about it," he paused and lowered his voice as a waiter passed by, "I know how this guy thinks. It'd be the first place he'd go." Harv looked at his watch and then at Nickerson. "Can you show me your basement?"

Carrie retrieved two flashlights from the office while Nickerson got a crowbar from his tool kit.

"I'm going to hook up the battery pack to my weapon, take it down to the launch, and motor out to the floating raft." Buzz headed toward the tower room. "I can get a direct shot at that rocky area from the water."

"If we can find that tunnel, I can sneak up on Burke from behind and nab him," said Harv.

"Sounds a little dangerous," said Carrie.

Harv smiled. "I'll have the element of surprise going for me. I'll be fine."

The kitchen help continued their chores as Nickerson opened the cellar door and made his way down the stairs with Carrie and Harv close behind.

"We've got four main areas down here," said Nickerson. "We've got two big storage rooms, a wine cellar, and a place we call the labyrinth."

"It's a bunch of small rooms and little hallways," said Carrie, "but it's on the opposite side from the water."

"OK, so we eliminate the labyrinth." Harv followed Nickerson down the main hallway.

Carrie turned on the lights in each room while Harv and Nickerson tackled the first storage area.

They wedged flashlights behind tables and chairs, stored against the cement walls. Nickerson raked his crowbar over the old masonry, banging on the walls, listening.

"There's nothing here." Carrie peered behind a ping-pong table, stored on its side. "I've seen these walls and these rooms many times."

"I know," said Nickerson, "but we've got to eliminate every possibility."

The second storage room was bigger. They removed books, pots, pans, and other items from large shelves along the wall. Then they moved the shelves and investigated the space behind them.

Nickerson banged the walls with his crowbar.

Harv looked at his watch. He knew night was fast approaching and Burke would make his move soon.

They walked to the wine cellar.

"This is the oldest part of the foundation," said Nickerson. "It was here decades before any Nickerson bought the place." He turned on a light. "Be careful not to break any of the bottles. Some of this stuff's expensive." He removed a few selected specimens and pounded the case's wooden backing with his crowbar.

Harv and Carrie removed more wine bottles from the racks and carefully placed them on the floor while Nickerson pounded and listened.

They moved methodically to the back of the cellar where the shelf cases were dusty and bare. The old wood creaked as cases were rotated away from the walls and flashlights scanned the emptiness behind them.

Nickerson continued banging with his crowbar.

Harv and Carrie probed with their flashlights through the dusty air.

Then they heard the sound. Nickerson's crowbar hit the empty wooden shelf case at the deepest end of the cellar. It was a hollow, empty sound, a different sound from what they'd been hearing.

"You hear that?" Nickerson whacked the back of the case again. Then he hit the adjacent case. "Hear the difference?"

"Yeah." Harv walked over. He placed his flashlight down and helped Nickerson move the big structure away from the wall.

Carrie was the first to walk around behind with her light. Then she stopped. She stood with her mouth open, saying nothing as Nickerson grabbed the other light and moved in behind her.

"Well I'll be damned." Nickerson flashed his light on the recessed doorway and the ancient wooden door in front of him. "You ever see this before?"

Carrie just shook her head, staring blankly. "I had no idea."

Harv continued sliding the case outward until it was at right angles to the wall, then walked around behind it.

Nickerson stepped down into the recessed opening and tried turning the doorknob. "It's locked." Looking closely at the patch job on the boards, he said, "This plywood's a lot newer than the rest of the door." He stepped back and gave the door a kick with the bottom of his foot, cracking the old wood around the patch. "Whoever put on this plywood sure as hell wasn't a Nickerson or we'd know about it."

Harv leaned back and kicked his foot completely through the crack Nickerson had created. "No," he said as the old wood splintered in front of him, "but it might have been a Burke." He brought his foot back out through the hole he'd made.

Nickerson gave one last kick, sending plywood and fragments of old door flying into the space beyond. He reached through the opening, struggled with the latch, then smiled as the locking mechanism moved. "It's locked from the inside."

The hinges squeaked as Nickerson opened the door and walked forward.

Carrie stepped closely behind him. "This is directly beneath the original house."

"I had no idea this was here." Nickerson's light explored the old stone walls.

Harv looked at his watch, then stepped down into the doorway and entered the room. Nickerson gave him the crowbar and flashed his light around the perimeter. Harv could see it was a rectangular room with very old stone walls. Carrie moved off to the left, rubbing her hand against the stones. Nickerson went to the right.

Harv stepped over a collapsed old chair and walked straight to the other side. The pile of stones against the far wall didn't get his attention at first. Not until the glimmering lights revealed a dark area above them—a dark area he was able to stick his crowbar through.

"Hey, guys, I think I've found something." He pulled a stone out of the wall with the crowbar as Carrie and her uncle moved in behind him. He borrowed Nickerson's flashlight and stuck it through the opening.

"You see anything?" Carrie aimed her light at the hole while Harv looked through to the other side.

Light danced off the old support beams, and Harv smelled the distinctive aroma of fresh salt air. He removed more stones and leaned through the opening as far as he could, groaning as a stone dug into his ribs.

Wriggling back out of the hole, he smiled and wiped cement dust off his face. "I think we found ourselves a tunnel."

Harv stepped back to let the others look through.

"I can't believe it," said Carrie, bringing her head back out of the hole. "There's definitely something back there."

"I'm going in," said Harv.

"You sure you wanna do that, son?" said Nickerson. "If he's in there, he's gonna be dangerous."

"I can't have this guy roaming around loose." Harv looked at his watch. "If he's in here, I need to get him."

Carrie insisted on coming with him, but Harv convinced her to stand guard over the opening. "Anyone other than me pokes his head through this opening, you whack 'em over the head. You're good at that."

She gave a stiff smile, grabbed his arm, and leaned into him. "You just be careful."

Nickerson looked at his niece. He stared a second. "I'm takin' the launch out," he said. "If Burke's there, and he tries to scoot out to the big boat, maybe I can head him off, or call Ned."

"That might not be a bad idea." Harv looked up, then he smiled and disappeared into the hole.

Holding a flashlight in his left hand, he wiped cobwebs away with the crowbar in his right. He crept forward. Several times a rock would move under his weight, causing him to fall sideways and lean against the wall. Something small scurried by in front of him. The smell of cool salt air became more pungent, and he soon saw a light area up ahead through the darkness. Reaching the opening, he noticed several bent and broken vines. He felt the exposed ends. The damage was fresh.

Harv moved quietly now. The bent vines left a reasonably good opening. Something dug into his shoulder blade. He heard waves crashing on the rocks, and saw a light shining. Emerging from the cave, he noticed a big spotlight coming from the water.

Then it came. A rustling sound, a movement off to his right.

Reflexes took over. Harv's right arm shot upward with the crowbar, deflecting a log headed down on him. Wood splintered as he rolled away to the edge of the rocky hill. The flashlight bounded off into the sea. His legs churned to get a foothold. Hoisting himself onto the ledge, he turned and looked up into the face of Peter Burke.

"You're the most annoying bastard I've ever met." Burke stood expressionless, withdrawing his gun from the holster. He had a detached, business-like air. "How the hell did you find the tunnel?"

"Your friend Smith is real talkative." Harv looked

down and stepped away from the steep slope leading down to the water. "How the hell did you get here?"

Burke laughed. "Looks like we both have our little secrets." He looked out at the water. "A guy I know brought me into the woods. I know every path and trail that leads to this place."

"Yes, this tunnel. The only place that no one knew existed."

"Except now *you* know, and that's a real problem."

Harv was between Burke and Buzz out on the floating raft and knew he had to buy some time and figure out how to change positions.

"Let me guess about the guy who gave you a ride—a guy named Chavone?"

Burke's eyes widened. "You're too smart for your own good sometimes, Harv. You know about this place. You know about Chavone." He waved at the spotlight coming from a boat out on the water.

"So, that *is* your boat out there," said Harv. "The *Sea Witch* I'm guessing?"

"You're a smart guy, Harv." He shook his head. "A huge pain in the ass right now, but smart. You could have been a rich man if you'd played the game right." Burke glanced quickly at his watch.

"I don't like your rules, Peter." It was practically dark, but he could see Buzz over his shoulder out on the floating raft. The spotlight danced along the rocks as a *Sea Witch* bullet smacked into a rock next to him.

Buzz turned toward the boat, switched his weapon to laser mode, maximum power, and laid a blue beam across the cabin. It knifed through the support struts, collapsing the roof on a forty-five degree angle. Sparks flew out in the early darkness.

As Burke looked to see what happened, Harv lunged at him, grabbing his gun arm with both hands. In the process, he slipped on the rocks, barely catching his footing on a slightly lower ledge. Peter jammed his free left hand into Harv's shoulder and pressed down from his elevated position. Harv strained under the force of Burke's weight as he struggled to stay on the hill. He looked down at the roiling water below, pushing upward and moving to his left. He reached out blindly for a foothold. Gradually, he maneuvered several feet over to a better position on the far side of Burke, giving Buzz a clear shot. Burke continued to push.

The boat, with its cabin roof askew, hovered out on the water, its spotlight illuminating both men like some bizarre movie set.

Water slammed against the rocks below. Harv looked up at Burke's cold eyes staring down at him and clutched his attacker's gun arm with both hands.

Buzz switched his weapon to electrical mode and maneuvered the blue light up the rocky hill. As it hit the middle of Peter's back, Buzz pulled the trigger, stunning his target, causing him to flinch. Burke shook his head.

Seizing the opportunity, Harv dropped his opponent's arm and used both hands to pull himself back up onto the higher ledge.

Moving the power level up, Buzz zeroed in on Peter again.

Harv crouched low, looking for an opening.

As Burke pointed his gun, Harv saw the man's entire body stiffen, then collapse like a marionette whose strings had just been cut.

A *Sea Witch* bullet caught the raft next to Buzz's left foot. He hopped to his right, switched back to laser mode, and laid another blue beam across the boat's cabin. It severed the remaining support struts, crashing the roof down like a pancake on the confused boatmen. Although he was concerned about destroying evidence, Buzz felt obliged to strafe the craft with two more passes, creating an explosion of sparks, popping the spotlight into a shower of glass.

The *Sea Witch* turned its bow away from shore.

Harv walked over, patted Burke down, and retrieved two flash drives from his inside jacket pocket. Peter didn't move. Harv felt his heart, and it was still beating. His legs twitched.

With the spotlight gone, Nickerson had to rely on the launch's hand lantern to negotiate the rocky shoreline as he approached. "Harv," he yelled, "you OK?"

Harv stood up. "Yeah, everything's fine." The lantern's light danced up the hill and found Harv waving from a ledge. "You have a rope you could toss up? I have a package for you."

CHAPTER 37

"You can go right down, Mr. Gallagher," the young man said as Harv signed the ADI register Wednesday morning. "Mr. Weitz is expecting you."

"Wow, no waiting. That's a first." Harv put the pen down. "Where's Jimmy Jarvis these days? He usually works Wednesday morning."

"Beats me; I'm filling in for him."

Harv pinned on his visitor badge and descended the elevator to the security floor. Artificial light flooded the hallway and reflected off the stainless steel fixtures as he made his way to Chuck's office.

"Well hello, Mr. Gallagher." Shirley looked up and smiled from her desk in Weitz's reception room. "Can I get you some coffee?"

"No thanks, Shirley, I've had enough stimulation for a while." Harv took a seat on the couch.

"Well if there's anything you want, just let me know." She walked over and placed two new *Business Week* magazines on the coffee table in front of him. "Mr. Weitz will be with you shortly."

After getting over his initial shock at Harv's sting operation, Chuck had asked Harv to drop by his office at ten o'clock Wednesday morning to wrap things up.

As Harv picked up a magazine, his phone went off.

"Hi, it's me," came the familiar voice.

Harv smiled and sat up. "Well, Miss Nickerson, what a pleasant surprise."

"I'm just calling to tell you that you left your sunglasses and hat here."

"Oh, thank God. I was afraid I was going to have to get a replacement outfit when I come up there."

Carrie laughed. "So you're definitely coming up?

"I have a standing policy, Carrie. Any time someone says I can stay at their beautiful inn for free, I always accept."

"Good. Mom meant it when she said it. We're so appreciative. That offer goes for Buzz as well you know."

"He's coming up too."

"Great."

"He's bringing up his girlfriend; is that OK?"

"Of course." Carrie paused a moment. "Are you bringing up anyone?"

"Who would I bring up?

"Oh, I don't know. I was just wondering."

"I think I'll just be coming up myself. Anyone else I might have brought up . . . Let's just say some things have changed."

"Change can be good sometimes."

Harv looked around the office. "Sheila called me yesterday and told me her mother doesn't exactly approve of me."

Carrie laughed. "Gee, I can't imagine why."

"I can tell you for a fact I don't approve of her either. Anyway, we've decided to step back and re-evaluate things."

"Good . . . I mean it's good to step back and look at

things objectively; maybe see things in a new light. Coming up here will be good for you."

"I'm really looking forward to it."

"Me too." She paused a second. "So, when do you think you'll be coming up?"

"Day after tomorrow. You have any vacancies?"

"Absolutely."

"I'm already on vacation mode starting today. I just have to see Chuck, then finish up my ADI invoice. Tie up a few loose ends at the office."

Sitting there looking around Chuck's waiting room, Harv was aware how different his perception of the place was now from the first time he saw it. Compared to Peter's office, Chuck's suite had seemed plain and depressing. Now, the place came across as powerful, honest, and friendly.

Harv heard voices outside the door. He finished his conversation with Carrie, put his phone back in his pocket, and looked up to see Chuck walking in with William Cobb.

"Harv, thanks for coming by." Chuck smiled. "You've met Bill Cobb."

Harv stood up and extended his hand to ADI's silver haired president. "Yes, we met the day this all started. It's a pleasure to see you again, sir."

"The pleasure's all mine, son." Cobb gave Harv's hand a vigorous shake.

"We were going over the case in the secure room, and Bill wanted to see you again." The secure room was a specially engineered conference room across the hall from Chuck's office. It had a secure phone to the Pentagon and to the regional FBI office.

"You've done us quite a favor, son," said Cobb

"Well, it was an adventure."

"More than you bargained for, I'm sure." Cobb smiled.

"Just a touch."

"I've got to run, but I wanted to see you again and thank you personally." Cobb looked quickly at his watch. "And Harvey, Ted Bass will be calling you to set up a time to come in and see him. He's going to be taking over our Marketing operation and could use your help."

"Great. I'll be on vacation next week, but when I get back I'll make sure we get together."

Cobb thanked him again before departing. Chuck then led him into his office, closed the door, and motioned for Harv to sit down.

"Smith is singing like a canary," said Chuck, picking up his phone. "Shirley, can you hold my calls?" He pointed to Harv, asked if he wanted coffee, and Harv shook his head. "Turns out the guy had no idea about the kind of people Burke was associating with. He was in over his head and was slowly beginning to realize it."

"Hopefully he'll spill enough to convict Peter."

"I'm afraid Mr. Burke has a lot more serious problems than being convicted. The last I heard he was still in a coma up at the hospital in Maine." Weitz leaned forward . "Harv, I want you to know if and when Burke does recover, you'll be protected."

Harv took a deep breath. "I have to be honest with you, Chuck. I know you're the best at what you do, and I hear you say I'll be protected, but I've just alienated and thoroughly pissed off one of the smartest, wiliest bastards on the planet."

"I hear you, Harv, but believe me we'll keep you safe. Let's just take it one step at a time."

Chuck turned on a voice recorder, and they talked in detail about the sting operation. Chuck told Harv they had recovered a pistol at the apartment of a guy in New York City and matched it to Harv's bullet. "This guy, Nick his name was, this guy admitted Burke hired him to whack you."

Harv was impressed to hear they had already picked up a boat named The *Sea Witch* in Saint John, Canada and were almost positive it was the same one Harv had seen.

"It sure sounds like your boat," said Chuck. "Cops up there said the craft looked like it had been through a hurricane. They had it all planned out. Putting blueprints, plans, prototypes on what I'm guessing is the *Sea Witch*, then up to Saint John, Canada."

Chuck retrieved some files from his desk, flipped through them, and then resumed his seat. "This is where Smith's lawyer shut him up yesterday. There's still a few details we need to fill in. But basically, according to the files, it's Saint John, then out to the rest of the world. Believe it or not France is even a player, although they do most of their spying on Germany."

Harv shook his head.

"It was a nice little concept, bringing in middle men and buyers from all over the world, putting them up in style at the Seaview, then exposing them to our stolen technology like a trade show. People and merchandise could go in and out of that place unseen thanks to the tunnel." Chuck continued to examine the files while talking. "They were going to build some nice stairs up that hill to the tunnel opening. Covered stairs. Peter was obsessed with drones and aerial surveillance. That tunnel was going to be finished off with lighting, flooring, the works. The plan was to sell to the highest bidder. Make the deal right there on the spot then pack off the merchandise for transport."

"I've got a question for you," said Harv. What's the deal with Cove Realty refusing to sell or rent waterfront properties? That always seemed weird to me."

Chuck smiled, put down his manila folder, and leaned back. "That was a real bone of contention between Peter and Smith. Burke was paranoid about any authority or competitor seeing anything at all relating to his activities. The Stewart Place obviously had the best view so they had to buy that property and mothball it, but Peter just took it over-the-top and didn't want to facilitate any rentals or sales that might possibly see anything at all out on the water that could compromise his operation. "

"A little extreme."

"Of course, but this is Burke we're talking about. It's just Peter being extra cautious, extra manipulative." He shook his head. "Smith was furious about it, but Burke was calling the shots in their little operation and got his way."

Chuck looked at his watch and pulled a large envelope out of his file. "Harv, I've got to wrap this up soon, but one reason I wanted you to come in this morning is to show you this." He opened the envelope, removed an eight-by-ten color photograph, and shoved it toward Harv along the desktop. "Does this look familiar to you?"

Harv leaned over the desk. "It's a dress"

"Look closely at it. Does it look familiar?"

Harv looked. "Just a gray dress."

"Does it look like any other gray dress you may have seen?"

"Wait a minute. The mystery woman I chased was wearing a gray dress." He looked closely. "Long sleeves, same shade of gray." He looked at Chuck. "Is this the same dress? Did you find the woman?"

"So it looks like the same dress to you?"

"At the time I was more interested in catching the woman than analyzing her clothing. But yeah, this picture looks like the dress. What's the story?"

"We found this dress in Jimmy Jarvis's apartment."

"Jimmy Jarvis, the security guard?"

"That's right."

"So Jimmy somehow knows our mystery woman?"

Chuck smiled. "Jimmy *is* our mystery woman."

"What the hell?" Harv stared at Chuck.

"Jimmy is part of this little troop of characters and dressed up like a woman to steal the wave accelerator."

"That was Jimmy?"

"Turns out Jimmy's from Corvellisville. Town right next to Back Hill Cove. He's from there. Family's there. That purse you recovered he stole from the back of his sister's closet. Went to Tufts. Had to drop out. Got a job here as a security guard. Peter found out he's from the area up there. Introduced him to Smith, and they sucked him into their little operation. He was hoping he could get a full-time job with them and live in his home town."

Weitz shuffled through some papers in his file.

"Smith's records showed a lot of phone calls to Jarvis's number. When asked about it, Smith admitted Jimmy was involved. We got a warrant, searched Jimmy's apartment, and found some incriminating information plus this dress."

Harv looked at the photo again. "Hell, that *is* the dress." He pushed the photo back to Weitz. "And Jimmy's involved with Peter's operation?"

"We nabbed Jimmy yesterday, confronted him with the evidence, and he confessed on the spot. Apparently the guy is way over his head with college loans. Really needed the money.

"Unbelievable." Harv looked at the photo again.

"He's been doing low-level, flunky jobs for Burke. Some of the things that have disappeared around here we think we can pin on Jimmy. Spent a lot of time up in Maine strategizing with Burke and Smith."

"So, that was Jimmy Jarvis I was chasing."

"If it makes you feel any better, Harv, Jimmy was on the freshman track team at Tufts back when he was a full-time student."

"It does. I thought I was losing it." Harv looked at his watch.

"Harv, I know you've got to go, and I've got an appointment, but I want to tell you how appreciative we are of everything you've done. If you'd told me before-hand what you were planning to do, I'd have told you not to do it," he stood up and walked toward the door, "but in hindsight, I guess I'm glad you didn't tell me. We owe you a lot."

"Wait till you get my bill before you get too sappy." Harv stood up.

"I'm sure it'll be fair."

"Oh, it'll be fair all right. High but fair."

They both walked to the door.

"Call me when you get back from vacation. I'll update you on things." said Chuck. "I promise I won't call you on vacation."

"You won't be able to; this is a real vacation this time. My phone's going to be turned off, and no one's going to know where I am. In fact, I'm going on pre-vacation mode right now." He pulled his phone out of his pocket and turned it off.

Chuck laughed. "Don't worry, I won't call the landline either."

"What landline? You have no idea where I'm going to be, remember?"

"That's right. How could I possibly call you on a landline when I have no idea where you'll be?" He opened the door. "You can relax for a while; what I got from you today should be all I need."

Harv said goodbye to Chuck and to Shirley and headed through the reception door to the corridor just as Chuck's phone rang.

"It's Lloyd Bannister in Legal," said Shirley.

Chuck walked back into his office and shut the door.

After a brief period of quiet, Shirley could hear Chuck's voice come rumbling through the wall. She tried not to listen. As she continued typing, Weitz burst out of his office, walked through the reception area and out into the hall.

"Damn," he walked back inside. "Shirley, this is important. Call the security guard at the main door. I need to talk to him immediately."

Without speaking, Shirley looked up the number and made the call while Chuck headed back to his office and closed the door.

Shirley immediately buzzed him. "Security officer Sagan on line one for you," she said.

Chuck picked up the phone and sat down at his desk. "Sagan, this is Chuck Weitz speaking."

"Yes, Mr. Weitz."

"A young man just left my office about a minute ago. Name's Harvey Gallagher. You must have him logged in around ten this morning."

"Let's see . . . Yes, sir. Harvey Gallagher from Gallagher Associates at nine fifty one A.M."

"He hasn't signed out yet has he?"

"No sir. Still got an open space here by his name."

"Great. Listen, Sagan. He's about to come by and sign out within the next few minutes. When he does, tell him to call me immediately at extension two three five. Got that?"

"Yes sir. Extension two-thirty-five."

"Tell him it's very important."

"I'll do it, sir."

Chuck hung up and buzzed his other phone. "Shirley, Harv Gallagher is going to be calling me in the next minute or two. When he does, ring me immediately, even if I'm on the phone, OK?"

"Yes sir. A problem, Chuck?"

"I'll tell you in a bit, Shirley." He hung up and called Cobb. During the next two minutes Chuck spoke in quick, muffled tones. As he hung up, the phone on Shirley's desk rang.

"Yes, Mr. Gallagher . . . I know. Let me connect you directly to Mr. Weitz." She pressed the phone button. "Mr. Gallagher on line two."

Chuck picked up his phone. "Jesus, you're a slow walker."

"Hey, for someone who wasn't going to call me, you've got a quick dialing finger."

Chuck laughed. "Harv, I was wondering if you could stand a little good news before you go on vacation?"

"Well, my day hasn't been too shabby so far but sure, I could use a little."

"I just got a call from our corporate attorney who tells me Burke didn't make it."

"What?" Harv yelled into the phone then looked around the foyer and lowered his voice. "He's dead?"

"Apparently your friend, Riley, shot enough electricity into him to overload his circuits, and he expired about an hour ago."

Harv walked a few paces away from the security desk. "Buzz isn't in any trouble is he?"

"Trouble? hell no. We have evidence that Burke conspired to have you shot and was trying to kill you on that hill. Your friend is a hero here."

"Thank God." Harv looked around the foyer.

"I wanted to catch you before you left for wherever the hell you're going."

"Hey, this doesn't change anything does it? I still won't have to come in and testify or anything will I?"

"With what we've got from Smith, your video, and those files, you probably won't have to do much more than give a deposition after you get back."

"This is incredible." Harv walked back to the security desk.

"The only reason I wanted to talk to you was to blow a little sunshine up your skirt before you left for vacation. Now get the hell out of here, OK?"

"Hey, Chuck, thanks."

"No, thank *you.*"

Harv smiled. "I'll see you sometime."

"Yeah, kid, you have a good one."

Harv said goodbye and hung up the phone. Then he signed out, took a deep breath, and walked out the big glass door to start his vacation.

www.ingramcontent.com/pod-product-compliance
Lightning Source LLC
Chambersburg PA
CBHW030002290326
41934CB00005B/196